DR DIANE URQUHART is lecturer in modern Irish history at th
the University of Liverpool. She is a graduate of Queen's Univ
fellow of the Institute of Irish Studies at Queen's. She has also worked as a researcher for the Women's History Project. She is the author of *Women in Ulster Politics, 1890–1940: A History Not Yet Told* (Dublin, 2000).

DR MARIA LUDDY is Reader in history at the University of Warwick and Director of the Women's History Project. She has written extensively on the history of women in Ireland.

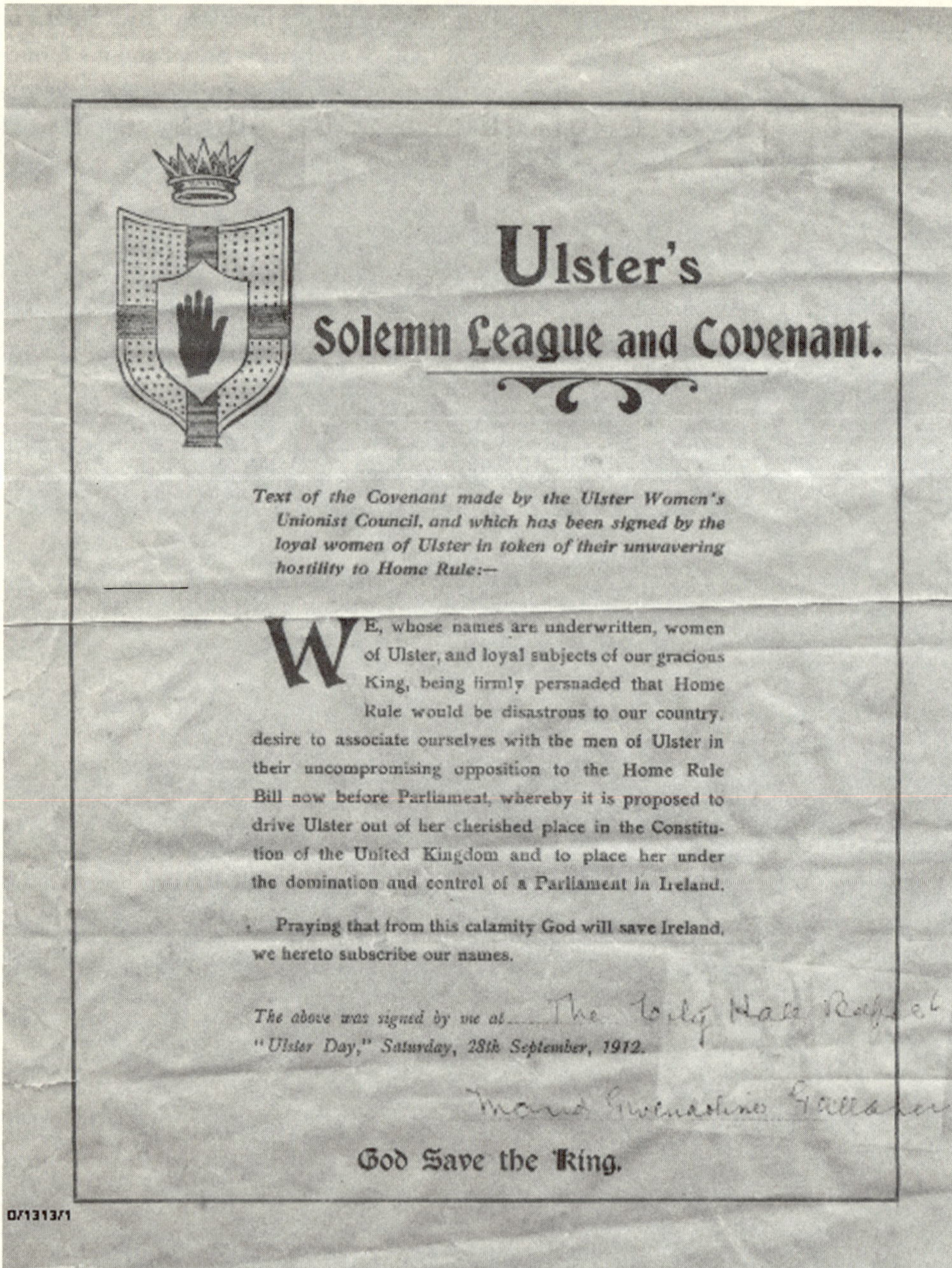

Ulster's
Solemn League and Covenant.

Text of the Covenant made by the Ulster Women's Unionist Council, and which has been signed by the loyal women of Ulster in token of their unwavering hostility to Home Rule:—

WE, whose names are underwritten, women of Ulster, and loyal subjects of our gracious King, being firmly persuaded that Home Rule would be disastrous to our country, desire to associate ourselves with the men of Ulster in their uncompromising opposition to the Home Rule Bill now before Parliament, whereby it is proposed to drive Ulster out of her cherished place in the Constitution of the United Kingdom and to place her under the domination and control of a Parliament in Ireland.

Praying that from this calamity God will save Ireland, we hereto subscribe our names.

The above was signed by me at The City Hall Belfast
"Ulster Day," Saturday, 28th September, 1912.

Maud Gwendoline Gallagher

God Save the King.

D/1313/1

Printed text of the Ulster Women's Unionist Council Covenant signed by Maud Gwendoline Gallagher, City Hall, Belfast on 'Ulster Day', 28 September 1912
D/1313/1, PUBLIC RECORD OFFICE OF NORTHERN IRELAND

THE MINUTES OF THE

ULSTER WOMEN'S UNIONIST COUNCIL AND EXECUTIVE COMMITTEE

1911–40

EDITED BY

DIANE URQUHART

GENERAL EDITOR

MARIA LUDDY

THE WOMEN'S HISTORY PROJECT

IN ASSOCIATION WITH

IRISH MANUSCRIPTS COMMISSION

2001

Printed by ColourBooks Ltd., Dublin
Design and production by Dunbar Design

ISBN 1-874280-93-2

CONTENTS

LIST OF ILLUSTRATIONS

ACKNOWLEDGEMENTS

The Women's History Association of Ireland undertook the organisation of the Women's History Project in September 1997. We would like to record our thanks to the WHAI and to the managing committee of the Women's History Project. Funding provided by the Department of Arts, Heritage, Gaeltacht and the Islands made the Project possible. We would like to thank the Minister, Ms Silé de Valera TD, for her support. Special thanks must also go to Brigid MacManus, Conor O'Malley and Joe Meleady of the department. The Women's History Project is grateful for the support received from the Irish Manuscripts Commission, particularly from Professor Geoffrey Hand, chairman of the Commission.

The Women's History Project owes particular thanks to the Ulster Women's Unionist Council for granting permission to publish these minutes. We are also most grateful to the Deputy Keeper of the Records, Public Record Office of Northern Ireland and the Trustees of the Museums and Galleries of Northern Ireland for permission to reproduce photographic and pictorial material. As editors, we wish to express our gratitude to the staff of the following institutions; the Public Record Office of Northern Ireland, in particular Dr Anne McVeigh and Dr David Lammey, the library of the Queen's University of Belfast, the Sidney Jones Library of the University of Liverpool and the Ulster Museum, especially Pat McLean.

We would like to thank our colleagues, Catherine Cox, Dr Leeann Lane and Orla Fitzpatrick of the Women's History Project, Dublin. On a personal note, Diane would like to thank her former colleagues in the School of Modern History of the Queen's University of Belfast, as well as her current colleagues in the Institute of Irish Studies of the University of Liverpool, for their support and good humour.

DIANE URQUHART
MARIA LUDDY

PREFACE

The Women's History Project began work in September 1997. The aim of the Project is to survey, list and publish historical documents relating to the history of women in Ireland. The Project, under the directorship of Dr. Maria Luddy, is managed by a committee appointed by the Women's History Association of Ireland. The Management Committee is made up of archivists, librarians, history teachers as well as academic historians. The work undertaken by the Women's History Project includes:

Jean Agnew and Maria Luddy (eds.), *The Drennan-McTier Letters, 1776–1819*, 3 volumes (The Women's History Project/Irish Manuscripts Commission: Dublin, 1998/1999).

A Directory of Sources for Women's History in Ireland (Women's History Project/Irish Manuscripts Commission, 1999) available on CD-ROM, which incorporates the results of a survey of over 250 private and public repositories in the Republic of Ireland and Northern Ireland.

A Directory of Sources for Women's History in Ireland is also available on the World Wide Web at http://www.nationalarchives.ie/wh

'If Ever You Go To Dublin Town' Photographs of Elinor Wiltshire (Women's History Project/National Library of Ireland; Dublin, 1999).

Material relating to women in the files of the Department of the Taoiseach, 1922–1966, will be available on the World Wide Web by 2001.

The work of the Project has and will continue to open up new areas of study allowing for a greater understanding of the diverse experiences of women in Irish history.

Síle Chuinneagáin, Caitriona Crowe, Myrtle Hill, Phil Kilroy,
Rena Lohan, Margaret MacCurtain, Christine Meek,
Eilís Ní Dhuibhne, Mary O'Dowd, Collette O'Flaherty,
Rosemary Raughter, Elizabeth Steiner-Scott, Bernadette Whelan

JUNE 2001

INTRODUCTION

Having arrived at a serious crisis in our nation's history, we believe it to be the duty of the women of Ulster to form themselves into an association ... we will stand by our husbands, our brothers and our sons in whatever steps they may be forced to take in defending our liberties against the tyranny of Home Rule.[1]

The establishment of the Ulster Women's Unionist Council on 23 January 1911 was a significant event in the history of women's political activism in Ireland. This organisation quickly developed into a strong, active and democratic body that bound the unionist women of Ulster together in one common aim – resistance to home rule for Ireland. Within a year of its establishment the organisation was easily the largest female political group Ireland had ever seen, with an estimated membership of 115,000–200,000 members. Yet in spite of its size and the public nature of its work, the UWUC has largely been overlooked not only by historians of women, but also by historians of unionism and of early twentieth-century Ireland.[2] Therefore, with the exception of a few quotations in secondary publications, this is the first time that any of the records of the UWUC have been reproduced at length.

Unionist women were involved in the anti-home rule campaign from the time Gladstone introduced the first Home Rule Bill to the Commons in 1886. This bill proposed to establish an Irish legislature with restricted powers and although it was quickly defeated, the unionist reaction was still one of shock and disbelief. This sparked an unprecedented coming together of unionists as opposition to the bill overcame former denominational, class and, to some extent, gender divisions. Unionist women, unable to express their political distaste for home rule by means of a parliamentary vote, instead petitioned, demonstrated, fundraised and canvassed

1 *Belfast News-Letter*, 19 January 1912.

2 The only work on the UWUC is Nancy Kinghan, *United We Stood: The Story of the Ulster Women's Unionist Council, 1911–74* (Belfast, 1975); Diane Urquhart, *Women in Ulster Politics, 1890-1940: A History Not Yet Told* (Dublin, 2000); *idem.*, "The female of the species is more deadlier than the male'?: The Ulster Women's Unionist Council, 1911–40' in Janice Holmes and Diane Urquhart (eds), *Coming into the Light: The Work, Politics and Religion of Women in Ulster, 1840-1940* (Belfast, 1994), pp 93–123; *idem.*, 'In defence of Ulster and the Empire: The Ulster Women's Unionist Council, 1886–1940', *Galway Women's Studies Centre Review*, 4 (1996), pp 31–40. For Ulster women's early activism against home rule see Maria Luddy, 'Isabella M. S. Tod 1836–1896' in Mary Cullen and Maria Luddy (eds), *Women, Power and Consciousness in 19th Century Ireland* (Dublin, 1995), pp 197–230.

for unionist candidates.[3] This was essentially auxiliary work and in many respects it set the tone for women's later involvement in the anti-home rule campaign of the early twentieth century. In spite of this, these early forays of women into unionist politics were significant, introducing many women to direct, if ancillary, political work for the first time. But following the defeat of the bill in June 1886 the sense of crisis gradually ebbed and this was not regained until the early 1890s when Gladstone's second Home Rule Bill was passing through the Commons. Again unionists galvanised themselves into action to oppose home rule: addressing parliament and holding mass public demonstrations, such as the Belfast Convention of June 1892, with women petitioning and demonstrating in increasingly large numbers. One of the largest female unionist petitions dating from this time contained close to 20,000 signatories. This was conveyed to parliament in April 1893 in a carriage belonging to Theresa, 6th Marchioness of Londonderry, a future president of the Ulster Women's Unionist Council.[4] Throughout March and April of 1893 female unionists also assembled in significant numbers to publicly express their resolve to resist home rule. This provides another indication of the escalating popularity of unionism: 1,000 women met in Strabane on 20 March to register their opposition, whilst 700 and 500 women attended meetings in Omagh and Raphoe respectively in the following week.[5]

The increasingly public profile of unionist women at this time fits into the wider context of women in British politics as the 1880–90s saw a proliferation of mixed sex and, more commonly, women-only political associations. The Conservatives' Primrose League and the Women's Liberal Federation were founded in 1883 and 1886 respectively, with the Women's Labour League following in their wake in 1906. The reasons for the establishment of these political associations are less feminist than pragmatic. The Corrupt and Illegal Practices Act of 1883 forbade the payment of political canvassers and this legislation, coupled with the extension of the electoral franchise in the following year, encouraged party organisers to look for a source of unpaid and volunteer political labour. Women seemed to fit this remit perfectly.

The inauguration of the UWUC in January 1911 was certainly welcomed as a valuable addition to the unionist campaign, but it was also an important turning point for female unionists. The establishment of a formal and permanent association gave women an opportunity to work together in a more systematic and co-ordinated political campaign. This was very apparent at the inaugural meeting of the UWUC that was heralded to mark:

3 The Liberal prime minister, W. E. Gladstone, introduced the first Home Rule Bill to the House of Commons in April 1886. The bill proposed the establishment of an Irish legislature with restricted functions but was defeated in the Commons in June 1886. Gladstone also introduced the second Home Rule Bill in January 1893. It only passed its third reading in the Commons with the repeated use of closure but was subsequently rejected by the House of Lords in September 1893.

4 Kinghan, *United We Stood*, p. 8.

5 Gordon Lucy, *The Great Convention: The Ulster Unionist Convention of 1892* (Lurgan, 1995), pp 55–56.

> the beginning of real and solid work and a thorough organising of the women of Ulster … to begin work at once, to canvass voters, to trace removals, and to endeavour to bring every single voter to the polls during elections, so that every seat in Ulster shall be won for the Union … the women of Ulster will be in no way behind the men in striving for so noble a cause.[6]

It was therefore apparent that the UWUC already had a clear idea of the type of campaign it wanted to wage. But if the UWUC's initial plan to rent a room to accommodate between forty and fifty people in January 1911 is any gauge then it seems that the organisation's initial expectations of success were conservative. In spite of this apparent prudency, the UWUC's membership figures bear witness to the fact that the organisation became hugely popular within a relatively short period of time. Much of the explanation for this popularity lies in the fact that the years of 1911–14 were seen as a crisis point in the history of unionism. The Parliament Act of 1911 removed the last constitutional bulwark against home rule by limiting the power of the House of Lords to a two-year veto. From a unionist perspective this constitutional change meant that any forthcoming home rule bill could no longer be defeated outright by the Lords as had been the case in 1893, but its implementation could now only be delayed.[7] In consequence, from 1911, the unionist campaign was broadened. Furthermore, the fact that the UWUC was led by members of Ulster's aristocratic élite, such as the organisation's early presidents, Mary Anne, 2nd Duchess of Abercorn, Theresa, 6th Marchioness of Londonderry, Rosalind, 3rd Duchess of Abercorn and Lady Cecil Craig, added respectability to the organisation.[8]

The following figures give an indication of the swift popularisation of women's involvement in unionist politics: during the first month of the UWUC's existence over four thousand women joined its West Belfast branch alone and by the end of 1911 thirty-two branches had been formed throughout Ulster with a collective membership of 40,000–50,000. Two years later, in 1913, the press were quoting membership figures of between 115,000–200,000. Although a margin of exaggeration is to be expected, the sheer scale of the UWUC's activities, attendance at their public demonstrations as well as signatories to their petitions, all suggest huge membership figures.

Many of the most active members of the UWUC were upper/middle class in social origin and this can be explained by the practicalities of political work. Throughout Britain it was women from these social classes who possessed the time and economic

6 *Belfast News-Letter*, 24 January 1911.

7 The Liberal government of H. H. Asquith introduced the Parliament Act of 1911.

8 Mary Anne, 2nd Duchess of Abercorn was the first President of the UWUC and retained this position from 1911–13. She was succeeded by Theresa, 6th Marchioness of Londonderry who was President from 1913–19. Theresa Londonderry was replaced by Rosalind, 3rd Duchess of Abercorn, who was President from 1919–22. She was succeeded by Lady Cecil Craig, later Viscountess Craigavon, who was President of the UWUC from 1922–42. See Appendix III for details.

freedom to participate in political life. Furthermore, the UWUC's ruling body, the Executive Committee, not only met on week days but also during normal working hours and this obviously precluded much working women's involvement. Many of the leaders of women's unionism were also connected to the unionist movement by familial and marital ties. For example, the spouse of the first UWUC president, Mary Anne, 2nd Duchess of Abercorn, was a unionist MP for Co. Donegal from 1860, the leading spokesman for unionism in the House of Lords from 1895 and the first president of the Unionist Association of Ireland. Some women, like the UWUC's second president, Thesesa, 6th Marchioness of Londonderry, were also politically astute and very well connected. Theresa Londonderry was the leading Tory political hostess of the late nineteenth and early twentieth century, promoting both her husband's and her son's political careers by entertaining royalty and the socio-political élite. Described by one contemporary as a woman 'who went for life, hammer and tongs, she collared it, and scragged it and rooked it like a highwaywoman in a tiara',[9] she was also an early and influential patron of the unionist leader, Edward Carson, and of the Tory leader, Andrew Bonar Law. Such connections meant that she was able to ask both the unionist and Tory leadership for advice on the implementation of UWUC policy and secure influential speakers for public meetings. The UWUC also acknowledged that it was as a result of Theresa's Londonderry's 'unceasing efforts' that their Ulster-based organisation was able to act on a much wider stage, bringing the organisation's work to the attention of 'leaders of the Unionist Party in England' and gaining 'so many openings in Great Britain for its workers'.[10]

But the glamour and political acumen of these upper-class women should not overshadow the importance of women working at a local level amongst the various women's unionist associations that were established throughout Ulster. Indeed it seems that many working-class women were active – signing petitions, canvassing, attending demonstrations and coming into unionist headquarters in the Old Town Hall and later in Glengall Street in Belfast to help disseminate newspapers, leaflets and propaganda espousing the unionist cause. The sheer scale of this work, as the minutes of the Ulster Women's Unionist Council clearly reveal, was often staggering.[11]

The UWUC was essentially an auxiliary organisation, formed to help the all-male Ulster Unionist Council oppose home rule, promote unionist propaganda and preserve the legislative union between Great Britain and Ireland. As Theresa, 6th Marchioness of Londonderry, remarked the Women's Unionist Council was formed:

> to express the feelings of the people of Ulster, who have fought with every means in their power to remain associated with England ... We banded ourselves together to see how we might best organise ourselves to impress our

9 E. F. Benson cited in Brian Masters, *Wynyard Park* (Teeside, 1973), p. 58.

10 *UWUC Year Book* (Belfast, 1920).

11 For instance, by September 1913 10,000 leaflets and newspapers were being sent weekly to Britain under the auspices of the UWUC.

> fellow-countrymen in England with the fact that Ulster will not consent to the tearing asunder of this country.[12]

Thus the UWUC's aim was not to rival men in politics. Rather the organisation wanted to complement the work of male unionists in the pursuit of a common goal – the defeat of home rule. The UWUC identified this as their sole concern. Not only were unionist women workers issued with a card to be read out at the start of each political meeting emphatically stating that only the union would be discussed, but the UWUC wrote to other political associations informing them of the same. Indeed, as far as can be ascertained from the surviving records of the UWUC and from newspaper coverage of their public demonstrations and activities, it seems that the decision to speak only on the subject of home rule was firmly adhered to.

A range of anti-home rule arguments was aired as unionist men and women alike objected to home rule on religious, economic, imperial and constitutional grounds. There were widespread fears amongst unionists that a Dublin parliament would be dominated by the Catholic religious majority and that the civil and religious liberties of Protestants would be subsequently overlooked. In addition to this, Ulster, especially Belfast, had prospered economically under the union, and this fuelled unionist claims that a home rule parliament would be ruinous to Ulster's industrial and commercial interests.[13] Unionists also forwarded the argument that the integrity of the empire would be harmed by home rule, opening the floodgates for the ruination of Britain's imperial position, and that it was unconstitutional to impose a home rule parliament upon Ulster. Perhaps of more interest, however, is the fact that as well as working alongside the UUC to promote these arguments in the hope of convincing Britain of the fallacy of its Irish home rule policy, the UWUC also developed a gendered argument in opposition to home rule. Here the sanctity of the unionist home featured strongly, with women's political action being portrayed as an extension of their maternal and protective instincts:

> If our homes are not sacred from the priest under the existing laws, what can we expect from a priest-governed Ireland … let each woman in Ulster do a woman's part to stem the tide of Home Rule … the Union … meant everything to them – their civil and religious liberty, their homes and children … once the Union was severed there could be no outlook in Ulster but strife and bitterness … Home was a woman's first consideration … in the event of Home Rule being granted, the sanctity and happiness of home life in Ulster would be permanently destroyed.[14]

The activities of the Women's Council in the early twentieth century bore many

12 UWUC Minutes, 28 January 1919 (Public Record Office of Northern Ireland, D/1098/1/3). Hereafter PRONI.

13 For details of Ulster's nineteenth–century economic expansion see Liam Kennedy and Philip Ollerenshaw (eds), *An Economic History of Ulster, 1820–1939* (Manchester, 1985) and Jonathan Bardon, *A History of Ulster* (Belfast, 1992).

14 Minute book of Lurgan Women's Unionist Association, 13 May 1911 (PRONI, D/3790/4).

similarities to the type of auxiliary work women conducted during the earlier home rule crises of 1886 and 1893. However, the establishment of the Council and the popularisation of unionism from 1911 onwards meant that this work could now be conducted on a much wider scale. Petitioning, for instance, remained a key activity. To cite just one example: in 1911 in response to the *Ne Temere* papal decree of Pius X, which declared mixed marriages null and void unless solemnised according to the rites of the Roman Catholic Church, the UWUC 'decided to prepare a petition to Parliament from the women of Ulster'[15] and 'to ask the Dublin women to join in getting signatures for the petition ... when the petition has been signed it should be issued in the form of a leaflet and distributed in England and Scotland, as an appeal to the women of Great Britain and Scotland for help.'[16] The huge scale of this work is well illustrated by the fact that by late April 1912 this petition measured 'almost one mile in length' and by the time it was presented to parliament by Sir John Lonsdale on 11 June 1912 it held the names of 104,301 women.[17] But the work of the Women's Council was in no way limited to petitioning. The Council was also an important fundraising body, collecting substantial monies for the Carson Fund which was launched in January 1912 to finance anti-home rule propaganda. Furthermore, members of the Council attended mass meetings in their droves. Even a brief analysis of attendance figures at these meetings again highlights the level of enthusiasm that unionism could arouse in the early twentieth century. For example, 10,000 women attended an UWUC meeting in Belfast in late 1912 and an estimated 25,000 women greeted Carson on his first visit to West Belfast in 1913.[18] Members of the UWUC also worked as so-called 'unionist missionaries' in Britain, co-operating with English and Scottish women's political associations, like the Conservative's Primrose League, the Women's Protestant Union and the Women's Amalgamated Unionist and Tariff Reform Association, conducting electoral registration work, canvassing and publicising the unionist cause. Indeed between April and May 1914 fifty-six UWUC members left their homes to conduct work of this type. The time that these women spent away from home varied from as little as four days to as much as five weeks or more at the zenith of the third home rule crisis. These workers were often specifically asked to speak by other political organisations which suggests that they were effective propagandists. They were certainly not diffident, as in 1912 the UWUC averred that their speakers were 'most anxious to address Radical Audiences rather than meetings of convinced Unionists'.[19] The UWUC was also unrelenting in the propaganda campaign it waged against home rule, sending thousands of leaflets and newspapers to Britain, America and the colonies. From June 1913 to March 1914, for instance, literature was sent to 14,902

15 UWUC Executive Committee Minutes, 25 September 1911(PRONI, D/1098/1/1).

16 *Ibid.*, 10 April 1912.

17 *Ibid.*, 30 April 1912. The figure for the total number of signatories is cited in Kinghan, *United We Stood*, p. 20.

18 UWUC Annual Report for 1913 (PRONI, D/2688/1/3).

19 UWUC Active Workers' Committee Minutes, 15 November 1912 (PRONI, D/2688/1/3).

electors in sixty-five English and Scotch constituencies.[20] This was all part of the UWUC's maxim that, with regards to home rule, 'Prevention is better than cure'.[21]

The unionist leadership was conscious of the significance of maintaining unity in order to present a favourable public image to the English electorate, and consistent attempts were made to present unionists as a respectable community with valid reasons for resisting home rule. The scheme for organising the by now infamous 'Ulster Day' on 28 September 1912 was one of the most striking examples of this. On this day unionist men and women signed the Ulster Solemn League and Covenant and Women's Declaration respectively, outlining their solidarity as well as their determination to resist home rule.[22] The signatories to these documents provide one of the best examples not only of the scale of unionist opposition, but also of the comparative strength of women's unionism: a total of 234,046 women signed the Declaration compared to 218,206 male signatories to the Covenant.[23]

Yet even with such widespread opposition by 1913 it seemed as if constitutional means were insufficient to defeat home rule. As a result a 90,000 strong Ulster Volunteer Force (UVF) was formed in January 1913 with the intention of convincing British public opinion of unionists' determination to defeat home rule by military means if necessary. An equally disciplined female force of volunteers backed this military body of men and played an active part, especially in the UVF Nursing, Driving and Signalling Corps. The UWUC helped administer the activities of these women, drafting schemes to train women, organising instruction classes in first aid and securing medical equipment and supplies for UVF medical units which were established throughout Ulster in preparation for civil war with Britain.

By the end of July 1914 it seemed as if unionist determination to resist home rule by military means would be put to the test. The UWUC, although unnerved by the prospect of violence, remained resolute to support whatever course of action was needed to defeat home rule. However, the political climate was suddenly and significantly altered by the outbreak of the First World War. Unionists called an immediate political truce. While the third Home Rule Bill passed through all of its parliamentary stages, it was never implemented. The war put the whole home rule question into cold storage and by the time it ended the political situation in Ireland had altered to such an extent that home rule was no longer an acceptable political solution to the 'Irish problem'.

During the First World War, in tangent with the unionist truce, the main political activities of the UWUC were suspended. Indeed, during the conflict the priorities of the UWUC changed and work was scaled down accordingly. In contrast to the

20 UWUC Executive Committee Minutes, 19 May 1914 (PRONI, D/1098/1/2).

21 *Ibid.*, 21 April 1914.

22 Although the wording on the women's declaration uses the term 'Covenant', this term was rarely used by the UWUC. Instead, perhaps to differentiate between the male and female signatories, the UWUC consistently use the term declaration and I have followed their lead.

23 Figure for female signatories cited in UWUC Executive Committee Minutes, 16 January 1913 (PRONI, D/1089/1/1). Figure for male signatories cited in A. T. Q. Stewart, *The Ulster Crisis. Resistance to Home Rule, 1912–14* (London, 1967), p. 65.

pre-war period, the UWUC's Executive Committee met only on an average of twice per annum, whilst its Advisory Committee, a body formed in April 1912 and made up of twenty-three UWUC members whose role it was to assist the UWUC's full-time and paid secretary, met weekly, then fortnightly, and then only monthly to deal with any political business that arose. Now the focus of the organisation was on war work which the UWUC perceived as a practical expression of their oft-proclaimed loyalty to Britain. Thus the UWUC became involved in recruiting for both Voluntary Aid Detachments and soldiers for the Ulster and imperial forces, asking 'each member, each in her own district to place herself at the disposal of the recruiting officers.'[24] In tangent with this, during the war the UWUC protested against the exclusion of Ireland from military conscription which was implemented under the terms of the Compulsory (Military) Service Acts of 1916 and 1918. The Women's Council opined that Ireland should join Britain's war effort in a common bond of service to the empire. The organisation also believed that it was their 'duty to see that their families and dependants [of men in military service] are cared for, and that any want and suffering which may result shall be minimized as much as possible.'[25] To fulfil this aim the organisation became engaged in extensive charitable work, co-operating with bodies like the Soldiers' and Sailors' Families Association, visiting the families of men who were serving in the forces and making arrangements to care for those who were discharged from the forces on medical grounds. In August 1914 the Women's Council also inaugurated the Ulster Women's Gift Fund for Soldiers, which by the end of the war had raised in excess of £100,000. Indeed unionist headquarters in Belfast were converted into premises where women sorted, packaged and dispatched food and comforts and assembled military dressings not only for Ulster regiments but also for other army and navy units and for hospitals. In addition to this, the UWUC initiated a Prisoner of War Fund in 1916, financed the purchase of a fully equipped ambulance for the Ulster Division serving in France and in the years 1914–16 were responsible for financing the running of the UVF hospital in Ville de Pau, Cabinet du Maire, in France.[26]

Although it seems that most women accepted that the change in the UWUC's priorities were dictated by wartime conditions, the question of home rule and the uncertainty of their post-war political situation were never wholly forgotten. Hints of this can be found in the UWUC records where, for example, in 1917 the Women's Council 'urged that members … should in their private capacity try to reach as many Colonial Soldiers as possible, and instruct them in the Home Rule question'.[27] Work of this sort, conducted on an individual, as opposed to a group basis, meant that the unionist political truce could be maintained, whilst some

24 UWUC Executive Committee Minutes, 8 February 1916 (PRONI, D/1098/1/2).

25 UWUC Minutes, 18 August 1914 (PRONI, D/1098/1/3).

26 The UWUC financed the running of this hospital until the end of 1916 when the French authorities decided to move the hospital nearer to the war front and provide the necessary financial support for its operation.

27 UWUC Advisory Committee Minutes, 2 January 1917 (PRONI, D/2688/1/7).

didactic work could be carried out. Indeed, members of the UWUC were actively encouraged to continue in this vein as the following extract from a letter, dated January 1917, from Richard Dawson Bates to Theresa Londonderry illustrates. He emphasised that in spite of 'the fact that they [women unionists] are doing war work, they should not lose sight of the main object of the association, namely, the defeat of Home Rule.'[28]

Such duality was again apparent early in 1918 with the passage of the Representation of the People Act which granted the electoral franchise to women aged over thirty. This prompted the UWUC to become involved in the registration of women voters, spending £5000 paying 'preferably women' electoral canvassers and inspectors.[29] This was obviously perceived as fundamentally important work as the Council expended such a sizeable amount at a time when it was experiencing some financial difficulties as a result of many local associations failing to pay affiliation fees during the war. This, coupled with the scale of the electoral campaign mounted by the UWUC, caused the organisation to sink into the red. Yet electoral work remained a priority. Twice weekly classes on the workings of the proportional representation electoral system were held under the auspices of the UWUC and from March 1919 women unionist candidates standing in district and county council elections received official and financial support from the UWUC. This type of support grew from the end of March of the following year and women unionist candidates in poor law elections were offered the same support. Several years later the Council even depicted 'Poor Law work … [as] women's work.'[30] However, on the question of women coming forward as candidates in the first Northern Ireland parliamentary election of 1921 the UWUC were not so forthcoming, expressing the opinion:

> that the time was not ripe for this, and the essential thing in the first Parliament was to preserve the safety of the Unionist cause, that too much organisation and construction work would be necessary for which perhaps women had not the necessary experience, and except in the case of outstanding qualifications, men candidates were preferable.[31]

This stance can partially be explained by the organisation's integral conservatism as it had never advocated votes for women believing that its one political objective was to oppose home rule. However, in addition to this, neither the unionist leadership nor the Ulster Unionist Council encouraged female parliamentary candidates. Edward Carson clearly expressed this in February 1921 when advising an UWUC meeting that 'in choosing candidates to choose the man who they

[28] Richard Dawson Bates to Theresa, 6th Marchioness of Londonderry, 3 January 1917 (PRONI, D/2846/1/1/8/65).

[29] UWUC Executive Committee Minutes, 18 June 1918 (PRONI, D/1098/1/2).

[30] UWUC Minutes, 6 May 1930 (PRONI, D/1098/1/3).

[31] UWUC Executive Committee Minutes, 25 January 1921 (PRONI, D/1098/1/2).

[32] *Northern Whig*, 7 February 1921.

thought would best represent their views.'[32] Such views were prevalent. Over a decade later, the UWUC expressed the belief that 'it would be helpful to the Unionist cause if more women would come forward to Local Government and Town Council work'.[33] While they employed female trainee political organisers in their headquarters and funded scholarships to train unionist women in politics, economics and citizenship, they did not openly promote women candidates for election to the Northern Ireland or Imperial Parliaments.[34]

Yet to assess the significance of women's enfranchisement solely in terms of the number of women who were elected to parliament is to overlook the fact that possessing a vote cast women in a new political light. No longer could any astute politician overlook them. Indeed, the impact of the Representation of the People Act of 1918 became quickly apparent within unionist ranks. In the immediate aftermath of women's partial enfranchisement unionist leaders gave the Women's Council permission to re-organise and continue as a separate organisation. Moreover it seems that the granting of votes to women boosted the confidence of the UWUC as it was only in the aftermath of the Representation of the People Act that the UWUC issued an uncharacteristically vehement appeal, demanding a definition of their status within the unionist movement:

> During the last 4 years of war, our opinion on any one political matter has never been asked. We ... have been mute, under what we consider has been a very insidious and slow disintegration of our power ... we have held fast to our Unionist opinions, and our voice has been heard and acted upon although perhaps the 'Ulster Unionist Council' may have thought us an entirely negligible quantity ... what is the position of the Ulster Women's Unionist Council? It has none – we are nothing ... is it right or just that we should be in this position[,] that we should remain in this position – are we wise to re-organise and spend the large sum of money involved and trouble ourselves and expend our health and strength if we have no recognition? ... [We] realise many anxieties, difficulties, and dangers ... have to be faced by the Men with regard to the Vote for Women, and its possibility on future elections. But ... we have not been treated as comrades ... We must have more power for immediate action ... we have mediated and thought to do [what] will be of supreme importance in keeping our people together, in educating women's opinion and to bring the war to a final and satisfactory conclusion ... let us stand out now for the rights and liberties of the Ulster Women's Unionist Council. Let us fight under the motto of our old banner 'Union is Strength'.[35]

33 UWUC Minutes, 26 January 1932 (PRONI, D/1098/1/3).

34 In the period 1921–40 a total of three women sat in the Northern Ireland Parliament: Dame Dehra Chichester (later Parker), Julia McMordie and Margaret Waring. All three were unionist representatives and active members of the UWUC. Dehra Chichester was an MP for Londonderry from 1921–29 and for South Londonderry from 1933–60; Julia McMordie was an MP for South Belfast from 1921–25 and Margaret Waring was an MP for Iveagh in Co. Down from 1929–33. See Urquhart, *Women in Ulster Politics*, pp 175–198.

35 UWUC Advisory Comittee Minutes, 4 June 1918 (PRONI, D/2688/1/7).

This appeal, coupled with female enfranchisement, proved to be a catalyst for change as the UWUC was granted representation on the UUC and a joint committee of the Men's and Women's Councils was established to co-ordinate work between these two bodies from 1918.[36]

Perhaps bolstered by their representation on the UUC, and aided by the political work that had been conducted during the war, the UWUC succeeded in sustaining interest, support and members. In the immediate post-war period the organisation's didactic and propagandist work of the pre-war era was quickly and fully revived. The UWUC could, however, no longer rely solely on the old rallying cry of 'No home rule'. Instead the organisation had to work hard to sustain interest by launching new initiatives to make the UWUC appear both attractive and politically relevant in the new state of Northern Ireland. UWUC speakers continued to address political meetings, disseminate propaganda and new branches of the UWUC were formed. Although the period of acute crisis with regards to home rule was over, this was not totally replaced by a feeling of security in unionist ranks. UWUC propaganda from the inter-war years frequently highlighted the need for unionists to continue to be on their guard, emphasising:

> that no false sense of security will tend in any way to induce the relaxation of those efforts necessary to maintain our organisation at the highest state of perfection … if a time of crisis should again arise the loyal women of Ulster must be well prepared, and with this end in view should see that the necessary machinery is kept in smooth working order.[37]

With regards to the UWUC's new initiatives, in April 1919 the idea of producing a monthly paper for unionist women was mooted. This paper sought to combine the unionist message with the dominant domestic and maternalistic ideology of the inter-war period. The first issue of *Ulsterwoman* appeared on 12 July 1919, though its success was to be short-lived. 11,000 advance orders were received for the first edition of this publication, but this initial enthusiasm soon waned. With dwindling demand publication of *Ulsterwoman* was stopped in August 1920, at a financial loss of £120 to the Council. In spite of this loss, the UWUC were not deterred from launching a successor to *Ulsterwoman* several years later. Produced for the first time in October 1925 and entitled, *Northern Ireland, Home and Politics, A Journal for Women* this publication suffered a similar fate to its predecessor. It collapsed in June 1927 after demand fell.

More successful, however, was the UWUC's scheme of reorganisation that was launched in October 1923 with the aim of 'forming a connected chain from the organisation at Headquarters down to the most remote or scattered districts throughout the Six Counties.'[38] This rejuvenation involved speakers' classes, meetings that combined education with entertainment, and the holding of

36 The UWUC was granted twelve representatives on the UUC at this time.

37 UWUC Executive Committee Minutes, 21 January 1927 (PRONI, D/1098/1/2).

38 UWUC Executive Committee Minutes, 22 October 1923 (PRONI, D/1098/1/2).

Executive Committee meetings outside Belfast to increase interest in the work of the Women's Council at a local level. The organisation also expanded its objectives – promoting the purchase of empire produced products, hosting an annual speakers' competition from 1931 onwards and running Pioneer Clubs young girls from 1931–34, with the intention of interesting the women voters of the future in unionism. Overall, therefore, it seems that the UWUC managed to meet the challenges of the inter-war world. To take the year of 1930 as an example: over 7,000 propaganda leaflets were sent from under the auspices of the Council; UWUC speakers addressed over 160 meetings and over thirty new women's unionist associations were formed.[39] The education of women voters also remained a key element of the UWUC's work with 'the goal being that every woman elector should be given an opportunity of studying Unionist aims and ideals [so] the Unionist women of Ulster realise their political responsibilities and their power as citizens'.[40]

Work of this nature continued throughout the 1930s until the outbreak of the Second World War in September 1939. This prompted another suspension of the political activities of the UWUC. Once again war work came to the fore and the UWUC's Executive Committee met only once a year, with its Finance Committee being empowered to deal with all business for the duration of the war.

Although the UWUC must be viewed as an intrinsically auxiliary and conservative organisation, it is not without significance. The sheer size of the association and the scale of its activities are an effective illustration of the degree of political interest many women possessed in the early years of the twentieth century, even years before they possessed the right to vote. The UWUC was undoubtedly the largest female political force Ireland had ever seen. It made a significant contribution to the strength of popular unionism and its espousal of unionist principles, although having much in common with those of male unionists, was not mere imitation. When the gendered aspect of unionism developed by the Women's Council in an undeniably successful attempt to attract women into the organisation is considered, unionism is revealed as a wider political doctrine than is often acknowledged. The fact that many women remained faithful members of the UWUC not just over years, but over decades, alludes to the deep sense of political responsibility and perhaps enjoyment that they derived from membership of this body. The minutes of the UWUC provide a fine and not yet fully tapped source for both the history of unionism and the history of women in early twentieth-century Ireland. Indeed, it is hard to disagree with the astute observations of one contemporary who remarked in 1922 that unionist women were:

> No idle sightseers ... but a genuine political force ... When critical times for the Union arrived there was ... no apathy to be overcome by the Protestant women in Ulster ... [who] very quickly became a most effective organisation with that of the men.[41]

39 UWUC Annual Report, 1930 (PRONI, D/2688/1/9).

40 *Ibid.*, 1934.

41 Roland McNeill, *Ulster's Stand for Union* (London, 1922), p. 111, p. 37.

EDITORIAL NOTES

THIS CALENDAR IS BASED on three large, bound, typescript minute books of one of the most significant female political organisations in Ireland's history, the Ulster Women's Unionist Council (UWUC). The minute books date from the year of the UWUC's establishment in 1911 to 1940 and are deposited in the Public Record Office of Northern Ireland. The organisational structure of the UWUC during this period was divided into two sections: a Council and an Executive Committee. The former comprised of nominated representatives from various branches of the UWUC which were established throughout Ulster and were known as women's unionist associations. Each women's unionist association returned one representative to the Ulster Women's Unionist Council for every three hundred members enrolled and in 1929 a maximum quota of ten representatives for every women's association was fixed.[1] In addition, the wives of Ulster unionist peers and Ulster unionist MPs, as well as 'distinguished ladies who have rendered, or are likely to render, service to the cause, being residents in, or natives of, Ulster' were nominated as Council members.[2] From the 1920s women unionist members of the Northern Ireland House of Commons and Senate and of the Imperial Parliament, as well as three representatives from each district lodge of the Association of Loyal Orangewomen in Northern Ireland, were also given representation on the Council. The Council met annually, usually in mid January, and when specially convened, to debate both UWUC and unionist business. The Council minutes therefore represent the public face of women's unionism. Indeed, coverage of these Council meetings was often given in the Ulster press, especially in the early years of the organisation when women acting on a political stage were still viewed as something of a novelty.

By comparison, the minutes of the UWUC's Executive Committee represent the private face of women's unionism. This committee was the governing, decision and policy-making body of the UWUC. The Executive Committee met at least quarterly per annum and consisted of officer bearers, including an elected President, five Vice Presidents, a Chairman, Vice Chairmen, an Honorary Treasurer and Assistant Honorary Treasurer.[3] In addition to this, twenty provincial representatives, the

1 See Appendix II for details.

2 Draft constitution of the UWUC, January 1911 (PRONI, D/1098/1/3). This constitution is reproduced in Appendix I.

3 See Appendix III for a list of UWUC office bearers from 1911–40.

wives of Ulster unionist peers and of Ulster unionist MPs were appointed to the Executive Committee and each women's unionist association elected two, and later five, representatives onto this body. Moreover, if any women's unionist association enrolled over two thousand members they were entitled to nominate an extra committee member for every five hundred additional members. The Executive Committee also had the power to co-opt a maximum of twenty women likely to be of 'service to the cause' to its ranks.[4] In a similar vein to the Council in the 1920s, the Executive Committee also gave representation to the Association of Loyal Orangewomen.

The records of both the Ulster Women's Unionist Council and its Executive Committee are classed under reference number D/1098/1 in the Public Record Office of Northern Ireland: D/1098/1/1 is the UWUC Executive Committee minute book dating from 24 January 1911 to 21 October 1913. These minutes detail the inauguration, development and early work of the UWUC. D/1098/1/2 is the UWUC Executive Committee minute book dating from 18 November 1913 to 26 April 1940. These Executive Committee minutes provide a full account of the UWUC's activities at the height of the third and most severe home rule crisis of 1912–14 and during the First World War of 1914–18. The minutes also detail the UWUC's reaction to the partition of Ireland and the establishment and workings of a separate Northern Ireland Parliament from 1921–40. D/1098/1/3 is the Council minute book dating from 18 January 1912 to 26 April 1940. This minute book covers annual and specially convened UWUC meetings and gives detailed information on the activities of the Council up to the outbreak of the Second World War.

Additional miscellaneous documents relating to the UWUC, including photographs, newspaper reports, records of UWUC sub-committees and affiliated women's unionist associations are available in the Public Record Office of Northern Ireland and a list of all such records is appended to this calendar.[5] Although every effort has been made to locate minute books for the UWUC in the post-1940 period, the whereabouts of these later minute books remains unknown.

In this calendar every effort has been made to identify individuals mentioned in the text and footnotes giving brief biographical details have been added, wherever possible, to the minutes. For some titled and well-known persons this was a comparatively easy task. For others, who are mentioned only by a surname in the minutes, it is impossible to provide (with any degree of accuracy) biographical details. In addition to this, one of the challenges of women's history is that women are frequently only referred to in connection to their spouses. Therefore the date of a marriage is often much more readily available than a woman's date of birth or death, or details concerning her career.

The main sources for the biographical data included in this calendar are as

4 Draft constitution of the UWUC, January 1911 (PRONI, D/1098/1/3). See Appendix I.

5 See Appendix V for details.

follows: *Burke's Peerage*, *Dod's Peerage*, *Debrett's Peerage*, *The Dictionary of National Biography*, *Who Was Who* and *Thom's Irish Who's Who*. The latter was produced as a one-off edition in 1923 and has proved invaluable in compiling biographical information. Information has also been gathered from various histories of unionism and of late modern Ireland which are listed in a select bibliography at the end of this calendar.

The calendar that follows is a synoptic version of the minutes of the UWUC rather than a transcript. The original spelling, lay out and punctuation have been preserved throughout and, where possible, the minutes have been reproduced in full. All quotation marks in the calendar are also contained in the original minutes and were often used to quote an extract from a letter that was read aloud at UWUC meetings, to denote a motion being proposed and highlight the names of various newspapers and journals. Occasionally letters read at Council or Executive Committee meetings are attached to the original minutes and such correspondence, where relevant, has been footnoted in this calendar in an attempt to give a full picture of the nature and significance of the work of the UWUC in early twentieth-century Ireland. However, additional information to assist the reader, insert a missing word or qualify certain pieces of legislation has been added to the calendar. Such editorial additions can be identified as they are contained within parenthesis. The minutes have also been edited to avoid repetition and this is identified in the text by elisions. Lists of members attending UWUC meetings, which for the annual meetings of the organisation can run up to several hundred women, have also been omitted. Again these omissions are indicated by elisions in the text.

This is the first time that any of the minutes of the UWUC have been reproduced at any length. This calendar will introduce many of those who are perhaps unaware of the importance, or even the very existence, of the UWUC to an organisation which in many ways is unique to the history of early twentieth-century Ireland. Above all, the calendar that follows is not just of relevance to those interested in women's history, but those interested in the political workings of Ireland at a pivotal point in her history.

CHRONOLOGY

1886	25 January	Irish Unionist Parliamentary Party established.
	8 April	W. E. Gladstone introduces the first Home Rule Bill to the House of Commons.
	8 June	Gladstone's Home Rule Bill defeated in the House of Commons.
1893	January	Unionist Club movement established.
	13 February	Gladstone introduces the second Home Rule Bill to the House of Commons.
	March	Ulster Defence Union established to co-ordinate the activities of the anti-home rule campaign.
	1 September	Home Rule Bill passes in the House of Commons.
	8 September	Home Rule Bill defeated in the House of Lords.
1904	2 December	Beginnings of an organisation for Ulster Unionist MPs (known as the Ulster Unionist Council from March 1905).
1905	3 March	Ulster Unionist Council launched.
1908	2 August	*Ne Temere* papal decree of Pius X on mixed marriages.
1910	21 February	Sir Edward Carson elected chairman of the Irish Unionist Parliamentary Party.
1911	January	Unionist Club movement revived.
	23 January	Ulster Women's Unionist Council established.
	18 August	Parliament Act passed. This removed the House of Lords' power of absolute veto and replaced it with a two-year delaying power.
1912	January	The Sir Edward Carson Unionist Defence Fund established to finance anti-home rule propaganda in Great Britain.
	11 April	Third Home Rule Bill introduced to the House of Commons.

	28 September	Solemn League and Covenant and Women's Declaration subscribed to in Ulster. The former was signed by 218,206 men and the latter by 234,046 women.
1913	16 January	Home Rule Bill passes its third reading in House of Commons.
	30 January	Home Rule Bill defeated in House of Lords.
	31 January	Ulster Volunteer Force formally established.
	7 July	Home Rule Bill passes in the House of Commons.
	15 July	Home Rule Bill defeated in the House of Lords.
	24 September	Provisional Government of Ulster set up, backed by the Ulster Volunteer Force.
1914	24–25 April	Larne gunrunning to arm the Ulster Volunteer Force.
	25 May	Home Rule Bill passes in the House of Commons.
	23 June	Government of Ireland (Amendment) Bill which allowed for the temporary exclusion of parts of Ulster from the Home Rule Bill.
	8 July	Government of Ireland (Amendment) Bill altered by the House of Lords to permanently exclude all Ulster is shelved by the government.
	4 August	Great Britain and Germany go to war.
	15 September	Home rule suspended in advance of its enactment.
1916	12 June	Ulster Unionist Council agree to immediate implementation of home rule if six Ulster counties were temporarily excluded.
1918	6 February	Representation of the People and Redistribution of Seats Act grants the parliamentary vote to women aged thirty and over.
	11 November	Cessation of the First World War.
1920	25 February	Government of Ireland Bill introduced in the House of Commons.
	20 March	Ulster Unionist Council accepts the Government of Ireland Bill.
	24 June	Ulster Unionist Council decide to revive the Ulster Volunteer Force.
	23 December	Government of Ireland Act sets up a six-county parliament and administration in Northern Ireland.

1921	4 February	Sir Edward Carson resigns as unionist leader and is succeeded by Captain James Craig.
	24 May	Northern Ireland general election. Ulster unionists win 40 out of 52 seats.
	22 June	Northern Ireland Parliament opened by George V.
1925	3 April	Northern Ireland general election.
	7 November	Report of the Boundary Commission leaked to the press.
	3 December	Agreement to maintain the existing border between Ulster and the rest of Ireland.
1929	22 May	Northern Ireland general election.
1935	22 October	Death of Edward Carson.
1938	9 February	Northern Ireland general election.
1939	3 September	Start of the Second World War (ends May 1945).
1940	24 November	Death of James Craig.
	25 November	John Andrews succeeds James Craig as Prime Minister of Northern Ireland.

Miss Whitaker, Honorary Secretary of West Belfast Women's Unionist Association canvassing women in Belfast to sign the Ulster Women's Unionist Council Declaration, September 1912
INF/7A/2/20, PUBLIC RECORD OFFICE OF NORTHERN IRELAND

ULSTER WOMEN'S UNIONIST COUNCIL EXECUTIVE COMMITTEE MINUTES 1911–13[1]

[1] This minute book is held by PRONI under reference number D/1098/1/1.

24 January 1911

The first Meeting of the Executive Committee of the Ulster Women's Unionist Council was held in the Parlour of the Y.M.C.A. Hall, Belfast[2] ... Mrs Wheeler[3] informed the Committee how the formation of the Association came about ... A vote of thanks to Mrs Mercier-Clements[4], Mrs McMordie[5] and Mrs Moore,[6] the Unionist Council Press etc., for their trouble in arranging the Public Meeting on the 22nd [January 1911] ... [Office bearers of the U.W.U.C., including the post of President, were elected.[7] It was proposed by Lady Jaffe[8] and seconded by Mrs

2 This meeting was chaired by Mrs Sarah A. Finlay, Honorary Secretary of the UWUC from 1911–12. Twenty–one members attended this meeting. A list of attendees and apologies received is included in the minutes, unless otherwise specified.

3 Mrs Edith Wheeler was an Honorary Secretary of the UWUC from 1911–12. She was one of the most active members of the UWUC from the inauguration of the organisation until her death in 1922. She was married to George Wheeler, a well–known unionist solicitor. Edith Wheeler was also the sister of Alice Milligan, the acclaimed poet, Irish language enthusiast and playwright. See Diane Urquhart, *Women in Ulster Politics, 1890–1940* (Dublin, 2000), p. 88.

4 Mrs Edith Mercier Clements was Assistant Honorary Treasurer of the UWUC from 1911 until her death in 1920.

5 Julia McMordie was born in Hartlepool in 1860 and was educated at Christchurch. In 1885 she married R. J. McMordie, five times Lord Mayor of Belfast. An active member of the UWUC, she was a Vice Chairman of the organisation from 1911–19 and a Vice President from 1919–41. She was elected as a unionist member to the Northern Ireland Parliament, representing the Willowfield district of Belfast in 1921 and held this position until 1925. McMordie was an Honorary Burgess of the City of Belfast and during World War I acted as President of St. John's Voluntary Aid Detachment for Belfast. She was granted a CBE in 1919 and was a member of Belfast City Council from 1917 and an Alderman on this body from 1920. She was a Lady of Grace of the Order of St John of Jerusalem and also served as a JP in Belfast. She died in 1941. See *Thom's Irish Who's Who, 1923* (Dublin, 1923), p. 154: Urquhart, *Women in Ulster Politics.*

6 Mrs Moore was possibly the wife of James Moore, a member of the Ulster Unionist Council.

7 This position was offered to Theresa, 6th Marchioness of Londonderry. However, she did not accept this offer and Mary Anne, 2nd Duchess of Abercorn became the first President of the UWUC. Theresa, 6th Marchioness of Londonderry, was the eldest daughter of Charles John Talbot, the 19th Earl of Shrewsbury. She married Charles Vane–Tempest Stewart, the 6th Marquis of Londonderry, in 1875. Theresa was a Vice President of the UWUC from 1911–13 and President of this body from 1913–19. She was also a Primrose League Dame and was appointed to the Senate of The Queen's University of Belfast in 1909. She was widowed in 1915 and died on 16 March 1919. The 2nd Duchess of Abercorn was born Lady Mary Anne Curzon, the 4th daughter of Richard William Penn, the first Earl of Howe. In 1869 she married James Albert Edward Hamilton (1838–1913), unionist MP for Co. Donegal from 1860–80, the chief spokesman for Ulster unionism in the House of Lords from 1895 and the first President of the Ulster Unionist Association. Their family residence was Baronscourt in Newtownstewart, Co. Tyrone. Like her husband, the 2nd Duchess was involved in unionism and from 1911–13 and she served as the first President of the UWUC. She died on 10 May 1929. See Urquhart, *Women in Ulster Politics*: H. Montgomery Hyde, *The Londonderrys: A Family Portrait* (London, 1979).

8 Lady Paula Jaffe was the daughter of M. Hertz. In 1879 she married Sir Otto Jaffe, the chairman of Jaffe Brothers Limited, linen merchants, President of the Ulster Reform Club, High Sheriff of Belfast in 1901 and Lord Mayor of Belfast in 1899–1900 and 1904–05. *Dod's Peerage, Baronetage, Knightage, etc., of Great Britain and Ireland for 1921* (London, 1921), p. 468.

Workman[9] that] there should be a limited number of Vice-Presidents, to work with the Executive Committee. A Sub-Committee was appointed to elect Vice-Presidents, and to arrange for representatives from country branches, and to lay the names before the next Executive Committee.
SUB-COMMITTEE to consist of several members, Mrs Ewart,[10] Mrs Finlay, Mrs Mercier-Clements, Mrs Ward, Mrs Andrews,[11] Miss Henderson,[12] and Miss Sinclair. Miss Sinclair to act as Hon. Secretary to Sub-Committee.

HONORARY SECRETARIES

It was decided that Mrs Mosse, Mrs Finlay and Mrs Wakefield Richardson, be asked to act as Honorary Secretaries.
Mrs Finlay consented to act, if either of these are unable to act, the Committee decided to give Miss Sinclair power to ask Miss Henderson, Norwood Tower, and Mrs H. C. Kelly, Strandtown ... The loan of a desk was kindly offered by Mrs Riddell. It was decided to appoint a Sub-Committee to find a suitable room to hold 40 to 50 people, rent up to £25 a year. Sub-Committee to consist of two Members – Mrs McMordie and Mrs Wheeler ... In former years capital was formed by donations from the Council and the Executive Committee, followed by regular annual subscriptions.
It was decided by the Committee to advertise for a Secretary in the 'Irish Times', 'Whig' and 'Belfast Newsletter'.

30 January 1911

The 2nd Meeting of the Executive Committee of the Ulster Women's Unionist Council was held in the Y.M.C.A. Parlour ... at 11-30 a.m. [Theresa] the Marchioness of Londonderry being in the Chair[13] ...By request of the Committee,

9 Mrs Workman was probably a member of the Workman shipbuilding family, the owners of the Workman Clark shipyard on the River Lagan in Belfast. At its peak this shipyard was the 6th largest in the UK. It closed in 1935 as a result of the world–wide recession.

10 Mrs Ewart was probably a member of the prominent linen merchant family in Belfast and wife of Herbert Ewart, JP, and member of the Ulster Unionist Council.

11 This was probably Lizzie, the daughter of James A. Pirrie of Little Clandeboye, Co. Down. In 1870 she married the Rt. Hon. Thomas Andrews, Deputy Lieutenant and High Sheriff of Co. Down (1843–1916), a flax spinner in Comber, Co. Down. He was President of the Ulster Liberal Unionist Association from 1892, one of the promoters of the 1892 Unionist Convention, a member of the Ulster Defence Union from 1893 and a Chairman of Down County Council from 1902. *Whitaker's Peerage, Baronetage, Knightage and Companionage* (London, 1935), p. 115.

12 Miss Florence E. Henderson was an Honorary Secretary of the UWUC from 1911–12.

13 Twenty–one members were present at this meeting.

as Mrs Thomas Sinclair[14] was unable to be present, Captain Craig M.P.[15] kindly attended the Meeting, to lay before it a draft constitution drawn up by Mrs Sinclair aided by Mr Sinclair and himself.

After lengthened discussion, on the motion of Lady Londonderry[,] seconded by Lady Ewart,[16] the constitution[17] was passed with the following amendments;–

That the affiliation fee for 1911 be 3 guineas per annum instead of 5 guineas, and that the country branches be asked to add a donation this year to their affiliation fee to help start the U.W.U.C. throughout Ulster. Passed.

That there be one Vice President and 20 County Representatives, these to be elected by the Executive.

It was reported to the Meeting that by Lady Londonderry's desire, after consultation with the signatories of the original circular convening the Public Meeting at which it was decided to form the Association, Mr Sinclair telegraphed Her Grace [Mary Anne] the Duchess of Abercorn, asking her to become President of the Council to which she consented.[18]

14 Mrs Elizabeth Sinclair was the daughter of William Richardson of Brooklands, Belfast and the second wife of Rt. Hon. Thomas Sinclair (1838–1914). Thomas Sinclair was a merchant and the leader of the Ulster Liberal Party from 1868. In 1886 he became a Liberal Unionist and was President of the Ulster Liberal Unionist Association from 1886–90. He was Vice President of the Ulster Defence Union in 1893 and chairman of its council. In 1896 he became a Privy Councillor and served as President of Belfast Chamber of Commerce in 1876 and 1902. He was also a member of the Standing Committee of the Ulster Unionist Council. Mrs Sinclair was a Vice Chairman of the UWUC from 1912–19. *Who Was Who, 1897–1915*, vol. 1 (London, 1920), p. 652.

15 Captain Charles Curtis Craig (b. 1869), was elected unionist MP for S. Antrim in 1903. He was a Deputy Lieutenant for Co. Down and served in the Ulster Division during World War I. He was the elder brother of James Craig, who, born in 1871, became a stockbroker before embarking on an army career. James Craig was captain of the Royal Irish Rifles in South Africa from 1900–01. He returned to Ulster to become a unionist MP for East Down in 1906 and for Mid-Down in 1918. James Craig was also a Grand Master of the Co. Down Orangemen and Quartermaster General of the 3rd Ulster Division from 1914–16. He was knighted in 1918 and was appointed Secretary of the Ministry of Pensions in 1919 and to the Admiralty from 1920–21. He became the leader of the Ulster Unionist Party in February 1921 and first Prime Minister of Northern Ireland in June of the same year. Craig held both of these positions for life. He was created Viscount Craigavon in 1921 and died in 1940. *Thom's Irish Who's Who*, pp 49–50.

16 Lady Mary Warren Ewart was the daughter of Robert Heard of Kinsale. In 1876 she married Sir William Quartus Ewart, 2nd Baronet of Glenmachen, a Deputy Lieutenant of Belfast, a JP for Co. Down and High Sheriff of Co. Antrim in 1897. She was a Vice Chairman of the UWUC from 1911–20. Lady Ewart was widowed in 1919 and died in 1929. *Thom's Irish Who's Who*, p. 75; *Dod's Peerage*, p. 304.

17 This draft constitution is reproduced in Appendix I.

18 Lady Cecilia Caroline Bingham was the only daughter of the 4th Earl of Lucan. She married James Albert Edward, the 3rd Duke of Abercorn, on 1 November 1894. Her husband was Treasurer of the royal household from 1903–05 and an MP for Londonderry City from 1900–12. In 1917 he was appointed HM Lieutenant for Co. Tyrone and was a member of the Senate of Northern Ireland from 1921. He was appointed Governor of Northern Ireland in 1922 and retained this position until 1945. The 3rd Duchess of Abercorn was a Vice President of the UWUC from 1914–19 and President from 1919–22. Their family home was Baronscourt in Newtownstewart, Co. Tyrone. Before her death on 18 January 1958 the Duchess was granted a DBE and an honorary LLD from The Queen's University, Belfast. *Dod's Peerage*, p. 2; *Thom's Irish Who's Who*, p. 1.

At the unanimous desire of the Meeting, [Theresa] the Marchioness of Londonderry consented to be Vice-President.

The Hon. Secretary reported that Miss F. Henderson, Norwood Tower, would act as the second Hon. Secretary, and it was decided to ask Miss Tracey,[19] Ballybogey House, Dervock, Co. Antrim, to be the third. This was proposed by Mrs Riddell, and seconded by Miss Ferguson. After lengthened discussion, the Committee decided that the paid Secretary should be a man, and the Hon. Secretary was instructed to write to this effect to those ladies who had answered the advertisement.

It was decided that a salary of from £180 to £200 per annum should be offered, this to include rent of office, furniture [and] telephone.

A Sub-Committee to consist of Lady Londonderry, Mrs Finlay, Miss Henderson, Mrs McMordie, Mrs Mercier-Clements, Mrs Wheeler and Miss Sinclair, was appointed to meet at 2-45 p.m. on February 1st. to interview applicants for the post, and lay the names before the Executive.

The Hon. Treasurer having asked for funds, the following donations were promised;–

Lady Londonderry	£50
Miss Connor[20]	£20
Lady Ewart	£10
Lady Jaffe	£10
Mrs Andrews	£10
Lady Anderson[21]	£10
Mrs Moore, Finaghy	£10
Mrs McMordie	£10
Mrs Clarke	£10

Lady Londonderry having agreed to accept the post of Chairman the following were appointed Vice-Chairmen;– Lady Ewart, Mrs McMordie, Lady Jaffe.

Proposed by Lady Londonderry
Seconded by Lady Anderson

An earnest appeal be made to Unionist Women in Ulster to form Associations which shall be affiliated with the U.W.U.C. and to communicate with the Hon. Secretaries.

19 Miss E. A. M. Tracey was an Honorary Secretary of the UWUC from 1911–12.

20 Miss E. Connor was Honorary Treasurer of the UWUC from 1912 until her death in 1930. She was awarded an OBE after World War I.

21 Lady Wilhelmina Anderson was the daughter of Rev. Andrew Long of Monereagh, Co. Donegal. In 1890 she married Sir Robert Anderson, 1st Baronet, the chairman of Anderson and McAuley Ltd., John Arnott and Co. Ltd., Milford Weaving and Finishing Co. Ltd., William Ross and Co. Ltd., Vulcanite Ltd., City Estates Ltd., Baltic Firewood Co. Ltd. and the director of Laganvale Brickworks Ltd. He was Sheriff of Belfast in 1903, a JP and an alderman in Belfast, Lord Mayor of Belfast from 1908–09 and High Sheriff for Co. Monaghan in 1911. Lady Anderson was a Vice Chairman of the UWUC from 1911 until she resigned this post in 1918. *Dod's Peerage*, p. 20.

Lady Londonderry desired the Committee to note that she wished a copy of the agenda of each Meeting of the Executive Committee to be sent to her some days before the date of the Meeting, so that she may have an opportunity of expressing her opinion on it – She particularly requests that a telegram be sent to her, at the same time that the agenda is posted advising her that it was coming … Lady Londonderry also is of [the] opinion that the Council should urge the Ulster case against Home Rule mainly on social and economic grounds, by which course the charge of Ulster bigotry will be avoided.

But of course when occasions like the Belfast mixed marriage case occur they should be properly dealt with.[22]

31 January 1911

The adjourned Meeting was held in the Y.M.C.A. Parlour … at 4 p.m. The Marchioness of Londonderry being in the Chair[24] … It was proposed by Lady Londonderry and seconded by Mrs McMordie that the Executive earnestly hope that a branch of the Ulster Women's Unionist Council will be started at once in every Parliamentary Division in Ulster … A list of twenty names of ladies was submitted to the Executive, and the Hon Secretary was instructed to write and ask them would they be willing to become the Provincial Representatives of the Council.

Proposed by Miss Sinclair,
Seconded by Mrs Finlay,

That the wives of Ulster peers, having seats in Parliament, and the wives of Ulster Unionist Members of Parliament be immediately co[-]opted members of the Executive Committee, as specified in paragraph 6 of the Constitution … On the motion of Mrs Wheeler seconded by Mrs McMordie it was resolved that a list be kept by the Secretary of ladies willing and able to speak in English or Scotch constituencies at election or other times.

It was moved by Lady Londonderry and seconded by Mrs Finlay that a vote of thanks be sent to the Ulster Unionist Council for the cordiality with which they have welcomed the formation of the Ulster Women's Unionist Council.[25]

1 February 1911

[The meeting of the Executive Committee of the UWUC was adjourned.][23]

22 This is a reference to the 1910 McCann case. In response to the 1908 *Ne Temere* papal decree which declared mixed marriages null and void if they were not sanctioned by the Roman Catholic Church, a Belfast Catholic man left his Protestant wife, taking their children with him. This case received considerable press attention.

23 This is noted in the UWUC Executive Committee minutes of 30 January 1911.

24 Seventeen members were present and there were three apologies.

25 Members of the UWUC Finance Committee and Affiliation Committee were also appointed at this meeting.

17 February 1911

The Third Meeting of the Executive Committee was held in the Y.M.C.A. Parlour … at 11-30 a.m. … The Chair was taken by Mrs McMordie, Vice-Chairman[26] [The appointment of a secretary for the UWUC was discussed] and the terms of the advertisement were then discussed. It was finally decided it should take the following form;–

ULSTER WOMEN'S UNIONIST COUNCIL

Wanted immediately a gentleman to undertake the duties of paid Secretary. Must have had practical experience of political organization. Apply with testimonials and references, to the Hon. Secretaries, Ardmora, Myrtlefield Park, Belfast and the Hon. Secretary was instructed to have it inserted three times in the 'Belfast Newsletter'[,] 'Northern Whig' and 'Irish Times' the Sub-Committee arranging to meet on Friday, February 24th. to examine the applications, and to report on them to a meeting of [the] Executive to be held on the following Monday, February 27th.

27 February 1911

The Fourth Meeting of the Executive Committee was held in the Y.M.C.A. Parlour … at 11.30 a.m. … Lady Ewart (in the Chair)[27] … [It was resolved that] for the purpose of carrying out section 3, Clause D of our Constitution which in certain contingencies requires consultation of the Women's Unionist Council with the Ulster Unionist Council; and further for the purpose of carrying out the final clause in section 3 of said Constitution which enacts that, – 'It is desirable that the Women's Unionist Council should, in all its operations keep in close touch with the Ulster Unionist Council' the Executive Committee hereby requests the Ulster Unionist Council to nominate a Consultative Committee of its members to whom the Executive of the Women's Unionist Council can at all times refer as circumstances may require, proposed by Mrs. Finlay and seconded by Mrs Andrews and passed unanimously.

A circular was then read by the Hon. Secretary which it was suggested should be sent to the Provisional Representatives and wives of Ulster Unionist M.P.s asking them to take steps at once to form Branches in their respective Parliamentary Districts, and also to raise funds for the work of the Ulster Women's Unionist Council. This was approved of and the Hon. Secretaries were instructed to have copies of the circular sent to these ladies along with copies of the Constitution.

REPORT OF SUB-COMMITTEE RE. SECRETARY …

Twenty-three applications for the post of Secretary were received and considered. These were gradually reduced to three. These gentlemen were summoned by telephone and interviewed, when one of the three was finally eliminated. On a vote

26 Sixteen members were present at this meeting.

27 Twenty members were present at this meeting and there were three apologies for non–attendance.

being taken between the remaining two, Mr. Hamill was chosen by 6 votes to 2.[28] While Mr. Hamill has no actual experience of political organization, his whole manner and appearance, impressed the Committee very favourably. He is 25 years of age, a strict teetotaller, a member of the Presbyterian Church, and has a brilliant College record behind him. By the outline he gave of what he considered would be expected of him in the way of organising work, he seemed to have considered the subject well, and to have a clear grasp of it. Mr. Hamill has an office in Ocean Buildings with Telephone installation. A good room is to be had beside his office which would be large enough to accommodate the Executive for meetings.

29 March 1911

The fifth meeting of the Executive Committee was held in the U.W.U.C. office … at 12 o-clock … (Lady Dixon[29] in the chair)[30] … A letter was read from Mrs George Wheeler asking for permission to use the Committee Room for a series of lectures on practical work. It was unanimously agreed to allow Mrs Wheeler to use the room, she to submit the names of speakers who were to address the different meetings. A letter was also read from Mrs Wheeler containing a list of ladies willing to work in England and Scotland; but consideration of this letter was postponed as the matter was to come up again in resolutions 8 and 11 … A letter from the Secretary of the Ulster Unionist Council was read, stating that the Council as requested by the Ulster Women's Unionist Council, had appointed the following gentlemen to act as a Consultative Committee, Right Hon. Thomas Sinclair D.L.; Right Hon. Thos Andrews D.L.; Col. R.G. Sharman Crawford D.L.,[31] Major Crawford[32] and Mr W. R Young.[33]

The Secretary then read the following report of work done since the last meeting of the Executive Committee.

28 John Hamill retained the position of UWUC Organising Secretary until 1928.

29 Lady Edith Dixon, née Clark, the wife of Sir Thomas Dixon, Lieutenant of Belfast. Both were renowned for their charitable works which included the Sir Thomas and Lady Dixon Hospital established in their former home, Cairndhu House in Larne, Co. Antrim. Lady Dixon served as a JP, was awarded an OBE after World War I and was the first woman Mayor of Larne. She was widowed in 1950 and died in 1964. *Thom's Irish Who's Who*, pp 62–3.

30 Twenty–one members were present and there were seven apologies for non–attendance.

31 Colonel Robert Gordon, the Rt. Hon. Sharman–Crawford (b. 1853), was an MP for E. Belfast in the Imperial Parliament from 1914–18, an MP for Mid Down in the Northern Ireland Parliament from 1921 and a member of the Northern Ireland Senate from 1921. He was awarded a CBE in 1919 and was a JP for Co. Down. *Thom's Irish Who's Who*, p. 229.

32 Major Frederick Crawford (1861–1952), a Boer War veteran who was the key figure in the establishment of a secret subcommittee of the Ulster Unionist Council which considered importing weapons to Ulster in 1910. In 1914 Crawford was responsible for organising the importation of 25,000 weapons and 3 million rounds of ammunition for the Ulster Volunteer Force from Germany which were landed at Bangor, Larne and Donaghadee on 24–25 April. See S. J. Connolly (ed.), *The Oxford Companion to Irish History* (Oxford, 1998), p. 125.

33 Rt. Hon. William Robert Young (b. 1856), of Galgorm Castle, Co. Antrim, the manager of J. and R. Young Linen Merchants in Belfast and a JP for Co. Antrim. *Thom's Irish Who's Who*, p. 266.

REPORT OF WORK DONE SINCE THE LAST MEETING
OF THE EXECUTIVE COMMITTEE.

500 copies of the Constitution have been printed and copies sent to each member of the Executive. Copies have also been sent to each of the Provincial Representatives and wives of Ulster M.P.s together with a copy of a letter read at the last Executive, asking them to take steps to form branches of the Council in their respective districts ... Branches are being formed in the following divisions: –

NORTH DERRY.

In arranging for a meeting to be held in Coleraine on March 15th to organize a branch there, of which Lady Bruce[34] is President, Mrs Hugh T. Barrie,[35] wrote to Mrs Finlay Hon. Secretary to know if the Secretary of the U.W.U.C. could attend the meetings to help them. This was arranged ...

A letter was sent by the Secretary to Mr Dawson Bates,[36] asking about the possibility of the Unionist Associations of Ireland[37] helping us with funds for sending women workers and speakers to England and Scotland. Mr Bates replied saying that the Committee regretted that they could not give the Ulster Women's Unionist Council any financial assistance as their funds were earmarked.

As the Secretary informed Mrs Finlay[,] Hon. Sec.[,] that he had received very few replies to the circular letter sent to Provincial Representatives and wives of Ulster Unionist M.P.s she instructed him to send the following letter to those who had not replied.

Dear Madam,

With reference to the letter sent to you along with copies of the Constitution of March 8th, we should be glad to hear from you what steps you are taking to form

34 Lady Ruth Isabel Bruce, the third daughter of Haughton Charles Okeover. In 1903 she married Sir Hervey Ronald Bruce, 5th Baronet of Downhill, JP and Deputy Lieutenant in Co. Londonderry. Lady Bruce was the President of North Derry Women's Unionist Association. She died in 1915. *Thom's Irish Who's Who*, p. 18; *Dod's Peerage*, p. 122.

35 Mrs Catherine Barrie was the wife of Rt. Hon., later Sir, Hugh Thomas Barrie (1860–1922), MP for N. Londonderry from 1906, the owner of a grain and produce business in Co. Londonderry. He led Ulster unionists during the 1917 convention and was later appointed Vice President of the Department of Agricultural and Technical Instruction for Ireland. *Who Was Who, 1916–28*, vol. 2 (London, 1929), p. 58.

36 Sir Richard Dawson Bates was born in Belfast in 1877 and educated at Coleraine Academical Institution. This Belfast–based solicitor became secretary to the Ulster Unionist Council in 1905, replacing T. H. Gibson. Bates retained this position until 1921, when he was appointed as the first Minister for Home Affairs for Northern Ireland. This key ministry had responsibility for some of the most controversial issues in Northern Ireland, including electoral affairs, law and order and local government. Bates remained at the Ministry of Home Affairs until 1943 and he acted as a legal adviser to the UWUC for many years. Connolly, *Oxford Companion to Irish History*, p. 40.

37 The Unionist Associations of Ireland were active from 1907, co–ordinating a propaganda campaign between southern and Ulster unionists via its Joint Committee. The Joint Committee was wound up with the unionist truce that was declared on the outbreak of World War I. The committee was not revived after the cessation of the conflict in 1918. See Patrick Buckland, *Irish Unionism, 1885–1923. A Documentary History* (Belfast, 1973).

a branch of the Ulster Women's Unionist Council in your Parliamentary Division.

As we are receiving requests from Women's Unionist Associations in England and Scotland to be 'linked up' with our branches you will see how important it is that branches should be formed and affiliated without delay.

Stamped envelope enclosed for reply.

We remain
Yours faithfully,

The Hon. Secretaries.

EAST BELFAST

Mrs McMordie, had a meeting in the East Belfast Unionist association room on 16th March, and sub-committees were formed to arrange for public meetings in the different wards of the Division.

NORTH ANTRIM

Mrs Kerr-Smiley[38] is calling a meeting in Ballymoney on 3rd April.

SOUTH ANTRIM

Mrs Charles C. Craig,[39] writes that she is taking steps to form a branch and will report progress later.

EAST ANTRIM

Mrs McCalmont,[40] has been away from home but will organize meetings in Larne, Ballyclare, Whitehouse & Carrickfergus.

CO. FERMANAGH

Lady Erne,[41] has arranged to have a meeting in Enniskillen on 19th April, and has asked Mrs Finlay, to go to Enniskillen on the 18th to talk matters over, and to attend the meeting the following day.

SOUTH DOWN

The Countess of Kilmorey[42] writes that the South Down Women's Unionist

38 Maud Kerr–Smiley was the daughter of Ernest L. Simpson of N. York. In 1905 she married Peter Kerr–Smiley, MP for N. Antrim from 1910. *Thom's Irish Who's Who*, p. 125.

39 Lilian Bowring Craig was the daughter of John Wimble of Long Ditton, Surrey. In 1897 she married Charles Curtis Craig, MP for S. Antrim from 1903. *Thom's Irish Who's Who*, p. 49.

40 Mrs James McCalmont was President of E. Antrim Women's Unionist Association and a Vice Chairman of the UWUC in 1922. She died in 1922. Information compiled from UWUC minutes (PRONI, D/1098/1/1–3).

41 Florence Mary, 4th Countess of Erne, the daughter of the 3rd Earl of Enniskillen. In 1870 she married John Henry George, the 4th Earl of Erne and MP for Enniskillen from 1868–80 and for Co. Fermanagh from 1880–05. He was Lord of the Treasury from 1876–80 and the Chairman of Fermanagh County Council in 1899, 1905 and 1908. The Countess of Erne died in 1924. *Thom's Irish Who's Who*, p. 74; *Dod's Peerage*, p. 298.

42 Ellen Constance, the 3rd Countess of Kilmorey, the 2nd daughter of Edward Holmes Baldock, MP for Shrewsbury. In 1881 she married Francis Charles Needham, the 3rd Earl of Kilmorey, a representative peer for Ireland from 1882–1915, Deputy Lieutenant, JP and High Sheriff for Co. Down in 1871 and MP for Newry 1871–74. The Countess of Kilmorey was widowed in 1915 and died in 1920. *Thom's Irish Who's Who*, p. 126; *Dod's Peerage*, p. 491.

Association was formed previous to the meeting in Belfast, and is progressing favourably.

CO. MONAGHAN

Lady Rossmore,[43] is ill and would like someone else to take up the work.

The Countess of Dartrey[44] has been abroad but will see what she can arrange.

MID ARMAGH

The Countess of Gosford[45] is in Cannes and can do nothing. Mrs J. B. Lonsdale,[46] cannot undertake to form a branch as she lives in London and is very seldom in the constituency; she will subscribe £3.3.0. per annum. Lady Stronge[47] also [away] from home but sent list of ladies who might help.

EAST TYRONE

Lady Ranfurly,[48] is unable to undertake any organization work.

NORTH BELFAST

Mrs Robert Thompson[49] is away from home and will not return till June.

Requests for Irish lady speakers and workers have been received from the Women's Amalgamated Unionist & Tariff Reform Association[50] London, through the Vice-President, and from the South Berks[hire] Unionist Association …

As there was not a unionist Member in West Belfast, the Secretary was instructed to send a copy of the circular letter re[.] the formation of branches to

43 Mittie, the 5th Countess of Rossmore, the daughter of Richard Christopher Naylor of Hooton Hall, Co. Chester. In 1882 she married Derrick Warner William, 5th Baron Rossmore, Grand Master of the Orange Order in Co. Monaghan in the 1880s. She was awarded an OBE in 1920 and was widowed in 1921. *Dod's Peerage*, pp 744–5.

44 Mary Frances, Baroness de Ros and the 3rd Countess of Dartrey. In 1878 she married Anthony Lucius Dawson, the 3rd Earl of Dartrey. *Thom's Irish Who's Who*, p. 55.

45 Lady Louisa Montagu, the 4th Countess of Gosford, the 2nd daughter of the 7th Duke of Manchester. In 1876 she married Archibald Brabazon Sparrow, the 4th Earl of Gosford, Lord of the Bedchamber to HRH Prince of Wales from 1886–1901 and Vice Chamberlain to HM Queen Alexandra in 1901. The Countess of Gosford was a former Lady of the Bedchamber to HM Queen Alexandra and was awarded a DBE in 1920. She died in 1944. *Dod's Peerage*, p. 368; *Thom's Irish Who's Who*, pp 93–4.

46 Mrs J. B. Lonsdale, wife of Sir John Brownlow Londsdale, 1st Baron Armaghdale and unionist MP for Mid Armagh. *Who Was Who*, vol. 2, p. 30.

47 Lady Ethel Margaret Stronge, the daughter of Col. and MrsBurges. In 1885 she married Sir James Henry, 5th Baronet Stronge, barrister, JP, Deputy Lieutenant in Co. Armagh and Grand Master of the Orange Lodge of Ireland. *Thom's Irish Who's Who*, p. 242.

48 The Hon. Constance Elizabeth, Countess Ranfurly, the daughter of 7th Viscount Charlemont. In 1880 she married Uchter John Mark Knox, the 5th Earl of Ranfurly, a Deputy Lieutenant and JP for Co. Tyrone, Lord in Waiting to HM, 1895–97, Governor of New Zealand, 1897–1904. He was appointed to the Privy Council of Ireland from 1905 and of Northern Ireland from 1923. *Thom's Irish Who's Who*, p. 214; *Dod's Peerage*, pp 713–4.

49 This was possibly the wife of Robert N. Thompson, MP.

50 The Women's Amalgamated Unionist and Tariff Reform Association (WAUTRA) was a conservative women's organisation which enjoyed close links with the National Union of Conservative Associations. After 1918 the organisation moved its headquarters to the Central Conservative Office as the Women's Unionist Association.

Mrs S. Cunningham.[51]

It was suggested by Mrs Finlay, and agreed to that where a Provisional Representative was unable personally to organize a branch she should be asked to nominate someone to do so in her place … Mrs Sinclair, suggested that some collecting cards should be sent to the Unionist Association in Dublin, for distribution in the South of Ireland; and this was agreed to.

7 April 1911

The sixth meeting of the Executive Committee was held in the U.W.U.C. office … at 11.30 a.m. … Lady Ewart (in the chair)[52] … A letter was read from Miss Graham Hope, Organizing Secretary of the Women's Amalgamated Unionist & Tariff Reform Association, London, offering to receive Irish Unionist workers in September and undertaking to arrange the work for them and pay their expenses; such workers to be of two classes; First, ladies capable at speaking at small cottage meetings, in village schools, or in ladies' drawing-rooms, possibly even at larger meetings; Second, women of any class who will be content to go from house to house talking to each individual occupier and explaining all the facts.

The Secretary then read the following.

REPORT OF WORK DONE SINCE LAST MEETING OF THE EXECUTIVE.

Since the last meeting of the Executive Committee held on 29th March meetings have been held in the following constituencies: –

NORTH ANTRIM:

On Monday 3rd April Mrs Kerr-Smiley held a meeting in the Town Hall Ballymoney, at which it was resolved to form the 'North Antrim Women's Unionist Association.' Mrs Kerr-Smiley has sent the Secretary a copy of the rules of the association from which it would appear that the association is to be affiliated to the Council, but otherwise no official information has been received.

EAST ANTRIM:

On Monday 3rd April Mrs McCalmont, had a meeting of ladies in Larne at which the Organizing Secretary was present. It was decided to form an East Antrim Association, to be affiliated to the Ulster Women's Unionist Council. A committee was formed to arrange for a public meeting in Larne soon after Easter; Mrs W. F. Coates undertook to form a branch in Carrickfergus and district and Mrs Kirkpatrick, one in Ballyclare; and Mrs McCalmont hopes to arrange for the starting of branches in the Whitehouse and Kells and Connor districts, and so to

51 Mrs Janet Cunningham, the daughter of Dunlop McCosh of Dalry, Ayrshire. In 1898 she married the Rt. Hon. Samuel Cunningham, a stockbroker and from 1921 a member of the Northern Ireland Senate. Janet Cunningham later served as a JP. *Thom's Irish Who's Who*, p. 53.

52 Twenty–three members were present at this meeting and there were nine apologies for non–attendance.

cover the whole constituency. A letter has been received from the Dowager Lady Smiley[53] stating that she cannot undertake any practical work as she is abroad for a great part of each year.

SOUTH ANTRIM:

Mrs Charles C. Craig writes to say she is having a meeting in Lisburn on 21st April to form a branch of the Ulster Women's Unionist Council, and that she also hopes to form a branch in Antrim.

The Secretary of the Ulster Unionist Council sent a list of 400 electors in Haddington and asked that ladies should be got to send newspapers and other literature to these people during the contest in that constituency; and several ladies have undertaken this work. On Wednesday 5th April Mrs Wheeler had a meeting of ladies willing to go as 'Missionaries' to English and Scotch constituencies. About a dozen ladies attended and a paper by Miss Ffolliott of Boyle was read, entitled 'Suggestions for Irish Unionist Missioners'; the paper was followed with close attention and all the ladies present took part in the discussion which followed.

With regard to the organization of branches in the various constituencies, Mrs Milliken suggested in the case of North Down as The Dowager Marchioness of Dufferin and Ava[54] was unable to help and as Mrs Mitchell-Thompson was too ill to undertake the work some other lady or ladies should be got to take the matter in hand. The Secretary was instructed to submit the following names of ladies in the constituency to Mr Mitchell-Thompson and ask him to nominate someone to act as Mrs Mitchell-Thompson's deputy in the matter, Mrs Dunbar-Buller,[55] Mrs McCance and Mrs Edwin Hughes.

Mrs Sinclair (Strabane) then proposed Motion No. 2 on the agenda. 'That the question of the 'big meeting' to be held in Belfast be discussed by the Executive'; and Mrs Wheeler seconded. A long discussion followed in the course of which it was agreed that it would be well to arrange to hold the meeting about the time of the Coronation; Mrs McMordie said the Colonial delegates to the Coronation [of

[53] Valerie, Dowager Lady Smiley, the youngest daughter of Sir Claude Champion de Crespigny, 4th Baronet. In 1903 she married Sir John Smiley, 2nd Baronet, who contested seats as a unionist candidate in W. Belfast in January 1906 and in December 1910. *Thom's Irish Who's Who*, p. 233; *Dod's Peerage*, p. 796.

[54] Hariot, Marchioness of Dufferin and Ava was born in 1843, the eldest daughter of Archibald Rowan Hamilton, Esq. of Killyleagh Castle in Co. Down. On 23 October 1862 she married Frederick Temple Blackwood, the 1st Marquis of Dufferin and Ava. Her husband was Governor General of Canada from 1872–78, British Ambassador to Russia in 1879 and to Turkey from 1881–82. He also served as Viceroy of India from 1884–88, British Ambassador to Italy from 1888–88 and to France in 1892. The family home was Clandeboye in Co. Down. Hariot was awarded the freedom of the city of Belfast in 1912. She was granted a DBE in 1917 and was a Lady of the Imperial Order of the Crown of India and a Lady of the Royal Order of Victoria and Albert. She was also awarded the George Cross of the Turkish Order of the Shefkat and the Persian Order of the Lion and the Sun. From 1921–36 she was a Vice President of the UWUC. She died on 25 October 1936. *Thom's Irish Who's Who*, pp 69–70.

[55] Georgina Dunbar–Buller, the only surviving child of George Dunbar, Deputy Lieutenant, JP and MP of Woburn, Co. Down. In 1890 she married Charles William Dunbar–Buller, Deputy Lieutenant, JP and High Sheriff of Co. Down. She died in 1920. *Thom's Irish Who's Who*, p. 70.

George V] were to be in Belfast on the first Monday in June, but as it was pointed out that the first Monday in June would be Whit Monday it was considered it would be impossible to get the Railway Co[mpany]'s to make arrangements to convey a large number of delegates to Belfast on that date. The Secretary was instructed to write to the Vice-President[56] and ask for her views on the question, at the same time pointing out that members of the country branches expected something of the kind, and that it would stimulate the enrolment of members, also that it would help our 'missionaries' in England and Scotland by calling attention to our work. Mrs Sinclair (Strabane) moved and Mrs G. H. Clarke seconded Motion No.3 on the agenda 'That steps should be immediately taken to provide, train and send out when and where required suitable women workers; and that being a most responsible business five members of the Executive be appointed to sit jointly with the men's five named representatives to consider the matter as a whole, and to report to the next meeting of the Executive. Mr Hamill to act as Secretary to this joint special meeting'. Passed unanimously. Mrs Thos. Sinclair proposed and Mrs Kelly seconded that the following be the five ladies above mentioned, Mrs Wheeler, Mrs Mercier-Clements, Miss Ferguson, Mrs Sinclair (Strabane) and Mrs Milliken. This was passed unanimously … Mrs Thomas Sinclair then proposed and Mrs Mercier-Clements seconded that the Wives of the Unionist Peers and of Ulster Unionist Members of Parliament be co-opted to the Executive Committee. This was passed unanimously.

21 April 1911

The seventh meeting of the Executive Committee was held in the U.W.U.C. office at 33 Ocean Buildings … at 11.30 a.m. … [Theresa] The Marchioness of Londonderry (in the chair) … Arising out of the minutes the question of the 'big meeting' was then discussed and the Vice-President expressed her opinion that as the papers would for the next month or two be full of news about the Coronation [of George V] and the various events connected therewith so that a demonstration in Belfast would not receive much, if any [press] attention, nor be properly reported.

After some discussion the following motion proposed by Lady Londonderry and seconded by Mrs Mercier-Clements was passed unanimously 'that unless a Home Rule Bill is in the meantime brought into the House of Commons we decide not to have the big meeting until the early autumn'. Correspondence was read which had passed between Mrs Thomas Sinclair and Mrs Arnold-Forster[57] on the subject of workers being sent to England by the Ulster Women's Unionist Council to work

56 Theresa, 6th Marchioness of Londonderry.

57 Mary, the wife of Hugh Oakley Arnold–Foster (1855–1909), unionist MP for West Belfast from 1892–1906 and for Croyden from 1906–09. He was appointed Secretary to the Admiralty in 1901 and Secretary of State for War, 1903–05. *The Dictionary of National Biography: The Concise Dictionary, Part II, 1901–70* (Oxford, 1982), p. 75.

under the Women's Amalgamated Unionist and Tariff Reform Association and it was agreed that the following letter should be sent to Mrs Arnold-Forster by the Vice-President:–

Dear Madam,

Your letters to Mrs Thomas Sinclair have been laid before the Executive Committee of the Ulster Women's Unionist Council, and I have been asked to reply as follows:–

As we understand that our members are being asked to speak solely on the question of Home Rule we have much pleasure in accepting the invitation extended to us by your association and shall be glad to work with you on the same lines as in 1893.[58]

Would you kindly let us know exactly what you propose with regard to Expenses?

We hope that your Committee will be most careful when advertising any of our speakers to make it quite clear that they are concerned solely with the question of the Union between Great Britain and Ireland and with nothing else.

Also with regard to any ladies you send over here, we shall be very pleased to receive and help ladies coming to acquire practical local knowledge on the question of the Union and will offer them hospitality; but as aforesaid under our Constitution we are precluded from touching any other subject …

A letter from Mrs Thomas Sinclair was read suggesting that cards be ordered of a size to fit an ordinary envelope giving the address of the Ulster Women's Unionist Council and the names of the office-bearers as printed on the Council's notepaper, and which could be sent to anyone requiring information about the Council. On the proposal of Mrs Thomas Sinclair seconded by Lady Dixon it was unanimously agreed that the Secretary be instructed to get these cards printed.

A letter from the Secretary of the Women's Unionist Association (west of Scotland) asking that arrangements should be made to send two ladies to work in Scotland for some time, and a telegram from Mrs Marshall, Greenock asking that an Irish lady be sent over to address a drawing-room meeting there on 26th April, were both referred to the Standing Committee re[.] workers and delegates.

The Secretary then read the following:–

REPORT OF WORK DONE SINCE THE LAST MEETING OF EXECUTIVE.

In accordance with the letter of the 6th April received from the Secretary of the Ulster Unionist Council the following six ladies went to Haddingtonshire to canvass on behalf of the Unionist candidate, Mrs & Miss Wetherall of Ballycastle[,] Co. Antrim, Miss Edith McCausland of Garvagh, Mrs George Wheeler, Mrs Mercier-Clements and Miss Katherine Grange of Belfast.

EAST ANTRIM: On the 10th April a meeting of ladies summoned by Mrs W. F. Coates was held in the Y.M.C.A. Carrickfergus. It was resolved to from a Carrickfergus Branch of the East Antrim Women's

[58] This is a reference to the fundraising, petitioning and canvassing work that unionist women conducted in opposition to Gladstone's second Home Rule Bill in 1893.

Unionist Association, and the Organizing Secretary who was present explained the necessary steps and details of organization. Public meetings are to be held in Larne, Carrickfergus and Ballyclare on the 2nd, 3rd, & 4th May, at which Mrs Sinclair of Strabane is to speak.

North Derry Women's Unionist Association has been affiliated to the Council.

EAST BELFAST: On Tuesday 11th April Mrs McMordie invited a number of ladies to meet at Cabin Hill. Mrs Sinclair of Strabane gave a most interesting address; and afterwards, in response to an appeal from Mrs Geo. Wheeler, several of those present volunteered for various kinds of active work.

The same evening a most successful public meeting, arranged by Mrs John Lowry, was held in Belmont Lecture Hall. Lady Ewart presided and the speakers included Mrs McMordie, Mrs Sinclair of Strabane, Mrs Mercier-Clements, Mr Charles Henderson and Rev. Dr. MacDermott.

At the close of the meeting more ladies volunteered for work; and a few days later the Secretary received from Mrs Lowry a further list of active workers.

CO. FERMANAGH: On the 19th April a meeting of ladies presided over by the Countess of Erne was held in the Town Hall[,] Enniskillen, at which Mrs Finlay one of the Hon. Secs. of the Ulster Women's Unionist Council was present. It was decided to form a Women's Unionist Association to be affiliated to the Council …

Mrs Finlay proposed and Lady Jaffe seconded motion No 3 on the agenda:–

'That it be an instruction to the Affiliation Committee to take steps immediately to put into force the resolution passed at the second meeting of the Executive, viz:– "That the Executive earnestly hope a branch of the Ulster Women's Unionist Council will be started at once in every Parliamentary Division in Ulster".'

This was passed unanimously.

Mrs Thomas Sinclair proposed and Mrs Finlay seconded motion No 4 on the agenda:–

'that steps be at once taken to collect funds for the Ulster Women's Unionist Council and cards be issued.'

This was passed unanimously and the Secretary was instructed to see about printing the cards.

This concluded the business.

5 May 1911

The eighth meeting of the Executive Committee was held in the office[,] 33 Ocean Buildings at 11.30 a.m. ... Mrs Mosse presided[59] ... The Executive Committee authorized the Standing Committee in case workers were asked for by the West of Scotland Unionist Association, or Newbury to apply to the Hon. Treasurers for funds for their travelling expenses ... the Secretary [Mr. J. M. Hamill] be instructed to write to the President [Mary Anne, 2nd Duchess of Abercorn] to ask her to take steps to start branches [of the Ulster Women's Unionist Council] in the Parliamentary Divisions in Co. Donegal ... it was resolved that a leaflet setting forth the advantages etc., of affiliation as suggested by Mrs Sinclair be printed at once and as cheaply as possible, and that the Secretary be instructed to send copies to the Hon. Secs. of all branches for distribution amongst their members ... it was resolved 'That a list of Ulster women living out of Ulster be kept in the office, with a view to their co-operation' ... Letters were read from the West of Scotland Unionist Association, the East & West of Scotland Liberal Unionist Association[60] and the North Derry Women's Unionist Association. In reply to the latter, the Secretary [Mr. J.M. Hamill] was instructed to ask them to contribute to the funds of the Ulster Women's Unionist Council, as they might find them selves (*sic*) able to do so. This concluded the business.

19 May 1911

The ninth meeting of the Executive Committee was held ... at 11.30 a.m. in the U.W.U.C. office[,] 33 Ocean Buildings Belfast ... Mrs McMordie (in the chair)[61] ... A letter was read from the Vice-President[62] enclosing a letter from the Hon. Mrs Ivor Maxse, Chairman of the Women's Amalgamated Unionist & Tariff Reform Association on the question of workers being sent to England in the Autumn. Mrs Maxse's letter stated that arrangements would be made by the branch secretaries of the W.A.U.T.R.A. to provide hospitality for our workers, to get up meetings and generally to give them every facility for their work; that a fund would be raised to pay the expenses of these ladies and that it was hoped that the Men's Unionist Associations of Ireland would assist; Mrs Maxse suggested that the ladies should receive as much as they did in 1894, that is to say the sum of about 10/- a week to cover wear and tear and other expenses. Mrs Maxse also stated that her association hope to send some of their most experienced lady speakers and missionaries to

59 Twelve members were present at this meeting and there were eight apologies for non–attendance.

60 The Liberal Unionist Association was created following the party split which occurred in Liberal ranks after W. E. Gladstone's conversion to home rule for Ireland in 1885. Liberals, who collaborated with Conservatives to oppose the 1st Home Rule Bill of 1886, were subsequently known as Liberal Unionists and a Liberal Unionist Party was formed in Britain in the months of May and June 1886. An Ulster Liberal Unionist Association was formed in June 1886. See Buckland, *Irish Unionism, 1885–1923.*

61 Ten members were present at this meeting and there were twelve apologies for non–attendance.

62 Theresa, 6th Marchioness of Londonderry.

Ireland in the course of the summer to study the Home Rule question; and they would pay these ladies fees, but they hoped that hospitality would be provided here. The committee instructed the Secretary to write saying that they had much pleasure in accepting the offer of the W.A.U.T.R.A. on the terms on which it was made.

A letter was read from Messers. Sharman D. Neill Ltd. suggesting that the Council should have a badge, and submitting designs. It was proposed by Mrs Wheeler, seconded by Mrs Finlay, that the Council should adopt the same badge as the Unionist Clubs, provided the latter did not object. The Secretary was instructed to write to the various affiliated associations asking how many badges each would be prepared to take, and if a sufficient number were guaranteed it was decided to order 2,000. The price of the badges was fixed at 1/– each … A report of the Affiliation Committee was then read. The report stated that two more branches had been affiliated – The Mid-Tyrone Women's Unionist Association and The Portadown Women's Unionist Association. The report also stated that an application for affiliation had been received from the Londonderry Women's Unionist Registration Association. As this association is already affiliated to the Women's Amalgamated Unionist & Tariff Reform Association and therefore presumably includes Tariff Reform among its objectives the Committee felt some difficulty in dealing with the application and decided to refer the matter to the Executive Committee.[63] Meanwhile the Secretary was instructed to write to the Derry Association asking for definite information as to their rules and objects. The committee decided to postpone discussion on the position of the L.W.U.R.A. until a reply had been received to the Secretary's letter … Mrs Wheeler proposed and Miss Ferguson seconded motion No. 3 on [the] agenda 'That the question of contributions from Branch Associations and of their finances generally be discussed.'

After some discussion it was decided that a recommendation should be made to the four Belfast Branches when formed that all surplus funds after payment of their own expenses should be handed in to the central office.

Mrs McMordie proposed and Mrs Wheeler seconded that to secure uniformity in the case of the Belfast Branches they should be recommended to insert as one of their rules that members should pay an annual subscription from one penny to five shillings.

This was passed unanimously.

Mrs McMordie suggested that the Secretary should draft a rule which might be adopted by all four Belfast Branches.

In the absence of Mrs Sinclair of Strabane, Mrs Wheeler proposed motion No. 4 'That a suitable form of message be drafted which the Secretary be empowered to send to public meetings etc., in England and Scotland when asked for'; Miss Connor seconded. Mrs Finlay moved as an amendment 'That the Secretary be authorised to send a suitable message when required.' Mrs Mercier-Clements

63 This difficulty can be explained by the fact that the UWUC's constitution stated that opposition to home rule was the sole objective of the organisation. See appendix I.

seconded this which was passed unanimously.

Motion No. 5 on [the] agenda 'That Lady Arthur Hill[64] be requested to assist in organizing programmes of patriotic music suitable for our meetings' was moved by Mrs Wheeler seconded by Miss Ferguson, and passed unanimously and the Secretary was instructed to write to Lady Arthur Hill on the matter.

7 June 1911

The tenth meeting of the Executive Committee was held in the U.W.U.C. office at 33 Ocean Buildings … at 11.30 a.m. [Theresa] The Marchioness of Londonderry (Vice-President) presided[65] … The report of the Standing Committee was then read; it stated that in response to the request from the South Berks[hire] Conservative Association, two ladies[,] Mrs Wetherall of Ballycastle and Miss Johnston of Londonderry have been sent to conduct an Anti-Home Rule campaign in South Berks[hire] and South Somerset. The Report contained the following recommendation to the Executive Committee 'That ladies going to speak for Branches on behalf of the Ulster Women's Unionist Council, get second class fare and a sufficient allowance to cover incidental expenses; and that this should also apply to the expenses of the Organizing Secretary when travelling on behalf of the Council.'

Lady Londonderry proposed and Mrs Craig seconded that slips be printed and given to every delegate on behalf of the Council to be used as an introductory paragraph; such slips to be worded as follows:–

'I want to make it clear that I am here as an Irishwoman to explain the dangers that will arise to your country and mine by the adoption of the Government policy of Home Rule and that I do not concern myself with the other questions in which the English Unionist may be interested.'[66] The following recommendations were also made by the Standing Committee and passed unanimously.

(a) 'That receipt forms, schedules of expenses and report forms for the use of workers sent to England and Scotland, similar to those used by the Ulster Unionist Council, be printed.'
(b) 'That Mrs Wheeler's class of 'Active Workers' be taken over by the Executive Committee for the future. Mrs Wheeler to continue to convene the meetings.'
(c) 'That during the summer months that Organizing Secretary should visit each of the Branches to stir up the local workers and keep them in touch with the central office.'

The Standing Committee further recommended 'That the Organizing Secretary be

64 Lady Annie Hill, the daughter of James Fortescue Harrison, a former MP. In 1877 she became the second wife of the Rt. Hon. Lord Arthur William Hill, a son of the 4th Marquess of Downshire. He was a Deputy Lieutenant and JP for Co. Down and a JP in Berkshire. He was also MP for Co. Down from 1880–85 and for W. Down from 1885–98 and 1907–08. *Thom's Irish Who's Who*, p. 111.

65 Fourteen members were present at this meeting and there were nine apologies for non-attendance.

66 For example, tariff reform.

instructed to visit the office of the Irish Unionist Alliance[67] in Dublin and the office of the Women's Amalgamated Unionist & Tariff Reform Association in London, and that in the latter case his visit should coincide with the Annual Conference of Branch Secretaries to be held on 4th July.'

After some discussion it was decided that it was not necessary for the Secretary to go either to Dublin or London at present.

Mrs Finlay proposed and Miss Ferguson seconded Motion No. 2 on the agenda:– 'That the question of the Affiliation of Irish Women's Unionist Associations outside Ulster with the Ulster Women's Unionist Council be discussed.'

The Vice-President suggested that it would be time enough to arrange this when an Association outside Ulster approached the U.W.U.C. on the matter … In the absence of Mrs Sinclair of Strabane, Mrs Wheeler proposed Motion No. 5 on the agenda:–

'That suitable postcards be ordered and kept in stock by Mr Hamill for members to purchase from him. The cards to be printed with the Red Hand, Union Jack or other such design as may be approved and the name of the Council.'

After some discussion the Committee decided that it would not be advisable to use such postcards as they would be too conspicuous in the post.

Lady Londonderry proposed and Mrs Thomas Sinclair seconded that a letter be sent to Mrs Arnold-Forster expressing the sympathy of the Executive Committee with her on the death of her father, Professor Story-Maskelyne.

This was passed unanimously.

This concluded the business.

16 June 1911

A Special Meeting of the Executive Committee of the Ulster Women's Unionist Council was held in the U.W.U.C. office[,] 33 Ocean Buildings, Belfast … at 11.30 a.m. … Mrs McMordie (in the chair)[68] … Mrs Finlay explained that the meeting had been called at the request of Miss F. E. Henderson and herself in view of the fact that the Parliament Bill would probably be introduced into the House of Lords on Monday 26th June 1911 and the Hon. Secretaries felt that a strong protest should be made by the women of Ulster against the inclusion of Home Rule in the operation of the Bill.

Mrs Finlay also reported that a resolution had been drafted and sent to the

67 The Irish Unionist Alliance was the successor of the Irish Loyal and Patriotic Union. Established in 1891 the Irish Unionist Alliance employed a special organiser to mobilise unionists in electoral constituencies, conducted electoral work and co–operated with unionist associations in England and Scotland. The Irish Unionist Alliance also had a Ladies' Committee which collected signatures for memorials, distributed propaganda and organised women with unionist sympathies into local associations. See Buckland, *Irish Unionism, 1885–1923*.

68 Fifteen women were present at this meeting and there were eleven apologies for non–attendance.

Secretaries of all the affiliated Associations with a request that those Associations should pass the resolution immediately.

Mrs Finlay proposed that the Executive Committee should pass the same resolution which read as follows:– …

'That the Ulster Women's Unionist Council protest in the strongest manner against the passing of any Home Rule Bill for Ireland as they know that the civil and religious liberty of the women of Ireland and the security of their homes can only be guaranteed under the Legislative Union of Great Britain and Ireland. Therefore they demand that the question of Home Rule in any shape or form be entirely excluded from the operation of the Parliament Bill; and they respectfully request the Unionist Members of the House of Lords to use every effort to secure this result. And that copies of this resolution be sent to the Marquis of Lansdowne,[69] the Marquis of Londonderry,[70] and the Irish Unionist Representative Peers.' [71]

Mrs Andrews seconded the resolution which was carried unanimously.

Mrs Mercier-Clements kindly offered to present a flag, to be displayed from the office window on public holidays etc.,

This concluded the business.

21 July 1911

The eleventh meeting of the Executive Committee was held … at 11-30 a.m. in the U.W.U.C. office[,] 33 Ocean Buildings Belfast … Lady Dixon (in the chair)[72] … [The] Secretary read the following report:-

REPORT OF WORK DONE.

Since the meeting of the Executive Committee on 7th June four new Women's Unionist Associations have been formed and affiliated to the Council – Antrim, South Belfast, Co. Monaghan and Mid-Armagh.

A letter was received from the Women's Amalgamated Unionist and Tariff Reform Association inviting the Secretary to attend the Annual Conference of the Association on 3rd & 4th July, and to speak in support of the proposal to have an

69 Henry Charles Keith Petty–Fitzmaurice, 5th Marquis of Lansdowne (1845–1927), served as Governor–General of Canada from 1883–88, Viceroy of India, 1888–94, Secretary of State for War, 1895–1900 and Secretary of State for Foreign Affairs from 1900–05. In 1903 he was appointed leader of the Conservatives in the House of Lords. *Who Was Who*, vol. 2, p. 606.

70 Charles Vane–Tempest Stewart, the 6th Marquis of Londonderry was Lord Lieutenant of Ireland from 1886–89, President of the Board of Education from 1902–05 and President of the Ulster Unionist Council. He was also HM Lieutenant for Co. Down from 1902 and for Belfast from 1900–03. He was a unionist MP for Co. Down from 1878–84. *Thom's Irish Who's Who*, p. 139.

71 The Parliament Bill was passed into law in August 1911 and removed the House of Lord's power of ultimate veto, replacing it with a delaying power. This removed the last constitutional bulwark against Home Rule.

72 Twenty members were present at this meeting and there were five apologies for non–attendance.

Anti-Home Rule Campaign in England & Scotland during the Autumn. In view of the decision come to by the Executive Committee the Secretary was unable to accept the invitation and there was not time to summon a meeting of the Executive Committee before the date of the Conference. The Secretary reported that matter to the Standing Committee re[.] Workers & Delegates; and as the Committee considered it most desirable that the Ulster Women's Unionist Council should be represented at the Conference in order to bring the work of the council prominently before the various delegates and members of the Women's Amalgamated Unionist & Tariff Reform Association, to arouse their interest and secure their co-operation when the Irish workers are sent over in the Autumn, the Secretary was instructed to send a statement of the facts to the Vice-President,[73] that she might take whatever steps she considered advisable.

The Vice-President wired back instructing the Secretary to attend the Conference, which he did.

He attended two private meetings of the Association and the large public meeting in the Queen's Hall. At the first private meeting Miss Austen Park, Treasurer of the W.A.U.T.R.A. introduced the subject of the Anti-Home Rule Campaign to be carried out in England & Scotland during the Autumn and the scheme was most enthusiastically received. The Secretary was also invited to various social functions in connection with the Conference at which he had the opportunity of discussing the Home Rule question and the work of the Ulster Women's Unionist Council with ladies from all parts of England and Scotland.

In addition to the various meetings held to form new Associations there was also a public meeting in Ballymoney on Monday 3rd July, at which the Council was represented by Mrs Sinclair (of Strabane) and Mrs Finlay (Hon. Sec.)

Mrs Mercier-Clements has presented a Union Jack and flag pole to the Council … A letter was read from the South Belfast Women's Unionist Association asking that the Committee of that Association might have permission to hold their meetings in the U.W.U.C. office, provided they arrange suitable times with the Secretary. Mrs Finlay proposed that this permission should be granted to the Committees of all four Belfast Affiliated Associations and this was unanimously agreed to by the Committee.

The Secretary then read the report of the Sub-Committee re[.] badges … The Committee decided to recommend the purchase of badges, provided that a suitable badge could be obtained which could be sold to members at 6d. each, and the Committee also consider that if the affiliated Associations undertook to purchase eight or nine hundred badges the Executive would be safe in ordering 1,000 to begin with.

The committee consider that it would not be advisable to allow the badges to be sold indiscriminately in a shop, but that the sale should be entirely controlled by the Central Office.

[73] Theresa, 6th Marchioness of Londonderry.

As regards the design for a badge, the Committee approve of a design submitted by the Secretary and recommend the Executive to adopt this design if ordering badges.

The Committee also recommend that the design selected for the badge should be registered to prevent its being copied and sold by outsiders.

After some discussion it was proposed by Mrs McMordie seconded by Mrs McCalmont and passed unanimously that the Secretary be instructed to order 1,000 badges of the design submitted.

The next business was to arrange the Autumn Campaign in England and Scotland and for the reception of delegates from the Women's Amalgamated Unionist & Tariff Reform Association on their visit to Ireland. The Secretary reported that when in London he had undertaken that the Council would send at least twenty workers to begin with, in the Autumn, this was approved of by the Committee.

A letter was read from the Secretary of the North Derry Women's Amalgamated Unionist & Tariff Reform Association, to the effect that, that Association intended to pay for, and send out its own workers. On the proposal of Mrs McMordie, seconded by Lady Dunleath[74] the Secretary was instructed to inform the North Derry Association that their workers could not be recognized by and sent under the auspices of the Council unless their names had been submitted to, and approved by the Standing Committee re[.] workers and delegates.

In connection with the visit of the delegates from the W.A.U.T.R.A. [to Ulster] the Standing Committee recommend that these ladies should be sent first to the North West of Ulster to see the condition of affairs in a Nationalist district, and should then be brought to the loyal districts in the East to contrast the prosperity, and industry which prevailed there and that for this purpose Mrs Sinclair of Strabane had kindly offered to entertain two of the ladies and show them round Donegal, Tyrone and Derry for ten days or a fortnight and it is hoped that the Derry ladies will arrange to take the remaining ladies; and that several members of the Executive Committee had kindly offered to provide hospitality for the English delegates during their stay in Belfast and the neighbourhood.

These arrangements were approved of by the Committee.

Mrs Wheeler then proposed Motion No.3 on the agenda:–

'That arrangements be made for a[n] Amateur Concert party with a good speaker on the Home Rule question to visit each organized branch during the coming Autumn & Winter and that notice of this be given to Branches early in September so that dates may be fixed.' Miss Tracey seconded and the resolution passed unanimously. Mrs McMordie proposed and Lady Jaffe seconded that Mrs Wheeler be asked to organize and arrange for the party and this was agreed to unanimously.

74 Lady Norah Dunleath, DBE, daughter of the Hon. Somerset Ward. In 1881 she married Henry Lyle Mulholland, Lord Dunleath, a JP, Deputy Lieutenant and Sheriff of Co. Down and MP for N. Londonderry from 1885–95. *Thom's Irish Who's Who*, p. 71.

Mrs Wheeler proposed Motion No. 4 on the agenda:–

'That arrangements be made to have literature distributed at the Scotch daylight boat'[,] this was seconded by Mrs Mercier-Clements and passed unanimously.

It was proposed by Mrs Andrews seconded by Mrs Riddell and passed unanimously that the arrangements for this distribution be left to the Standing Committee re[.] workers and delegates.

This concluded the business.

25 August 1911

The twelfth meeting of the Executive Committee was held ... at 11-30 a.m. in the U.W.U.C. office[,] 33 Ocean Buildings Belfast ... Mrs McCalmont (in the chair)[75] ... The business on the agenda was to make arrangements for:–

1 The holding of a Monster Demonstration of all women Unionists in Ulster, in connection with those to be held by the Men of Ulster on September 23rd and 26th.
2 The presentation of an address to Sir Edward Carson[76] in co-operation with all the other Unionist Organizations in Ulster.

Mrs Finlay (Hon. Sec.) who, at the request of the Secretary, was in charge of the business of the office during his absence on holidays, reported that she had had a communication from Captain Craig, in which he said Sir Edward Carson, K.C. M.P. was to visit Ulster on September 23rd and that a great demonstration was to be held at Craigavon to welcome him. As the various Unionist Organizations and the Orangemen had decided to present addresses to Sir Edward Carson at this meeting, Capt[.] Craig suggested that the Ulster Women's Unionist Council might like to do so also, and possibly hold a Women's demonstration of some sort on Wednesday September 27th, to follow the men's meetings.

75 Thirteen members were present at this meeting and there were twelve apologies for non–attendance.

76 Born in 1853 in Dublin and educated at Arlington House and Trinity College, Dublin, Edward Carson was called to the Irish bar in 1889. Government prosecutor in its case against the Plan of Campaign, 1889–91, he was appointed Irish Solicitor General in 1892. He was a unionist MP for Dublin University from 1892–1918. Carson was knighted in 1900 and served as Solicitor General from 1900–06. He was leader of the Irish Unionist Party from 1910 and moved for the exclusion of Ulster from the third Home Rule Bill in September 1913. In the same year he subscribed £10,000 to the Ulster Volunteer Force and claimed responsibility for the UVF's gun–running at Larne in the House of Commons in April 1914. He represented Ulster at the Buckingham Palace Conference in July 1914 and was appointed Attorney General in 1915, a position he resigned in October 1916. In December of that year he was appointed First Lord of the Admiralty. Carson joined the Cabinet in July 1917 but resigned in January 1918 upon discovering that the Prime Minister at the time, David Lloyd George, was drafting a Home Rule Bill for the 32 counties of Ireland. Carson was an MP for the Duncairn district of Belfast from 1918–21. He resigned as unionist leader in 1921 and served as Lord of Appeal from 1921–29. Created a life peer as Baron Carson of Duncairn in 1921, he died on 22 October 1935. See *Thom's Irish Who's Who*, p. 33 and A. T. Q. Stewart, *Edward Carson* (Dublin, 1981).

With regard to the question of a demonstration of Unionist Women a letter was read from Mrs Thomas Sinclair pointing out the serious risk of bringing a large number of women into the city [of Belfast] at the present time, owing to the prevailing industrial disturbance, as such a course might entail serious rioting which would tell very strongly against the Unionist Cause.[77] It was proposed by Lady Anderson, seconded by Mrs H. C. Kelly and passed unanimously that no demonstration should be held until the Home Rule scheme took a more concrete form and the [Home Rule] Bill was actually before the country. This re-affirming what had already been passed at a previous meeting by the advice of the Chairman of the U.W.U.C.[78]

It was unanimously decided to present an address of welcome to Sir Edward Carson. The Hon. Sec. in charge, read a letter from the Chairman in which she intimated her approval of the proposal, and her willingness to present the address. It was decided that two other representative ladies should be appointed to accompany the Chairman as a deputation from the Ulster Women's Unionist Council to Sir Edward Carson, but the selection of these two ladies was deferred till the Executive Meeting on September 8th, as so many members of the Executive were still away from home. The Hon. Sec. was asked to draw the attention of the Chairman to the date of the meeting at which the addresses were to be presented, viz:– September 23rd. and to ask her would it be convenient for her to be in Belfast on that day.

The Hon. Sec. submitted a rough draft for the proposed address. After some discussion Mrs McMordie, Mrs Wheeler, Miss Connor and Mrs Finlay were appointed a Sub-Committee to prepare the final form of the address of welcome and to confer with Captain Craig on the details of the necessary arrangements of the 23rd September.

8 September 1911

The thirteenth meeting of the Executive Committee was held in the U.W.U.C. office[,] 33 Ocean Buildings, at 11-30 a.m. … Mrs McMordie (in the chair)[79] … Mrs Finlay, (Hon. Sec.) read a letter she had received from Miss Tonge, one of the delegates sent over by the Women's Amalgamated Unionist & Tariff Reform Association, in which Miss Tonge stated that 'Ulster needed rousing'. In this connection Mrs Wheeler called the attention of the Committee to a letter which had appeared in the 'Irish News' a few days before. In it Miss Tonge was reported to have said at a meeting in Armagh that since her arrival in Ireland she had unfortunately come across a great deal of what appeared to her to be apathy and

[77] On 15 June 1911 a national strike of seamen led by the National Sailors' and Fireman's Union began. In Belfast seamen began strike action on 15 July and soon dockers came out in sympathy. From August to October 1911 Belfast railwaymen and women spinners in linen mills also took strike action. See Austen Morgan, *Labour and Partition: The Belfast Working Class, 1905–23* (London, 1991).

[78] Theresa, 6th Marchioness of Londonderry was the Chairman of the UWUC from 1911–13.

[79] Twelve members were present at this meeting and there were thirteen apologies for non–attendance.

indifference on the question of Home Rule, etc. Mrs Wheeler had written asking Miss Tonge for a correct version of her speech and she had replied that the quotation as given in the 'Irish News' was accurate. The Committee felt that Miss Tonge's attitude and statements were most unfortunate and calculated to do serious injury to the cause; and that any other ladies sent over here should be warned to be more careful as otherwise their visits would do more harm than good. The Committee also asked Mrs Finlay to write to Miss Tonge very strongly on the matter.

The report of the Standing Committee re[.] workers and delegates stated that at their meeting on Monday 4th September 1911, that Committee was informed that several men were anxious to be sent as workers to England & Scotland under the auspices of the Ulster Women's Unionist Council; but that the Committee felt that this was a matter which must be decided by the Executive Committee, and therefore wished to have it discussed at the meeting of the Executive committee on 8th September 1911.

The Committee felt that this question could not be dealt with hastily and therefore decided to postpone consideration of it till their next meeting, when it could be put on the agenda and gone into fully. The Sub-Committee appointed to arrange for the presentation of an address to Sir Edward Carson submitted a draft of the address, which was approved on the motion of Miss Andrews[,] seconded by Miss Connor. (Copy [of the] address at [the] end of [the] minutes)

The Committee recommended that the address should be plainly engrossed on parchment with one or two illuminated capitals. This was also approved of and the Secretary was instructed to arrange for the engrossment at a cost of from 10/1 to £1.

Miss Connor proposed that the Marchioness of Londonderry (Vice-President)[,] Mrs McMordie and Mrs Thomas Andrews should form the deputation to present the address to Sir Edward Carson.

This was seconded by Miss Thompson and passed unanimously.

Mrs Wheeler in proposing Motion No. 2 on the agenda asked to be allowed to divide it into two parts; she therefore proposed 'That a Financial Report up to date of money received from private individuals and Branches should be prepared and hung in the Council Room.' Mrs Mercier-Clements seconded this.

Mrs Finlay moved as an amendment 'That the subscription from Branches be hung up but not those of private individuals.'

This amendment not being seconded fell to the ground.

Mrs Wheeler's proposal was put to the meeting and passed.

Mrs Wheeler then proposed 'That a similar list be published in the papers.' Mrs Mercier-Clements seconded and the motion was passed unanimously.

After some discussion it was decided to postpone the publication until 15th October to give an opportunity for any outstanding subscriptions to be sent in.

On the proposal of Mrs McMordie and seconded by Mrs Finlay the details of the matter were referred to the Finance Committee.

Mrs Wheeler proposed and Miss Ferguson seconded Motion No. 3 on the agenda 'That all Branch Secretaries and Secretaries of Sub-Divisions be invited to Belfast to consult together and to be spurred on to make a vigorous Autumn Campaign in their districts.' This was passed unanimously.

It was decided to hold the Conference on Friday afternoon 22nd September 1911 in order to give those attending the opportunity of waiting for the Demonstration of welcome to Sir Edward Carson on 23rd September.

Mrs Wheeler proposed Motion No. 4 on the agenda 'To discuss our representation in the English press during the Campaign.'

A letter from Miss Austen Park of the Women's Amalgamated Unionist & Tariff Reform Association was read in which Miss Park said that Miss Graham Hope[80] was willing to communicate with various Unionist Newspapers in England offering to get them information as to the work of the Ulster Women's Unionist Council from the Secretary of the Council.

Mrs Sinclair of Strabane also forwarded a letter from Mr. O'Mahony offering to interest the Editor of the Daily Express in the work of the Council. On the proposal of Miss Ferguson the Committee unanimously decided to accept both offers ... The Secretary [Mr. J.M. Hamill] was also instructed to write to a number of English and Scotch papers appealing to Irish women in England and to communicate with him and assist the work of the Council.

Mrs Wheeler suggested that the Council should subscribe to the Press Cutting Agency and so get a record of all references to the work of the Council which appeared in the various papers; and Mrs Thos. Andrews kindly offered to pay the subscription.

Miss Tracey proposed and Mrs Finlay seconded Motion No. 5 on the agenda 'That notices should be sent to all Branch Secretaries after each meeting of the Committee informing them of all arrangements arrived at for the general working of the Association'.

This passed unanimously.

To the Right Hon.
Sir Edward Carson. K.C. M.P.
Chairman of the Ulster Unionist Parliamentary Party

Dear Sir,

On Behalf of the Ulster Women's Unionist Council, we desire to extend to you our heartiest welcome of the occasion of your visit to Ulster.

We recall with deep satisfaction and gratitude the splendid services you have rendered to the Unionist Cause, in Parliament, on the Platform and in the Press, ever since the Home Rule Conflict was thrust upon us in 1886. We feel we are now on the eve of a more critical struggle than either of the two preceding ones on behalf of the Union.

80 These UWUC minutes note that Miss Graham Hope was the Organising Secretary of the Women's Amalgamated Unionist and Tariff Reform Association.

It is therefore essential that Unionists all over the United Kingdom, should close their ranks, and join together in the most strenuous efforts to defeat the destructive policy of the Government.
We believe that in Wholehearted Union lies our strength, and in the exercise of it, we shall beyond doubt repeat the previous victories of 1886 and 1893.

We realise that the civil and religious liberty of the women of Ireland and the security of their homes can only be guaranteed under the Legislative and Administrative Union of Great Britain and Ireland; we are deeply conscious of our responsibilities and are determined to take our full share in the conflict that lies before us.

Confident of your continued powerful and effective advocacy of the cause we beg to subscribe ourselves on behalf of the Ulster Women's Unionist Council,

Your faithful friends,

Theresa Londonderry. Chairman
Sarah A. Finlay.
Florence E. Henderson. Hon. Secretaries
Eleanor A. M. Tracey.

22 September 1911

[Conference of UWUC Branch Secretaries, held in the hall of the Young Women's Christian Association, 9 Donegall Square East, Belfast, chaired by the Countess of Kilmorey]. Over thirty secretaries and officials attended from various women's Unionist Associations throughout Ulster and several members of the Executive Committee were also present. ... The Secretary [Mr J. M. Hamill] of the Ulster Women's Unionist Council explained that the meeting had been called by order of the Executive Committee. The Committee felt that at the beginning of the Autumn and Winter Campaign the active officials of the various affiliated Associations should be brought together and given an opportunity of exchanging ideas on the best methods of carrying on the work of their various Associations, and that they should realize that they form part of a large and vigorous body, all working together for a common object and bound together by common aims and interests. The Committee did not propose to put anything before the meeting for discussion but rather hoped that those attending would themselves suggest points of interest and would exchange their ideas on any thing brought forward.

The first subject proposed for discussion was the advisability of linking women's Unionist Associations in Ireland with similar Associations in England, and the Chairman called on Miss Johnston (Secretary of South Down W.U.A.) to open the discussion ... Miss Johnston suggested that the various affiliated Associations should be linked up with Associations in England in the ways the Men's Clubs had adopted.

Mrs Sinclair suggested that a list should be got of the Hundred constituencies in

England best worthy of attack, these should be dealt with first.

Mrs Lowry mentioned that in the last Anti-Home Rule Campaign [of 1893] much good had been done by sending newspapers and Unionist literature to public houses throughout England as both Radicals and Conservatives met there and discussed the question in a less partisan spirit than in their own clubs. The Secretary pointed out that as there were only between 25 and 30 Women's Unionist Associations formed in Ulster and if these were closely linked up with individual Associations in England they would be compelled to confine their efforts to a comparatively small area.

Lists of Radical voters were received from time to time in the central office and sent to such of the Branch Secretaries as were willing to take them; the members of the Branch Associations were then asked to send newspapers and literature to the address given on those lists. In this way the efforts of various Associations could be more widely spread and could be systematically directed from the central office ... Miss Clements, Secretary of (East Cavan W.U.A.) asked for suggestions on the best way to work up a district in which no one could be got to undertake the office of district Secretary, and in reply Mrs Sinclair gave a valuable outline of the best method to organize a constituency.

Mrs Sinclair brought forward the question of Mixed Marriages. She said that this was a question which effected women particularly and in connection with which women should make a special effort. Mrs Sinclair said that 10,000 women in Edinburgh were banded together in an effort to obtain a strict enforcement of that law of the land on this matter and the Unionist Women of Ulster should not be behind in their efforts. After considerable discussion it was suggested that a resolution should be drafted and sent to the papers on this matter. But on the proposal of Mrs Finlay seconded by Mrs Mercier–Clements it was considered better to recommend the Executive Committee to consider the question of Mixed Marriages and the advisability of presenting a petition to Parliament on the matter. This was unanimously agreed to ... In the evening Lady Crawford[81] kindly gave a reception at Mount Randal for those attending the Conference. Unfortunately the fear of trouble on the various railways prevented some of those who would have otherwise done so from waiting, but a considerable number availed themselves of Lady Crawford's kindness and spent a very pleasant evening.

25 September 1911

The fourteenth meeting of the Executive Committee was held in the U.W.U.C. office[,] 33 Ocean Buildings[,] Belfast, at 11-30 a.m. ... Mrs McMordie (in the chair)[82] ... The Secretary reported that, in the unavoidable absence of the Vice-President, the Countess of Erne had presented the address to

[81] Lady Annie Crawford, wife of Sir William Crawford (1840–1922), a JP for Belfast and Chairman of York Street Flax Spinning Company Limited in Belfast. *Who Was Who*, vol. 2, p. 243.

[82] Ten members were present at this meeting and there were eight apologies for non–attendance.

Sir Edward Carson on behalf of the Council.

A letter was read from Miss Graham Hope[,] Secretary of the Women's Amalgamated Unionist & Tariff Reform Association, expressing regret at the remarks made by Miss Tonge in Armagh, and also sending good wishes for the demonstration on 23rd September. A letter was also read from Lady Hervey Bruce (President of the North Derry Women's Unionist Association) saying that she had been asked to get up an Anti-Home Rule Meeting in Nottingham and asking would the Council help her with funds and speakers. The Secretary was instructed to consult the Secretary of the Ulster Unionist Council in the matter with a view to their co-operation ... Mrs Mercier-Clements proposed and Miss Tracey seconded 'That the best thanks of the Executive Committee be conveyed to Lady Crawford for her kindness in entertaining the Branch Secretaries and members of the Executive Committee on Friday 22nd September 1911'. This was passed unanimously.

In pursuance of the resolutions passed at the Secretaries' Conference the Committee proceeded to discuss the question of mixed marriages and the action to be taken by the Council in the matter.

On the proposal of Mrs Lowry seconded by Mrs King-Kerr the Committee unanimously decided to prepare a petition to Parliament from the women of Ulster. The following were selected as a Committee to draft the petition:–

Mrs Finlay, Miss Connor and Mrs Lowry with Mr. James Chambers K.C.M.P.[,][83] Mr. Dawson Bates, The Rev. Dr. MacDermot, The Right Rev. The Lord Bishop of Down, Connor & Dromore, The Rev. W. J. Rossington, The Rev. J. Rosenzweig, The Vice-President of the Methodist Conference, representatives of the Baptist, Congregational and Moravian Churches and the Secretary.

The next business was No.2 on the agenda 'To discuss the advisability of sending out men to work on behalf of the Ulster Women's Unionist Council'.

Mrs Mercier-Clements said that several men were anxious to do Unionist work in England but would prefer not to go under the Ulster Unionist Council; they asked to be paid nothing but their actual travelling expenses as they hoped to obtain hospitality through the various Unionist Clubs etc., in England. Mrs Mercier Clements also said that these men could be sent under the charge and control of a responsible lady and would be useful in working up meetings and would have special opportunities of reaching and interesting working men.

Mrs Mercier-Clements proposed and Mrs Wheeler seconded 'That men be employed on special service, when necessary, each case to be separately considered by the Executive Committee.'[84]

This passed unanimously.

The Secretary was instructed to write to Mrs Sinclair for full particulars of men in

[83] James Chambers was unionist MP for S. Belfast from 1910. He died in 1917. *Who Was Who,* vol. 2, p. 178.

[84] All Ulster Women's Unionist Council workers received travelling and subsistence costs.

North Tyrone who might be employed in this way … Mrs Lowry proposed, Mrs McCalmont seconded and it was carried unanimously that arrangements should be made for a special service and day of prayer on behalf of the Unionist Cause; and the Secretary was instructed to consult with the Secretary of the Ulster Unionist Council on the matter.
The business concluded.

13 October 1911

The fifteenth meeting of the Executive Committee was held … at 11-30 a.m. in the U.W.U.C. office[,] 33 Ocean Buildings, Belfast … Mrs James Craig (in the chair)[85] … With regard to Lady Hervey Bruce's request for help in organizing a Unionist Meeting in Nottingham the Secretary reported that as instructed by the Committee at their last meeting he had consulted the Secretary of the Ulster Unionist Council; that Mr. Bates had written to Mr. Cambray[,] Secretary of the Union Defence League[86] by whom meetings in England were arranged; that Mr. Cambray considered that if as mentioned by Lady Bruce, The Duke of Portland,[87] Mr. Walter Long M.P.[88] and Mr. H. T. Barrie M.P. took part the programme would be quite big enough and it would be a needless expense to send another speaker or speakers from here; and that he had written [to] Lady Hervey Bruce accordingly.

With regard to the proposed prayer meeting the Secretary reported that he had been advised that the proper course was to consult the Moderator of the General Assembly first on the matter … the Moderator said that owing to throat trouble he had cancelled most of his engagements and he would prefer that the Committee should not count on him when arranging the meeting. The Secretary was then instructed to approach the Primate and ask him to take part in the meeting … under the Constitution the annual meeting must be held in January and two months notice must be given to affiliated associations. The arrangements for the

85 Cecil Mary Norwell Diering was the only child of Sir Daniel Alfred Anley Turner, an officer of the King's Household. She married Sir James Craig in 1905 and had three children. Her husband became the first Prime Minister of Northern Ireland in 1921. Lady Cecil Craig was a Vice President of the UWUC from 1912–23 and from 1942–1960. In 1923 she became President of the UWUC. She retained this position until 1942. Lady Craig was widowed in 1940 and died in 1960. *Thom's Irish Who's Who*, pp 49–50. See also Urquhart, *Women in Ulster Politics.*

86 The Union Defence League was formed in February 1907 by Walter Long. It performed work of a similar nature to the Unionist Association of Ireland (UAI) and has been described as 'a hybrid British and Irish unionist propaganda organisation … often in danger of duplicating the work of the U.A.I.' Patrick Buckland, *Irish Unionism: Two. Ulster Unionism and the Origins of Northern Ireland, 1886–1922* (Dublin, 1973), p. 74.

87 William John Arthur Charles James, the 6th Duke of Portland (1857–1943), Lord Lieutenant of Co. Nottingham from 1898–1939 and Co. Caithness from 1889–1919. He was also Chancellor of the Most Noble Order of the Garter, 1937–43. *Dod's Peerage*, pp 697–8.

88 Walter Long, 1st Viscount Long of Wraxall (1854–1924). He was a Conservative MP from 1880–1921 and held numerous government posts including Chief Secretary for Ireland in 1905 and President of the Board of Agriculture with a cabinet seat, 1895–1900. He was also President of the Local Government Board from 1900–05 and from 1915–16, Secretary of State for the Colonies, 1916–18 and 1st Lord of the Admiralty, 1919–21. *The Dictionary of National Biography, 1922–30* (Oxford, 1937), pp 517–8.

annual meeting would therefore be part of the business for the next meeting of the Executive on Friday 27th October 1911, and at that meeting a suggestion would also be brought forward of having a large public meeting on the date of the annual meeting … The report of the Finance Committee was then read. The report stated that on 11th October there was a small credit balance at the Bank of £276 11 0 … Motion No. 3 on the agenda 'To consider our representation on the Committee of the London Women's Unionist Association' was then brought forward by Mrs Sinclair (Strabane). A lengthy discussion followed on the relations between the Ulster Women's Unionist Council and the Women's Amalgamated Unionist & Tariff Reform Association. Mrs Mercier-Clements proposed and Mrs Finlay seconded that the Secretary write to Mrs Wheeler and ask for her opinion on the value of working in co-operation with the W.A.U.T.R.A. and the advisability of continuing to do so.

27 October 1911

The sixteenth meeting of the Executive Committee was held … at 11-30 a.m. in the U.W.U.C. office[,] 33 Ocean Buildings, Belfast. Lady Dixon (in the chair)[89] … In connection with the proposed Prayer Meeting the Secretary read the following letter from the Primate:–

Dear Mr. Hamill,

I think in any crisis of National or Political life where there is always a grave danger of action being put to the credit of party bias, special prayers, and services of humiliation and intercession should be arranged for by the various religious bodies apart from political organizations which have their own great work to do and the members of which should also make known their bequests to God.

Yours truly,
John B. Armagh.

Mrs Clarke proposed, Mrs Finlay seconded and it was passed unanimously that the resolution to hold a Unionist Prayer Meeting be rescinded …

The Report of the Finance Committee was then read; it stated that on Wednesday 25th October there was a balance in the Bank of £488 8 8.

As some difficulty and delay seemed to have occurred in connection with the despatching of literature the Committee recommended that a stamped postcard should be inserted in each parcel of literature sent out, to be returned to the Secretary acknowledging receipt of the parcel.

The Committee decided to publish the list of contributors to the funds in the Evening Telegraph and Nomad's Weekly … The Secretary reported that he had received a request from the Ulster Echo that they should be allowed to publish a list of contributions. It was proposed by Mrs Finlay seconded by Mrs Wheeler and

[89] Thirteen members were present at this meeting and there were nine apologies for non–attendance.

passed that the Ulster Echo be instructed to publish the list provided that they do it on the same terms as other newspapers.

The next business was the arrangements for the Annual Meeting. A letter was read from the Vice-President[90] stating that she would be at Mountstewart from January 10th to the Meeting of Parliament so that any time up till then would suit her for the Annual Meeting.

The Vice-President also expressed her approval of the plan of having the Council meeting in the forenoon and the Public Meeting in the afternoon and asked what the Committee would like to do about speakers.

It was proposed by Mrs Riddell and seconded by Miss Tracey that the question of the exact date and the obtaining of speakers be left to the Vice-President … The next business on the agenda was Motion No. 3. 'To consider our representation on the London Women's Unionist Association'. This had been adjourned from the last meeting in order that Mrs Wheeler might report on the value of co-operating with the Women's Amalgamated Unionist & Tariff Reform Association and the advisability of continuing to do so.

Mrs Wheeler, who had just returned from work in England, gave as her opinion that in some cases the Branches of the Women's Amalgamated Unionist & Tariff Reform Association would certainly be of great assistance to our workers, but in other places the W.A.U.T.R.A. was itself a new organization and struggling for recognition. As we are such a short time at work Mrs Wheeler was of opinion that we should avail ourselves of the co-operation of the Women's Amalgamated Unionist & Tariff Reform Association where it seemed likely to be of use to us and that in other places we should work independently.

Motion No. 4. on the agenda 'That the question of the equipment of some of our active workers with selected Lantern Slides should be discussed.' was withdrawn by Mrs Wheeler, as the Secretary explained that the Ulster Unionist Council were arranging sets of slides for the use of workers.

The business concluded.

2 November 1911

A special meeting of the Executive Committee was held … at 11-30 a.m. in the U.W.U.C. office 33, Ocean Buildings, Belfast … Mrs Thomas Sinclair (in the chair).[91] [The meeting was called to discuss a replacement for the UWUC's Honorary Treasurer, MrsJohn Thompson, who was absent due to illness, and for the Honorary Assistant Treasurer, MrsMercier Clements, who was also absent] … on political business. [An Acting Treasurer, Miss Connor was appointed to replace the above officials until the Council's annual meeting in January 1912].

90 Theresa, 6th Marchioness of Londonderry.

91 Seven members were present at this meeting and there were five apologies for non–attendance.

10 November 1911

The seventeenth meeting of the Executive Committee was held … at 11-30 a.m. in the U.W.U.C. office[,] 33, Ocean Buildings, Belfast … Mrs G.H. Clarke in the chair[92] … A letter was … read which had been received by Mrs Wheeler from Mr Wm C Gillilan enclosing 100 copies of his song 'Stand Fast Ulster' as a gift to the Council … The report of the Standing Committee re[.] workers and delegates was then presented. The report stated that in accordance with the arrangement made with the W.A.U.T.R.A. twelve [UWUC] workers had been sent to England and Scotland, and three are going almost immediately. Three others volunteered, but work could not be arranged for them at suitable times and their visits had been postponed for a time.

At the last meeting Mrs Sinclair, of Strabane reported that she had been asked to conduct an Anti-Home Rule Campaign in the Newmarket Division of Cambridgeshire, and that she proposed to take with her Mr Morris St Clair, a conjurer and entertainer as the means of securing audience amongst the working classes.

The Committee unanimously approved of Mrs Sinclair's proposal and recommended the Executive Committee to make Mrs Sinclair a grant towards Mr St Clair's expenses of £5 …

Mrs Wheeler proposed Motion No 3. on the agenda 'That the Executive nominate a small committee to revise the Constitution and bring their suggestions before another Executive Committee previous to the General Meeting in January.' Mrs Riddell seconded and the motion was passed unanimously.

28 November 1911

The eighteenth ordinary meeting of the Executive Committee of the Ulster Women's Unionist Council was held … at 11-30 a.m. in the U.W.U.C. Office[,] 33, Ocean Buildings, Belfast … Lady Anderson (in the chair)[93] ... The Secretary laid before the Committee a Christmas card issued by the Unionist Clubs of Ireland[94] which a member of the Executive committee of the U.W.U.C. had left in the office.

Mrs Thos. Sinclair proposed that the following resolution be sent to the Secretary of the Unionist Clubs of Ireland:–

'That we the ladies of the Ulster Women's Unionist Council consider that the words

92 Twelve members were present at this meeting and there were seven apologies for non–attendance.

93 Eighteen members were present at this meeting and there were five apologies for non–attendance.

94 The Unionist Clubs were largely the creation of Lord Templeton of Castle Upton, Co. Armagh. Formed in 1893 at the time of the 2nd home rule crisis the Clubs were largely Ulster based with a central council in Belfast. The Clubs attempted to organise unionist opposition to home rule at both a local and national level. Unionist Clubs demonstrated and performed propaganda work as well as linking up with unionist associations in Britain. Although the Clubs declined in popularity from 1895 they were revived in 1911 at the suggestion of the Ulster Unionist Council. The movement augmented steadily and by February 1914 317 clubs had been established. See Buckland, *Irish Unionism, 1885–1923*, pp 194, 208.

on a card left at this office by a lady and bearing the address of Mayfair, Belfast might be more dignified and are unsuitable to be sent as Christmas cards over the country and calculated to do harm instead of good.'

Lady Jaffe seconded and after some discussion the resolution was passed.

Mrs Finlay (Hon. Sec.) read a letter which he had received from the Vice-President,[95] in which it was suggested that the Council might hold a bazaar in the Spring of 1912 to raise funds for the work of the Council.

After some discussion Mrs Finlay was instructed to reply to the letter saying that the Executive Committee was of the unanimous opinion that it would not be advisable to hold a bazaar at present.

Mrs Finlay (Hon. Sec.) reported the formation of an East Tyrone Ulster Women's Association.

A meeting had been held by Lady Ranfurly in Dungannon on Saturday 25th November 1911, which the Secretary was to have attended, but owing to a slight accident he had been unable to do so and Mrs Finlay had taken his place.

Arrangements had been made for the organization of the constituency and there seemed a good prospect that the Association would be a success ...

The Secretary was instructed to have a number of copies of the proposed revised Constitution printed and submitted to the various affiliated Associations in order that the delegates might be prepared to take this question as the first business at the Annual Meeting, and if the recommendations of the Committee were adopted the election of office-bearers might take place under the new rules.

Mrs Wheeler withdrew Motion No. 2 on the agenda and proposed that the question of mission work be referred to a joint meeting of the Finance Committee and the Standing Committee re[.] Workers & Delegates for consideration and report.

This was seconded by Mrs Finlay and passed unanimously.

Mrs Finlay proposed and Lady Anderson seconded that the following resolution be sent to Mr. A. Bonar Law M.P.[96]

'That the Executive Committee of the U.W.U.C. at this their first meeting after his election as leader of the Unionist Party, send their warmest congratulations to Mr. Bonar Law, and beg to assure him of their hearty co-operation and support in any work that may be undertaken for the maintenance of the Legislative Union of Great Britain and Ireland.'

Passed unanimously.

The business concluded.

95 Theresa, 6th Marchioness of Londonderry.

96 Andrew Bonar Law (1858–1923), unionist MP for Glasgow, 1900–06, for Dulwich, 1906–10 and for Bootle in 1923. In 1911 he was appointed leader of the opposition in the House of Commons and in 1918 was Leader of the Commons. He was Prime Minister and leader of the Conservative Party in 1922, but resigned office in 1923. *A Dictionary of Twentieth Century World Biography* (Oxford, 1992), p. 332.

4 December 1911

A Joint meeting of the Finance Committee and Standing Committee re[.] Workers and Delegates … was held … at 11 a.m. … Mrs Thos. Sinclair (in the chair)[97] … The business of the Committee was 'To consider the best method of conducting the Anti-Home Rule Campaign in England and Scotland, and the expenses of the same.'

The Secretary submitted a report as to Mrs Sinclair's work in the Newmarket division in Cambridgeshire. Mrs McMordie proposed, Lady Jaffe seconded and it was passed unanimously that Mrs Sinclair be sent a further grant of £15 for this work together with a letter conveying to her the cordial thanks of the Committee for her efforts on behalf of the Council.

The Secretary was instructed to send the following letter to Miss Nunn White, Secretary of the Women's Unionist Assoc. (West of Scotland)

'Dear Madam,

In view of the approaching Bye-Elections in North Ayrshire and Govan I have been instructed to ask you if workers from the Ulster Women's Unionist Council would be useful. Most of our ladies have just returned from work in England but it might be possible to induce some of them to back for these special occasions as speakers and canvassers.

Our Committee would pay travelling expenses if hospitality can be provided locally.

Kindly let me hear from you on this matter as soon as possible and please say in each case if the Candidate would help.

Yours faithfully,'

Mrs Finlay proposed the following resolution:–

'That this joint meeting of the Finance Committee and the Standing Committee re[.] Workers and Delegates recommends to the Executive Committee that each new opening occurring for workers shall be dealt with separately by the Finance Committee and the Standing Committee re[.] Workers & Delegates sitting jointly.'

Miss Ferguson seconded the resolution which was passed unanimously.

Lady Jaffe proposed and Mrs McMordie seconded the following resolutions:–

'That the Secretary be instructed to be on the watch for suitable openings for workers.'

This passed unanimously.

The business concluded.

5 December 1911

An extraordinary meeting of the Executive Committee was held … in the U.W.U.C.

97 Ten members were present at this meeting and there was one apology for non-attendance.

office[,] 33 Ocean Buildings, Belfast at 11-30 a.m. ... Mrs Thos. Sinclair (in the chair)[98] ... A report of the Finance Committee re[.] the expenses of the Annual Meeting was presented.

The Committee recommend that the cost of the meeting should not exceed the sum of £90 this calculation being based on the figures supplied by the Secretary of the Ulster Unionist Council.

The committee also recommend that a charge of one shilling should be made for admission to the Balcony of the Ulster Hall; only enough tickets being sold to fill the balcony.

Mrs McMordie proposed and Miss Connor seconded that the first four rows of the Area be reserved and numbered at 2/6. That the charge of one shilling be made for admission to the Balcony, and that after seats had been provided for the delegates[,] the orchestra and the remainder of the Hall shall be free.

Lady Ewart proposed the following amendment 'That only the one half of the Balcony on each side be sold at 1/–.' This was seconded by Mrs King-Kerr and carried.

The Motion was then put as amended and passed unanimously in the following form:–

'That the first four rows of the Area be reserved and numbered at 2/6. That a charge of 1/.- be made for admission to half the balcony on each side, only enough tickets being sold to fill half the balcony.'

Mrs Finlay proposed that the Unionist Clubs be asked to provide 150 stewards for the Public Meeting. Lady Ewart seconded this and it was passed unanimously ... It was decided that the Public Meeting should begin at 7-30 p.m.[,] doors to be open at 6-30 p.m.

The Secretary was instructed to ask the Duchess of Abercorn[,] President of the Council to Preside at the Public Meeting and failing her to ask the Vice-President[,] the Marchioness of Londonderry. He was also instructed to submit the names of the following gentlemen to the Vice-President and ask her if possible to get two of them to speak at the Public Meeting.

Mr. Bonar Law, Mr. Balfour,[99] Mr. F. E. Smith,[100] Mr. Walter Long, Lord

98 Eighteen members were present at this meeting and there were four apologies for non–attendance.

99 Arthur Balfour, 1st Earl of Balfour (1848–1930), was an MP from 1874–1922, President of the Local Government Board from 1885–86, Secretary for Scotland in 1886, Chief Secretary for Ireland in 1887, Conservative leader in the House of Commons and First Lord of the Treasury from 1891–92 and 1895–1902. He was also Prime Minister from 1902–05, First Lord of the Admiralty in 1915, Foreign Secretary from 1916–19 and Lord President of Council from 1919–22 and from 1925–29. R. F. Foster, *Modern Ireland, 1600–1972* (London, 1988), p. 413.

100 F. E. Smith, 1st Earl of Birkenhead (1872–1930), was a Conservative MP from 1906–18, Head of Press Bureau in 1914, Solicitor General in May 1915 and Attorney General in November 1915. He was also Lord Chancellor from 1919–22 and Secretary of State for India, 1924–28. Although he initially opposed home rule for Ireland he later supported a settlement based on Ulster exclusion. *The Dictionary of National Biography, 1922–30*, pp 782–4.

Willoughby de Broke[101] and Major Morrison Bell.

The Secretary was also instructed to invite the Marchioness of Tullibardine,[102] Miss Anna Richardson, Mrs Mercier-Clements, Mrs Lowry and Capt. James Craig to speak at the meeting.

It was decided that all local Unionist Members of Parliament should get platform tickets.

12 December 1911

The nineteenth ordinary meeting of the Executive Committee was held … at 11-30 a.m. in the U.W.U.C. office[,] 33, Ocean Buildings, Belfast. Mrs James Craig (in the chair)[103] … The Secretary reported that the Duchess of Abercorn had promised to preside at both the Annual Meeting of the Council and the Public Meeting on 18th January 1912; that no gentleman speaker had yet been secured for the latter meeting; and that the Marchioness of Tullibardine[,] Miss Anna Richardson, Mrs Lowry and Capt. James Craig had refused invitations to speak.

The first business on the agenda was the report of the Finance Committee re[.] the purchase of lantern slides for workers in England and Scotland. The Committee recommended to the Executive Committee that a set of 60 slides be purchased at a price not exceeding £3 5 0. for slides and a box.

Miss Connor proposed and Mrs Mercier-Clements seconded that the report be adopted. Passed unanimously.

Mrs Finlay proposed and Mrs McMordie seconded that the Secretary should if possible purchase a set of slides belonging to Mrs George Wheeler and which she had used when working in the Isle of Wight.

This was passed unanimously.

As Mrs Craig was in the chair, Lady Dixon proposed Motion No. 3 on the agenda 'That a monthly report as to mission work and the general work of the Council be sent to the various affiliated Associations.'

Mrs Finlay seconded the resolution which was passed unanimously.

Mrs McMordie proposed Motion No. 4 on the agenda. 'To recommend to the

[101] Richard Grenville, 19th Lord Willoughby de Broke (1869–1923), a JP for Co. Warwick and MP for the S. E. Division of Warwickshire, 1895–1906. *Dod's Peerage*, p. 918.

[102] Katherine Marjory, (1874–1960), 8th Duchess of Atholl and Marchioness of Tullibardine. She married John George Murray, Marquis of Tullibardine and the eldest surviving son of the 7th Duke of Atholl in 1899. Public service in many areas brought the Duchess recognition in the form of a DBE in 1917 and honorary doctorates from seven universities. She was a member of innumerable official committees and government commissions and was a prominent figure in Scottish Social Services, local government and an active supporter of the Conservative Party. She was elected to the House of Commons in 1923 as a member for Kinross and West Perthshire, the first Scottish woman and the second woman ever to receive ministerial office in 1924, as Parliamentary Secretary to the Board of Education. Throughout her life she worked for humanitarian causes and from 1944 was chairman of the British League for European Freedom, a position which earned her the nickname of 'The Red Duchess'. *Dod's Peerage*, p. 36.

[103] Ten members were present at this meeting and there were eight apologies for non–attendance.

Annual Meeting of the Council on 18th January 1912 that in addition to the members of the Executive Committee to be nominated by the various Affiliated Associations that the Executive Committee shall have power to co-opt a number of ladies not exceeding 20, who have rendered, or are likely to render service to the Cause.'

This was passed unanimously.

The business concluded.

4 January 1912

The twentieth meeting of the Executive Committee was held in the U.W.U.C. office 33, Ocean Buildings, Belfast … at 1-30 a.m. … Lady Ewart (in the chair)[104] … A letter was read from the Secretary of the Ulster Unionist Council stating that having regard to the low condition of their funds the Joint Committee could not undertake to supply literature free.

Mrs Thos. Sinclair proposed and Mrs Finlay seconded that the letter should be referred to a joint meeting of the Finance Committee of the Ulster Women's Unionist Council and the Consultative Committee of the Ulster Unionist Council to be called as soon as possible after the 18th January.

Passed unanimously.

Mrs Mercier-Clements proposed and Mrs McMordie seconded and it was passed unanimously that the Secretary be authorised to order literature up to the value of £10, pending a definite arrangement … The committee decided that it would not be advisable to publish at a large meeting the details of the Financial position of the Council but that a balancesheet … be kept in the office for the inspection of any members of affiliated Associations who might wish to see it.

A draft Manifesto to be proposed at the Annual Meeting was submitted by the Secretary.

Miss Ferguson proposed that the Manifesto be approved of and Mrs King-Kerr seconded and the resolution passed unanimously.

Mrs Mercier Clements proposed that the best thanks of the Committee be given to The Right Hon. Thomas Sinclair for the Valuable Assistance he had given in preparing the Manifesto. Mrs Riddell seconded this and it was passed unanimously approved of.

The next business was the arrangements for the Annual Meeting of the Council on the 18th January, 1912, and for the Demonstration in the Ulster Hall, on the same evening … The Committee decided that tickets should be printed for seven rows of half-crown seats.

It was suggested that a light dinner, (Price not to exceed 5/-. Wine extra) should be provided at the Ulster Hall for the convenience of holders of platform tickets who wished to get to the hall early.

104 Thirteen members were present at the meeting and there were four apologies for non–attendance.

The secretary was instructed to get quotations from caterers and arrange to have circulars sent out with all platform tickets.

It was decided to ask Mr. F. W. Moneypenny, M.V.O.[105] to assist the Committee in arranging the seats for speakers at the Public Meeting in proper precedence … The Secretary was instructed to ask the Right Hon. Thos. Sinclair to further assist the Committee by drawing up a resolution to be proposed at the evening meeting. The Secretary was instructed to have 5,000 copies of the Manifesto printed and a copy laid on each chair in for the Public Meeting.

The programme for the Public Meeting was also submitted and approved of … Mrs Finlay said that speaking on behalf of the Hon. Secretaries she would like to ask the Executive Committee to rescind the resolution of 29th March 1911 defining the duties and position of the Organizing Secretary. She said the that Hon. Secretaries felt that if the Committee would agree to rescind the resolution it would avoid the necessity of bringing the matter up at the Council Meeting.
She also said that on account of the resolution the Hon. Secretaries felt they could not sign the Annual Report for the year as it had deprived them of all responsibility for anything that had or had not been done.
Mrs James Craig seconded this proposal.

On a vote being taken three voted for the resolution and eight against. The Chairman declared the resolution lost.
The committee then proceeded to prepare a list of ladies to be recommended to the Affiliated Associations as suitable office-bearers for the coming year. In this connection a letter was read from the Secretary of the West Belfast Branch of the U.W.U.C. suggesting that Lady Clanmorris,[106] President of that Association should be nominated as a Provincial Representative.

The list of office-bearers finally prepared by the Committee was as follows:–

President:	The Duchess of Abercorn.
Vice-President:	The Marchioness of Londonderry.

Provincial Representatives:

Lady Bruce.	Lady Heygate.[107]
The Countess of Dartrey.	The Countess of Kilmorey.

105 Sir Frederick William Moneypenny, a JP for the City of Belfast, a City Chamberlain of Belfast, Gentleman Usher of the Black Rod in the Parliament of Northern Ireland, 1921–22. He was awarded an OBE in 1918 and a CBE in 1920. *Thom's Irish Who's Who*, p. 167.

106 Lady Matilda Catherine Maude Clanmorris, the only child and heiress of Robert Edward Ward of Bangor Castle, Co. Down. In 1878 she married John George Barry, 5th Baron Clanmorris (1852–1916), a JP for Co. Down and Galway. Lady Clanmorris was widowed in 1916 and died in 1941. *Dod's Peerage*, p. 179; *Thom's Irish Who's Who*, p. 37.

107 Lady Flora Heygate, daughter of John Walter of Bearwood, Berkshire. In 1888 she married Sir Frederick Gage, 3rd Baronet Heygate, a barrister, JP and Deputy Lieutenant for Co. Londonderry. Lady Heygate was widowed in 1940 and died in 1948. *Dod's Peerage*, p. 429.

The Dowager Marchioness of Dufferin and Ava.
The Marchioness of Ely.[109]
The Countess of Erne.
Lady Ewart.
The Countess of Gosford.
The Dowager Lady Smiley.
Lady Stronge.
Mrs Talbot.[113]
The Countess of Leitrim.[108]
The Countess of Ranfurly.
The Countess of Rossmore.
Mrs Saunderson.[110]
The Countess of Shaftesbury.[111]
The Marchioness of Hamilton.[112]
Lady Dunleath.
Lady Clanmorris.

Hon. Secretaries:

Mrs A. G. Finlay, Miss E. A. M. Tracey and Mrs G. H. Wheeler.

Hon. Treasurer: Miss Connor.

Hon. Assistant Treasurer: Mrs Mercier-Clements.

The business concluded.

6 February 1912

The 21st meeting of the Executive Committee was held ... at 2 p.m. in the Lecture

108 Violet Lena, 5th Countess of Leitrim, daughter of Robert Henderson, director of the Bank of England of Sedgwick Park, Horsham. In 1902 she married Charles Clements, 5th Earl of Gosford, HM Lieutenant Commander of the City of Londonderry from 1904–21 and Private Secretary to the Secretary of State for the Colonies from 1917. *Thom's Irish Who's Who*, p. 134.

109 Margaret, 5th Marchioness of Ely, daughter of F. A. Clark. In 1895 she married John Henry Loftus, 5th Marquess of Ely. *Thom's Irish Who's Who*, pp 72–3.

110 Probably Hon. Helena Saunderson, daughter of Thomas de Moleyns, 3rd Baron Ventry. In 1865 she married Colonel Edward Saunderson (1837–1906), the first leader of the Irish unionist movement. Saunderson was a Liberal MP for Co. Cavan from 1865–74, but in 1885 was returned as a Conservative candidate for N. Armagh. He held this seat until his death in 1906. Kate Newmann, *Dictionary of Ulster Biography* (Belfast, 1993), p. 234.

111 Lady Constance Sibell, 9th Countess Shaftesbury, elder daughter of the Earl of Grosvenor, the eldest son of the 1st Duke of Westminster. In 1899 she married Anthony Ashley–Cooper, 9th Earl of Shaftesbury, HM Lieutenant for Co. Dorset in 1916, Deputy Lieutenant and HM Lieutenant for Co. Antrim from 1911–16 and HM Lieutenant for Belfast City, 1900–11. He was Chancellor of Queen's University, Belfast, Lord Mayor of Belfast in 1907 and Lord Chamberlain in Her Majesty's Household. *Thom's Irish Who's Who*, pp 228–9.

112 Lady Mary Kathleen, Marchioness of Hamilton and later 4th Duchess of Abercorn. She was a sister of the 5th Earl of Erne and in 1928 married James Edward Hamilton, who succeeded to the title of 4th Duke of Abercorn in 1953. He was a Senator of Northern Ireland from 1949–62 and a County Councillor for Tyrone from 1946. He was also a High Sheriff and Lord Lieutenant for Co. Tyrone. The Duchess was a Vice President of the UWUC from 1952 until her resignation in 1965. *Burke's Genealogical and Heraldic History of the Peerage, Baronetage and Knightage* (London, 1953), pp 3–4; *Dod's Peerage*, p. 743.

113 Mrs Julia Elizabeth Mary Talbot, the only child of Sir Capel Molyneaux, 7th Baronet. In 1897 she married William John Talbot, JP and High Sheriff for Cos. Roscommon, Armagh and JP for Co. Galway. In 1917 he was appointed Lieutenant and *Custos Rotulorum* for Co. Roscommon. Julia Talbot was the President of Mid Armagh Women's Unionist Association and also served as a JP. She was awarded an OBE. She died in 1922. *Thom's Irish Who's Who*, pp 244–5.

Hall of the Young Women's Christian Association, 9, Donegall Sq. E.[,] Belfast … Mrs Thomas Sinclair (in the chair)[114] … Arising out of the minutes Mrs Sinclair of Strabane read the following statement as to the duties of the Honorary Secretaries:-

'As there are many new members here to-day it seems the right opportunity to explain in a few words the system we aim at.

All agree the Executive should keep in close touch with the affiliated Units represented on it and in close touch with all work done.

For this object they appoint Sub-Committees. The distinctive honour given by our new Constitution to Honorary Secretaries is that they are ex-officio members of every Committee … The Sub-Committee's system is highly recommended elsewhere; and we have every hope it will work thoroughly well here in this coming year. The more so, as we are all possessed with a common desire to be a credit to our country.'

A letter was read from Lady Arthur,[115] President of the Women's Unionist Assoc. of the West of Scotland. The letter suggested that suitable literature on the Home Rule question should be sent to all ministers in the United Free Church. The Secretary was instructed to write and inform Lady Arthur that a copy of the special number of the 'Witness', containing a report of the Presbyterian Convention had already been sent to all ministers of the U. F. Church, and ask if Lady Arthur would suggest anything further being done.

A letter was read from Miss M. Hamilton, Secretary of the South Belfast W.U.A. enclosing the following resolution:–

'That the delegates of the South Belfast W.U.A. to U.W.U.C. desire to place on record their implicit confidence in the Executive Committee of the Ulster Women's Unionist Council. They are of opinion that the action of certain office-bearers of the Council, in refusing to conform to the authorities of the Executive committee and at the same time continuing to hold office, does not make for the harmonious and sufficient working of the organization.[116] They further consider that the officers in question did not treat the delegates fairly or openly in allowing their names to go forward for re-election, without first making it clear on what terms they intend to hold office.'

[114] Sixty–four members were present at this meeting and there were seventeen apologies for non–attendance.

[115] Lady Janet Stevenson Bennett, daughter of Alexander Bennett McGrigor, LLD of Sterlingshire. In 1879 she married Sir Mathew Arthur, 1st Baron Glenarthur of Carlung, the chairman of the West of Scotland Liberal Unionist Association from 1893–1912, President of Glasgow Unionist Association in 1913 and President of the Scottish Unionist Association from 1912–14. He was also a member of the Executive Committee of the National Unionist Association from 1912–18 and a Deputy Lieutenant and JP for Ayr and Glasgow. Lady Arthur was later awarded an OBE. *Dod's Peerage*, p. 358.

[116] This is a reference to the three Honorary Secretaries of the Ulster Women's Unionist Council, MrsSarah A. Finlay, Miss Florence E. Henderson and Miss Eleanor A. M. Tracey, who felt that their position was marginalised by Mr John H. Hamill, the paid Organising Secretary of the council. Disputes finally led to the resignation of all three Honorary Secretaries in April 1912.

Signed on behalf of Delegates.

N. Lewis	(St. George's Ward)
M. O. Corbett	(Windsor Ward)
M. L. Walkington	(Cromac Ward)
V. Ainsworth Barr[117]	(St. Anne's Ward) …

The next business was the co-option of additional members of the Executive Committee in accordance with Par. 8 (c) of the Constitution.

The names of the following ladies were passed unanimously.

Mrs Wetherall, (Ballycastle)	Viscountess Jocelyn, (Bryansford)[118]
Mrs Sclater, (Hillsborough)[119]	Miss Barklie, (Larne)
Mrs Thos. Andrews, (Comber)	Mrs Geo. Preston,
Mrs Garrett Campbell,	Mrs James Moore,
Miss Riddell,	Mrs Kennedy, (Stewartstown)
Miss Bruce, (The Farm) …	

It be decided that the effect of the second clause of par. 8 (a) of the Constitution was that affiliated Associations are entitled to elect an extra representative for every 500 members at any time of the year. Passed unanimously … Mrs Thos. Sinclair then proposed Motion No. 18 on the agenda 'That in view of the large and increasing membership of the Ulster Women's Unionist Council and in order to promote its harmonious working, all suggestions or complaints as to the conduct of its business which any affiliated branch or individual members may feel called upon to make, shall be forwarded in writing, duly dated and signed, to the Hon. Secretaries by whom it shall be submitted to the Executive Committee.'

Mrs R.T. Martin seconded this motion.

Mrs King-Kerr moved the following amendment

'That the word 'Secretary' be substituted for the words 'Hon. Secretaries''. In moving this amendment Mrs King-Kerr dealt at considerable length with the differences of opinion which had arisen in reference to the respective positions of the Hon. Secretaries and the Secretary.

Considerable discussion followed in the course of which Miss Tracey, Hon. Sec. said that if the Executive would agree to pass Motion No. 21 she thought it would cover the whole ground, as it made clear the responsibility of the Executive and that there was no independent authority; and that she was sure none of the Hon. Secretaries wished for independent authority; and that it brought the position back to where it

117 Mrs Violet Ainsworth Barr, CBE, was an Assistant Honorary Treasurer of the UWUC from 1920–30, a Vice Chairman of the UWUC from 1923–25 and from 1933–47. She also served as Honorary Treasurer from 1930–47. She died in 1947. Information complied from UWUC minutes (PRONI, D1098/1/1–3).

118 Viscountess Elinor Jessie Jocelyn, the 2nd daughter of Joseph Charlton Parr, Deputy Lieutenant and JP of Heyes, Cheshire. In 1905 she married Robert Soame Joceyln, 8th Earl of Roden and Viscount Jocelyn. In 1919 he was elected as a representative peer for Ireland. *Dod's Peerage*, p. 737.

119 Mrs Sclater was the wife of Edward Sclater, JP and member of the Ulster Unionist Council. A. T. Q. Stewart, *The Ulster Crisis* (London, 1967), p. 75.

was before the passing of the resolution on 29th March, 1911. If the Committee agreed to that the Hon. Secretaries were willing to try to show they could work – always under the Constitution.

Accordingly, Motion No. 21. 'That in view of the gravity of the heavy work before us, the Executive Committee should meet on stated days (at least once a fortnight) for the next three months so as to keep well in knowledge and control of the work for which they are responsible to their Council and to the Public. And that considering the responsibility of the Executive the Secretaries be courteously reminded that there is no independent authority, and that the crisis is too serious to sanction any possible risk of friction or confusion in the working of this daily increasing business which the Executive must see properly carried out.' Proposed by Mrs Sinclair, Strabane, was passed unanimously.

Mrs Thos. Sinclair then withdrew Notice of Motion No. 18.

Mrs Thos. Sinclair proposed that congratulations should be sent to Their Majesty's, The King & Queen on their safe return from India, and also an expression of sympathy on the death of the Duke of Fife,[120] also that expression of sympathy be sent to Queen Alexandra[121] and to the Duchess of Fife.

Motion No. 20 on the agenda 'That children's and girl's clubs should be formed in connection with the Ulster Women's Unionist Council' was ruled out of order. The chairman explained that under par. 2 of the Constitution the scheme outlined by Mrs Talbot in proposing the resolution could not be taken up by the Council[122] … [The Executive Committee decided to accept] the Unionist Council's offer of offices with theirs in Old Town Hall, Belfast … [but] the office work of the Council be carried on as before at the office in Ocean Buildings, but that the Council should apply for the use of a large room in the Old Town Hall for Committee meetings[.][123]

20 February 1912

The 22nd meeting of the Executive Committee was held … in the Lecture Hall of the Young Women's Christian Association, 9 Donegall Square East, Belfast, at 2

120 Alexander William George, the 6th Earl of Fife who was made 1st Duke of Fife in 1889 on his marriage to Louise Victoria Alexandra Dagmar (1867–1931), the 3rd child of the Prince and Princess of Wales. The Duchess of Fife was Princess Royal of Great Britain and Ireland from 1905. *Dod's Peerage*, p. 317.

121 Queen Alexandra Caroline Mary Charlotte Louise Julia (1844–1924), Queen Consort of Edward VII. She was the eldest daughter of King Christian IX of Denmark. In 1863 she married Albert Edward, Prince of Wales, who succeeded to the throne in 1901. Queen Alexandra was widowed in 1910. *Burke's Genealogical and Heraldic History*, p. cxiv.

122 At this meeting members were appointed to the UWUC Affiliation Committee, the Emergency Committee, the Active Worker's Committee and the Sub–Committee re. the *Ne Temere* Petition.

123 The Ulster Unionist Council (UUC) offered the use of two rooms at a cost of £25 per annum, with 6 months rent free and with the UUC paying taxes, plus an additional £10 for coal, light and cleaning, with the occasional use of a room for committee meetings.

p.m. … Lady Dixon (in the chair)[124] … The Secretary reported that the balance at the Bank to date was £641.

The Secretary reported that Messrs. Henderson & Co., had quoted £5. 17. 6. as the Price of the Year Book recommended by the Executive Committee.

Miss Tracey proposed and the Countess of Kilmorey seconded that the Year Book should also include the names of the Presidents of the various Branches … Motion No. 8 on the agenda, 'That arrangements be made for a procession of women Unionists at Easter' was withdrawn by Mrs King-Kerr as the Committee considered that a procession of women would be most inadvisable.

Mrs Mercier-Clements proposed Motion No. 9 on the agenda 'That the Ulster Unionist Council be asked to provide accommodation at the Show Grounds for representatives of the Ulster Women's Unionist Council on Easter Tuesday.'

Mrs Robertson seconded the Motion which was passed unanimously … Mrs G. H. Wheeler proposed Motion No. 11 on the agenda. 'that an Ambulance Society be organized in connection with the Ulster Women's Unionist Council.' (Adjourned from the last meeting.) Mrs Murland seconded.

A letter was read from Capt. James Craig strongly approving of the proposal.

After some discussion Mrs Wheeler undertook to get fuller information about the St. John's Ambulance Society; and pending this the question was adjourned till the next meeting.

The business concluded.[125]

124 Fifty–three members were present at this meeting and there were thirty–one apologies for non–attendance.

125 A report of the UWUC Active Worker's Committee is attached to the minutes, stating, 'Since the last meeting of the Executive Committee the Active Worker's Committee have held two meetings.

Arrangements have been made to hold a series of training classes for workers and a large number of ladies likely to go to England or Scotland on behalf of the [U.W.U.] Council have been notified of these classes.

An application had been received from Unionist Agent in North Suffolk for the services of a lady speaker and canvasser for a month after Easter.

The Liverpool Women's Unionist Federation are holding a large Public Meeting in Liverpool on 19th March 1912 and Mrs Mercier–Clements has accepted an invitation to speak on the Home Rule question.

The Committee also desire to report that assistance has been given to various affiliated Associations in procuring speakers for local meetings and the Committee will be very grateful to any ladies who will volunteer for this kind of work, as some of the ladies on the list are likely to be overworked unless further volunteers come forward.' A report of the UWUC's Finance Committee is also attached to the minutes, stating, 'The Finance Committee have to report that at their last meeting on 15th February, 1912 the balance at the Bank was £797 1 2 … The Committee decided that the Hon. Treasurer should send a circular to those who subscribed to the funds of the Council in 1911 and also to the members of the Executive Committee for 1912 asking for subscriptions.

The committee recommend that a Year Book should be printed to include a list of office–bearers and Committees, the Annual Report for 1911, The Constitution of the Council and a list of the names and addresses of the Secretaries of the various affiliated Associations, but that the cost should not exceed £5.'

5 March 1912

The 23rd meeting of the Executive Committee was held in the Lecture Hall of the Young Women's Christian Association, 9 Donegall Square East, Belfast ... at 2 p.m. ... Mrs McMordie (in the chair)[126] ... [Mrs Robert Liddell of Donaghcloney,[127] Mrs Blacker of Carrickblacker, Portadown[128] and Mrs D. D. Reid, 7 Norfolk Crescent, Hyde Park, London[129] were co-opted onto the Executive Committee. A report from a special meeting of the Finance Committee was read stating]

1 ... Associations formed since 1st October, 1911, be asked to pay only one Affiliation Fee for 1911 and 1912; and that in future Affiliation Fees be due on 1st April of each year.

2 By instruction of the Finance Committee, the Hon Treasurer issued a circular to all members of the Executive Committee and to all who had subscribed to the funds of the Council last year.

From various letters received it appears that this circular has been misunderstood. It was not intended as a general appeal for funds but was addressed to these ladies as individuals.

Last year members of the Executive Committee paid a subscription direct to the central funds apart from any contribution they gave to their own local Association, and the Finance Committee thought that the members of this year's Committee would wish to do the same ...

In accordance with the notice she had given, Miss Connor then asked the Executive Committee to decide whether members of the Executive Committee were to pay an Annual Subscription.

After some discussion Mrs Robertson moved that members of the Executive be not asked for an official subscription but be left to do as they think best.

Miss Ferguson seconded the proposal which was passed ...

Business No. 8 on the agenda 'Statement dealing with the measures to be taken to keep the Executive Committee regularly and fully informed of the work done by the Central and Branch Organizations of the Council, with a view of promoting and extending its influence and usefulness.'

The Dowager Marchioness of Dufferin & Ava made the following suggestions:–

1 That a selection of the most important letters received at the office be read at each Committee meeting and a short report of the remainder of the correspondence

[126] Sixty–nine members were present at this meeting and there were thirty–two apologies for non–attendance.

[127] Charlotte Walton Liddell, daughter of John Arnott Taylor of Belfast. In 1896 she married Sir Robert Morris Liddell, a JP and High Sheriff for Co. Down, a JP for Armagh, Honorary Treasurer of the Ulster Unionist Council and managing director of William Liddell and Company, Belfast, London and New York. *Thom's Irish Who's Who*, p. 136.

[128] Eva Lucy Mary St. John, eldest daughter of Col. E. A. Fitzroy, Hale Place, Surrey. In 1903 she married Lieutenant Col. Stuart William Ward, a JP and Deputy Lieutenant for Co. Armagh and a Major from 1900. *Thom's Irish Who's Who*, p. 18.

[129] Possibly the wife of D. D. Reid, a member of the Ulster Unionist Council.

be prepared and read.

2 That provision should be made on every agenda for a report from each of the Sub-Committees.

3 That a report of the state of the funds specifying the Bank Balance, details of payments and all monies received from Branches, personal subscriptions etc., be given.

4 That a record of meetings held by the various Associations be given.

5 That a report be made regarding deputations and workers sent to England.

6 That the Committee be informed of literature which is most in demand.

7 That at each meeting of the Executive Committee a report should be read from one of the affiliated Associations stating the number of members, of any work done in the way of sending workers to Gt. Britain, circulating literature there or having Unionist voters placed on the Register. That these reports should be made in rotation.

Mrs Robertson, Mrs John Lowry, Mrs Sinclair and Mrs McClintock spoke in support of these suggestions ...

Miss F. H. Whitaker[130] mentioned that at present badges could not be obtained quickly enough ... The Secretary explained that the delay in getting badges at present was due to the fact that until the beginning of 1912 there was no great demand for badges; and the Finance Committee had not felt justified in ordering a large supply until they were sure the badges would be bought by the affiliated Associations.
The Chairman said the Finance Committee would in future be able to keep a larger stock in hand as the demand seemed to have increased.

Miss F. H. Whitaker moved Motion No. 10 on the agenda. 'That in future no person is employed by the U.W.U.C. unless he or she is a member of a Unionist Club and can be vouched for by the Executive Committee of the Club to which he or she belongs.' This was seconded by Miss Ferguson.

Considerable discussion followed dealing particularly with the case of one man who had been taken to England by a member of the Committee to assist her in a series of meetings.

Finally the Chairman pointed out that the proposal was already covered by the following resolution passed by the Executive Committee on 25th September 1911:–

'That men be employed on special service, when necessary, each case to be separately considered by the Executive Committee.'
The matter then dropped.

Miss Tracey proposed Motion No. 11 'That a vote of thanks be sent to the Secretary of the Y.W.C.A. for their generosity in granting us the use of their Hall at half price for the good of the cause.'
This was seconded by Mrs W. J. Allen[131] and passed unanimously.

130 Miss Francis H. Whitaker died in 1921.

131 Lady Maria Allen, daughter of John Ross. She married Sir William Allen, Honorary Secretary of the Ulster Unionist Council, MP for N. Armagh from 1917 and a JP and Deputy Lieutenant for Co. Armagh. He was knighted in 1921. Lady Allen also served as a JP and was a Vice Chairman of the UWUC from 1921–23 and from 1933 until her death in 1937. *Thom's Irish Who's Who*, p. 3.

The business concluded.

[Attached to the minutes is a report regarding the Easter Demonstration, from a meeting of the Sub-Committee which met on] Monday 4th March, 1912 at 12 o'clock in the U.W.U.C. office ... The Dowager Marchioness of Dufferin & Ava (in the chair) ... The Secretary laid before the committee letters which had been received from the Secretary of the Ulster Unionist Council with regard to accommodation for members of the Ulster Women's Unionist Council at the [Balmoral] Show Grounds.

[Letters attached to report:]

The Sub-Committee recommend the Executive Committee to accept the 250 seats offered at 5/– each.

They recommend that nine seats be offered to each affiliated Association, and that any seats which are not taken up in this way may be applied for by Associations wishing to send more than nine representatives.

The Sub-Committee further recommend that the matter of hospitality be considered and ladies in Belfast or the neighbourhood willing to give hospitality be asked to send in their names before the 12th March 1912.

The Sub-Committee also recommend that the question of a badge to be worn at the Demonstration be considered by the Executive.[132]

19 March 1912

The 24th meeting of the Executive Committee of the U.W.U.C. was held in the Lecture Hall of the Young Women's Christian Assoc. 9, Donegall Sq. E.[,] Belfast ... at 2 p.m. ... Lady Dixon (in the chair)[133] ... A letter was read from Mrs Mercier-Clements suggesting that copies of the Christian Advocate giving the report of the Methodist Convention held in Belfast on 14th March 1912, should be sent to every Wesleyan Methodist Minister in England.

Mrs Robertson proposed and Mrs King-Kerr seconded that the papers should be sent from the Office of the U.W.U.C. ... The Secretary reported that he had applied to the Railway Companies for permission to use the vouchers for Sub-Committees and Worker's Classes as well as for meetings of the Executive Committee, but that the request had been refused.

The secretary reported that he had received a claim for payment of income tax by the Council and that he was looking into the matter.

132 A letter from the UUC Secretary, Richard Dawson Bates, to the UWUC Secretary, John Hamill is attached to the minutes. Dated 1 March 1912 it states 'In answer to your queries:– (1) The Committee do not propose that the Ulster Women's Unionist Council should take any official part in the proceedings; (2) No further special accommodation will be provided for women in the Show Grounds, apart from the 250 reserved seats; (3) It is not proposed to allow women to take part in the March, which will consist of the Clubs and Orangemen. The grounds will, of course, be open to the general public.'

133 Seventy–two members were present at this meeting and there were twenty–four apologies for non–attendance.

A report of the Active Worker's Committee was read giving a list of meetings held since the last meeting of the Executive Committee and also of meetings arranged for future dates.

A report was also read of Campaign work done in England & Scotland up till the end of 1911.

A list of arrangements for linking was also given and a report stating that tours in North Suffolk and North Norfolk had been arranged for Mrs Dundas and Mrs Wheeler respectively.

Arising out of this report Mrs Sinclair made some suggestions with regard to orders for literature from country Associations.

Letters on the subject of linking and of openings for workers were read from Mr. H. Vernon Wilkins, Organizing Secretary of the Union Defence League, Major H. E. Tombe, Agent of the Unionist Associations of Ireland for the Northern Counties of England and Mr. Lewis B. Meredith, agent of the Unionist Associations of Ireland for the Eastern Counties of England.

A letter was also read from Miss J. B. Smyth, Secretary of the West Down W.U.A. reported that Mrs Smyth from Banbridge had addressed a meeting of 2,000 people at Macclesfield and was speaking at other places during her visit to England.

A report of the Finance Committee was presented and showed that the balance at the Bank on 5th March was £732 4 11.

A report of the Affiliation Committee stated that the West Down W.U.A. and the South Tyrone W.U.A. had been affiliated to the Council and that on 14th March the Secretary had attended a meeting in Ballymena when it was decided to form a Mid-Antrim Women's Unionist Association ...

A letter was read from Miss J. B. Smyth, Secretary of the West Down W.U.A. asking if it would be possible to present an address of welcome to Mr. Bonar Law either in Belfast or at Balmoral.

The Secretary reported that he had written to Mr. Bates and asked him if any opportunity could be given for presenting an address of welcome. Mr. Bates replied that no arrangements had been made for the Associations to present addresses of welcome to Mr. Bonar Law; and there would be only one address on Easter Tuesday, and that would be from the Unionists of Ulster.

It was proposed by the Marchioness of Dufferin & Ava and seconded by Mrs Robertson and passed unanimously that the Vice-President[134] be requested to arrange, if possible, for Mr. Bonar Law to receive an address from the Council. Mrs Thos. Sinclair proposed that the wording of the address and the arrangements for its presentation be left to the Demonstration Sub-Committee. Mrs R. T. Martin seconded the proposal which was passed unanimously

A letter was read from Miss F. E. Henderson stating that seats to view the procession were being let at the windows of the Samaritan Hospital, Lisburn Road. It was decided that any ladies wishing to have seats should apply to Miss Henderson direct.

134 Theresa, 6th Marchioness of Londonderry.

[The following resolution was passed] 'That the Executive Committee instructs the Honorary Secretaries to call a special meeting of the Ulster Women's Unionist Council on Wednesday, April 10th, 1912 at 11-30 a.m. and also to summon a special meeting of the Executive Committee for the same day at 3 o'clock p.m.; but that failing Lady Londonderry's presence on 10th April, no Council meeting should be held until she is able to attend.'[135]

10 April 1912

The 25th meeting of the Executive Committee of the Ulster Women's Unionist Council was held in the Minor Hall of the Young Men's Christian Association, Wellington Place ... at 11-30 a.m. ... The Marchioness of Londonderry, Vice-President (in the chair)[136] ... A letter was read from Mr. Joseph G. Reid, Secretary of the Methodist Convention stating that the Committee of the Methodist Demonstration against Home Rule had already issued 2,000 copies of the Demonstration number of the Christian Advocate amongst the Methodist Ministers in England.

A report of the Active Workers Committee was read. It contained a list of meetings held since [the] last meeting of the Executive Committee and a further list of meetings arranged for future dates ... Mrs Talbot stated that the League of Little Builders of the Empire had a balance in hand at the end of their Financial Year and that at her suggestion they had decided to make a donation of £5 to the Ulster Women's Unionist Council, provided the money could be earmarked to send a worker to England.

The Countess of Kilmorey proposed that Mrs Talbot's kind offer be accepted & the money earmarked accordingly. Mrs Sinclair of Strabane seconded and it was passed unanimously ... The Marchioness of Londonderry proposed and the Countess of Erne seconded that the Office of the Council be removed to the Old Town Hall.

After some discussion the Vice-President undertook to be responsible for any extra annual cost involved by the change and the proposal was then passed.

The Vice-President announced that she had received letters of resignation from the three Hon. Secretaries[137] and that as no suitable names had been suggested to fill the vacancies she proposed that the [Executive] Committee should recommend to the [U.W.U.] Council that a sub-committee be appointed to assist the Secretary [Mr. J.M. Hamill] and advise him on matters of policy etc.,

After considerable discussion the proposal was carried.

135 A list of twenty–five women's unionist associations that had affiliated to the UWUC is included in the minutes. These associations were situated in East and North Antrim, North, South, East and West Belfast, North, South, East and West Down, Lurgan, Portadown, South and Mid–Armagh, North, South, East and Mid–Tyrone, Londonderry and North Derry, Fermanagh, Lisburn, Monaghan, East and West Cavan.

136 One hundred and two members were present at this meeting and there were sixteen apologies for non–attendance.

137 See note 116 above.

The Vice-President proposed that it be a recommendation to the Ulster Women's Unionist Council that the Constitution be altered to allow of the election of two Vice-Presidents; and that [Hariot] the Dowager Marchioness of Dufferin & Ava be elected a Vice-President. Passed by acclamation.

Mrs Sinclair[,] Strabane, proposed that, all Ulster being now organized and represented on the Executive of the Ulster Women's Unionist Council, the Executive meetings should in future be held in various convenient centres such as Londonderry, Enniskillen and Portadown, in rotation with Belfast. Mrs Thos. Sinclair seconded. On a vote being taken the proposal was defeated.

Mrs Sinclair of Strabane proposed that in the case of our present Hon. Secretaries resigning it would be a fitting opportunity without personal offence, to abolish their office in which the working has led to regrettable friction, hindering our important work.

After some discussion Mrs Sinclair withdrew the motion[138] ...

[The minutes of a meeting of the Sub-Committee re. *Ne Temere* Decree held on 27 March are attached, and note as follows] when it was decided to draw up a petition from the Women of Ireland against Home Rule generally, but with particular reference to the ways in which the granting of Home Rule would affect the Women of Ireland. It was also decided to ask the Dublin women to join in getting signatures for the petition.[139] It was also decided to ask Mr. B. D. Megaw B.L. to assist the Committee when drawing up the petition.

The committee met again on the 28th & 29th March and on both occasions Mr. Megaw was present.

The draft petition was prepared ... and sent forward to the Emergency Committee for confirmation.

The Committee recommend that when the petition has been signed it should be issued in the form of a leaflet and distributed in England & Scotland, as an appeal to the women of Great Britain and Scotland for help.

'TO THE HONOURABLE THE COMMONS OF THE UNITED KINGDOM OF GREAT BRITAIN AND IRELAND IN PARLIAMENT ASSEMBLED.

The humble petition of the undersigned women of Ireland showeth.

That we are convinced that any legislation which would impair the existing Union between Great Britain and Ireland or result in the establishment of an Irish legislative body and an (independent) Irish executive responsible to it would be injurious to the common interests of our countrywomen, and we respectfully desire to call the attention of your Honourable House to certain of the grounds against such legislation which particularly affect women.

(a) Serious dangers would arise to our social and domestic liberties from entrusting

138 A report of the Finance Committee is appended to the minutes, stating, 'The Balance at the Bank on 1st April was £875–12–0.'

139 This petition was organised in response to the 1908 Papal decree, *Ne Temere,* of Pius X, which declared mixed marriages between Catholics and Protestants null and void if the marriage was not officially solemnized according to the rites of the Catholic Church.

legislative functions to a body of which a large permanent majority would be under ecclesiastical control.

(b) No legislative safeguards would avail to protect us against such dangers, as the Roman Catholic Church refuses to recognise the binding effect on any agreements which curtail her prerogatives and claims an uncontrolled jurisdiction in the provinces of education and the marriage laws, a claim which has been recognised in practice by the Irish Parliamentary Party.[140]

(c) The late iniquitous enforcement of the Ne Temere decree – a decree which specially affects the women of Ireland - and the slavish acquiescence of the Irish Nationalist members of Parliament in its operation, demonstrate that in an Irish Parliament the natural instincts of humanity would be of no avail as against the dictates of the Roman Church.

(d) The dominating power of ecclesiastics over education in Ireland, which is already excessive, would be largely increased and schools and colleges under the control of religious orders would be state favoured institutions under an Irish Parliament.

(e) There would be no prospect of beneficent legislation to ameliorate the conditions of life of unprotected women engaged in industrial work in many conventual institutions, as the Irish Nationalist members of Parliament steadfastly oppose such legislation.

(f) No valid reason has been advanced for depriving Irish women of the rights or privileges which they now enjoy.

We therefore pray the Honourable Commons of the United Kingdom of Great Britain and Ireland in Parliament assembled to reject any legislative proposals to disintegrate the United Kingdom and expose us to the disastrous consequences of such discrimination.

And so your Petitioners as in duty bound will ever pray etc.,

(Signatures follow) …

[A report from the Sub-Committee meeting of the 28 March regarding the Easter Demonstration is also appended, noting the following] when it was arranged to send 9 tickets to each affiliated Association which had applied for them and to distribute the extra tickets in proportion to the applications received.

The Committee also instructed the Secretary to send complimentary tickets to Mrs G. F. Stewart,[141] President of the Women's Committee of the Irish Unionist Alliance and Miss M. Austen Park, Treasurer of the Women's Amalgamated

140 The Irish Parliamentary Party (IPP) is often referred to as the nationalist party. The party grew from a loose association in the 1870s into a more cohesive and centralised party under Charles Stewart Parnell and his successors. The IPP's main aim was home rule for Ireland, but the fortunes of the party waned post 1918. Connolly, *Oxford Companion to Irish History*, pp 381–2.

141 Mrs G. F. Stewart was the wife of the Rt. Hon. George F. Stewart (1851–1928), MP, Vice Chairman of the Irish Unionist Alliance and Honorary Treasurer of the Joint Committee of Unionist Associations of Ireland. *Who Was Who*, vol. 2, p. 998.

Unionist & Tariff Reform Association.[142]

The Committee also drafted the address of welcome to be presented to Mr. Bonar Law on his arrival in Belfast ... It was decided that the address should be presented by Mrs R. J. McMordie, and that the deputation should consist of the three Hon. Secs. and the President of each affiliated Association.

Messrs, Carey & Thomson were instructed to engross and illuminate the address. On the 4th April a letter was received from the Secretary of the Ulster Unionist Council stating that the deputation to present the address must be confined to three ladies and the Secretary ... it was decided that the deputation should consist of Mrs R. J. McMordie (as originally arranged)[,] one Hon. Secretary and one Treasurer, as Lady Londonderry had specially asked that the Hon. Treasurer should accompany the deputation. It was decided to fill these two places by ballot and Mrs Wheeler and Miss Connor were drawn.

The Secretary reported that considerable dissatisfaction had been caused by the fact that the 250 seats allocated to the Council had not in any way been reserved. That similar tickets were being issued to other people free of charge and that many ladies had refused to pay 5/-, for their tickets. The Secretary had interviewed Mr. Bates on the matter and he had refused to make any other arrangements.

Mr. Bates informed the Secretary that only enough tickets were issued to fill the stands and that everyone would get a seat but no further concession could be made. He further stated that if the ladies were not satisfied with this arrangement any tickets returned on Saturday 6th inst., would not be charged for.

The Committee asked Mrs G. H. Clarke, & Mrs W. F. Coates to interview Mr. Bates but these ladies did not succeed in getting any better terms.

[A copy of the address to be presented to the Right Hon. A. Bonar Law, M.P. is also appended to the minutes, stating that] On behalf on the Ulster Women's Unionist Council, we desire to extend to you our heartiest welcome on the occasion of your first visit to Ulster, as leader of the Opposition.

We feel that we are now on the eve of a more critical struggle than either of the two preceding ones of behalf of the Union.

We believe that in wholehearted Union lies our strength, and in the exercise of it, we shall beyond doubt repeat the victories of 1886 and 1893.

We realise that the civil and religious liberty of the women of Ireland and the security of their homes can only be guaranteed under the Legislative and Administrative Union of Great Britain & Ireland; we are deeply conscious of our responsibilities and are determined to take our full share in the conflict that lies before us.

Confident in your powerful and effective advocacy of the cause we beg to subscribe ourselves on behalf on the Ulster Women's Unionist Council.

Your faithful friends,

[142] Letters accepting these invitations are appended to the minutes.

[A letter from Richard Dawson Bates to John Hamill, dated 3 April 1912, is also appended to the minutes, stating that] I should be glad if you will arrange for the Deputation representing your Council to be present at the Midland Railway at 11.45 a.m., on Easter Monday to present their Address to Mr. Bonar Law. The Deputation will have to be limited to three ladies and yourself. It is the only Address Mr. Bonar Law will receive, and it will have to be handed to him as he gets out of his Railway Carriage. Mr. Law will not, therefore, be able to make any Speech.

[A letter from Edward Carson addressed to Theresa Londonderry, dated 9 April 1912, is also appended to the minutes, stating that] I am extremely gratified with the success of the Women's Unionist Association and the work they have been doing and whose energies in straining every nerve to do all that is best for the cause. I really think we must in the end win a great victory. I am sure for this purpose every member of the Executive will see how essential it is that there … be the most absolute harmony in all your proceedings and as I have always been pressing upon our men to form a real brotherhood born of the Comm[ittee] … so I suggest that the ideal of a genuine and sympathetic union of absolute cohesion be aimed at by yr[.] Executive.

Will you please thank all of yr[.] members for me for all of the work they are doing tho' I do not get the opportunity of meeting them all personally I fully appreciate their incalcuable work.

30 April 1912

The 26th meeting of the Executive Committee was held … at 2-30 p.m. in the Lecture Hall of the Young Women's Christian Association, 9 Donegall Sq. E.[,] Belfast … Mrs McMordie (in the chair)[143] … [Noted] 'That the Executive Committee of the Ulster Women's Unionist Council at their first meeting since the appalling disaster to the Titanic[144] desire to express their heartfelt sympathy with the relatives and friends of those who perished on that occasion; and the Committee specially extend their sympathy to The Right Hon. Thomas and Mrs Andrews and the members of their family.'

The resolution was passed by the members standing and in silence …

A letter was read from Mr. Joseph G. Reid of the Methodist Convention asking the Executive Committee to assist the Committee of the Methodist Convention by purchasing a quantity of leaflets giving reports of the speeches of Sir William Whitla[145] and other gentleman.

143 Seventy–four members were present at this meeting and there were twenty–two apologies for non–attendance.

144 Ocean liner built by Harland and Wolff shipyard in Belfast which sank on its maiden voyage in April 1912 with the loss of 1,490 passengers and crew.

145 Sir William Whitla (1851–1933), Professor of Materia Medica at Queen's College, Belfast, knighted in 1902, President of the British Medical Association in 1909 and a member of the Irish Convention in 1917. He was also Pro–Chancellor of The Queen's University, Belfast and represented the university in the Parliament of Northern Ireland from 1918–22. *Thom's Irish Who's Who*, p. 260.

After some discussion the Secretary was instructed to try and obtain the leaflets free from the Ulster Unionist Council and failing that to order 2,000 from Mr. Reid.

A letter was read from Mrs Clegg, Secretary of the Ladies' Committee of the Irish Unionist Alliance ... reporting a gift of 3,000 copies of the Primate's Address to the General Synod in Dublin for distribution in England and Scotland.

The Secretary was instructed to send a letter of thanks to Lady Arnott.[146]

A letter was read from the Dowager Marchioness of Dufferin & Ava accepting the office of Vice-President ... Also a recommendation that a letter should be sent to all the Provincial Representatives asking them to assist in obtaining openings for canvassers and speakers in England and Scotland by bringing the work of the Council under the notice of English and Scotch Members and Agents ... The report of the Affiliation Committee stated that the Mid-Antrim Women's Unionist Association had been affiliated to the Council.

The report of the Advisory Committee was presented. It contained a recommendation to the Executive Committee to open a subscription list amongst the new Members of the Executive Committee for the furnishing of the New Offices in the Old Town Hall ... Mrs Robertson proposed 'That the Secretaries be requested to ask all Branch & District Secretaries to send in concise but full report[s] of all the work done in each Branch up to December 31st, 1911 and each fourth month thereafter, so that the Executive Committee be kept acquainted with the work done.

'That the Secretaries be also requested to summarise and abstract these reports and lay the results before the Executive meeting in May 1912, as regards the first set of returns for 1911, and every fourth month thereafter as regards the succeeding reports, and that the detailed reports be laid on the table for the inspection of any Members who desire to see them.'

Miss Ferguson seconded this.

On a vote being taken 14 voted for the proposal and 20 against. The Chairman declared the Motion lost ...

[A report of the Finance Committee is appended to the minutes, stating that] four canvassers were being sent to Norfolk and that the Council would have to pay not only travelling expenses but also part of the board and lodging of these ladies.

The Hon. Treasurer was authorised to give each of the four workers £10 (ten pounds) on account of their expenses.

21 May 1912

The 27th meeting of the Executive Committee was held ... at 2 p.m. in the Lecture

146 Lady Caroline Sydney Arnott, the eldest daughter of Sir Frederick M. Williams. In 1881 she married Sir John Alexander Arnott, 2nd Baronet of Woodlands, the chairman and managing director of the *Irish Times*, who was also a JP and Deputy Lieutenant. Lady Arnott was later made a DBE. *Dod's Peerage*, pp 29–30; *Thom's Irish Who's Who*, p. 8.

Hall of the Young Women's Christian Association, 9 Donegall Sq. E.[,] Belfast … Lady Dixon (in the chair)[147] … The Secretary reported that copies of 'Against Home Rule' should be purchased and sent to working men's Clubs in England & Scotland, and that the Committee had instructed him to get a quotation for 250 copies.

The Advisory Committee suggested that these copies might be supplied at wholesale price to any affiliated Associations wishing to send them to Clubs in constituencies with which they are linked. The publishers have offered to supply 250 copies @ 8d per copy being £8:6:8: for the lot.

It was proposed by Mrs Thomas Sinclair seconded by Mrs Robertson to order 250 copies … A letter was also read from Mrs Hill[,] 101 Fitzroy Avenue, Belfast proposing that an entertainment should be got up in the Ulster Hall for the benefit of Members of the various local Women's Unionist Associations … a Sub-Committee be appointed to meet Mrs Hill and consider the details of her proposal and report to the Executive Committee [which] should consist of two representatives from each of the Belfast Women's Unionist Associations and the Sub-Committee to choose its own Chairman.

[A report of a meeting of the Sub-Committee re. the *Ne Temere* Petition, held on 20th April 1912, is appended to the minutes, stating that] A letter was read from Sir John B. Lonsdale informing the Committee that the signatures to the Petition should be in his hands during the Whitsuntide Recess.

The Secretary reported that the Petition would have to be rolled by machinery to bring it within reasonable bulk as the slips when pasted together measured from 1,600 yards or almost one mile in length …

The Committee recommend to the Executive Committee that the Secretary take the Petition over to London and put it in the hands of Sir John B. Lonsdale hence avoiding any loss, risk or damage to the Petition in transit.

The Sub-Committee also recommend that Sir Edward Carson be asked to present the Petition.

The Committee further recommend that after the Petition has been placed in Sir John B. Lonsdale's hands a statement be sent to the Newspapers giving the number, length and other particulars as to the Petition.

18 June 1912

The 28th meeting of the Executive Committee was held … at 2 p.m. in the large hall of the Old Town Hall[,] Victoria Street, Belfast ... The Dowager Marchioness of Dufferin & Ava (in the chair)[148] … The Report of the Finance Committee showed a balance in the Bank of £627. [It was agreed] 'That a reserve fund of £300 be gradually formed and specially set aside, the fund earmarked for campaign work;

[147] Sixty–five members were present at this meeting and there were thirty–four apologies for non–attendance.

[148] Sixty–nine members were present at the meeting and there were thirty–four apologies for non–attendance.

the Finance Committee to report monthly how much can be set aside'. Passed unanimously.

Notice of Motion No. 11. 'That classes for Workers be held in various provincial towns to be conducted by suitable persons was 'in the absence of Mrs Mercier Clements' proposed by Mrs Wheeler and passed unanimously …

Mrs Pooler proposed and Mrs Robertson seconded that Notice of Motion No. 13 'That in as such as there is a large balance to the credit of the funds of the Ulster Women's Unionist Council, a substantial subscription be sent to Sir Edward Carson's fund for the Anti-Home Rule Campaign. The amount of subscription to be decided by the Finance Committee. [']

After some discussion Mrs Pooler asked to be allowed to withdraw the Motion until further subscriptions come in …

Active Worker's Committee.

REPORT

Since the last meeting of the Executive Committee held on the 21st May, the following arrangements have been made for workers:–

Mrs Malone went from North West Norfolk to Ellesmere, Shropshire where she is doing three weeks canvassing.

July 4th. Meeting at Newport, Shropshire.

July 11th Shropshire.

July 24th Market Drayton. Mrs J. C. White.

The following ladies are working in the Holmfirth Bye-Election Mrs Beattie, Mrs Courvoisier, Miss McKelvey, Miss Speers and Miss Ethel Webb, also Mrs Mercier-Clements.

Mrs Sinclair (Strabane) is working in the Newmarket Division of Cambridgeshire and Norfolk.

Arrangements are also being made for a Campaign in Yorkshire during the next few months.

An application has also been received from the West of Scotland for 4 canvassers in September, to be followed by a speaker later.

Miss Clara Johnston, Holywood, is working in Ross-shire on behalf of the Unionist candidate Capt. MacLeod.

The Committee desire to recommend to the Executive the adoption of Mrs Mercier-Clements' proposal to hold classes for workers in Provincial towns and also to recommend the adoption of Mrs Wheeler's proposal to establish a special reserve fund for a General Election.

16 July 1912

The 29th meeting of the Executive Committee was held … at 2 p.m. in the U.W.U.C. Committee Room No 4, Old Town Hall, Victoria Street, Belfast … The

Right Hon. The Countess of Erne (in the chair)[149] … A letter was read from the Secretary of the Chatham and Gillingham Women's Unionist Association enclosing a resolution passed at a meeting of the association on Thursday 20th June 1912 … That this meeting of the Executive Committee and Members of the Chatham and Gillingham Women's Conservative and Unionist Association, hereby expresses its admiration of the resolve of the Loyal Women of Ulster to stand by their menfolk in the resistance of Home Rule, and pledges itself to join hands with those loyal brothers and sisters in Ireland, to in every way resist any attempt of the separation of the two countries, but on the other hand to do all in its power to still further strengthen the Union of the Kingdom and the Unity of the Empire …

A letter was read from Mrs Sinclair (Strabane) who had been working in Cambridge and Norfolk enclosing a cheque for £8.18.6 which had been collected after one of Mrs Sinclair's meetings in Norfolk and given to her for the Campaign fund of the Council … The Secretary reported that he had a visit from Captain MacLeod[,] Unionist Candidate for Rosshire, and that Captain McLeod asked him to express to the Committee his appreciation of the services rendered by Miss Clare A[.] Johnston in Rosshire, and his thanks to the Committee for sending Miss Johnston … Mrs Mercier–Clements asked the Committee to consider the advisability of inviting a number of Radicals from England and Scotland to visit Ireland and consider Irish conditions for themselves ... and [it] passed unanimously that the Secretary [Mr. J.M. Hamill] be instructed to communicate with the Secretary of the Ulster Unionist Council on the matter.

The business concluded.

During the month of June the following Campaign work was done:–

N Norfolk	Miss Grange	1 month	£11. 19. 6
	Miss Hamill	1 month	13. 16. 8
Ross-shire	Miss Clare Johnston	5 weeks	5. 0. 0
Holmfirth	Miss Speers		2. 7. 9
Bye-election	Miss E Webb		3. 15. 0
	Mrs Beattie		4. 9. 9
	Mrs Courviosier		3. 8. 3
	Miss McKelvey		3. 16. 9
	Mrs Mercier-Clements		6. 0. 9½
Glasgow St Rollox	Miss H. Douglas	4 days	2. 8. 4
Oswestry	Mrs Malone	2 weeks	7. 7. 4
Cambridge & Norfolk	Mrs Sinclair	4 weeks	10. 0. 0
			£74. 10. 1½

[149] Forty–three members were present at this meeting and there were thirty–eight apologies for non–attendance.

During the first fortnight of July the following is the record:–

Ross-shire	Miss Clare Johnston
Cambridge & Norfolk	Mrs Sinclair
Shropshire	Mrs Murland, Mrs J.C. White
Crewe	Mrs Leatham, Mrs ffrench Beytagh
Hanley Bye-Election	Mrs Shaw Hamilton, Mrs ffrech Beytagh, Miss Leatham
Eddisbury Div. Cheshire	Miss C. M. Johnston

12 meetings in Ulster ...

FINANCIAL REPORT.

Cash in hands or at Bank £688 4 4.

17 September 1912

The 30th meeting of the Executive Committee of the Ulster Women's Unionist Council was held in the large Hall of the Old Town Hall, Victoria Street, Belfast … at 2 p.m. … The Dowager Marchioness of Dufferin & Ava (in the chair)[150] … The Chairman submitted a draft of the Women's Declaration to be signed on Ulster Day, which had been prepared by the Advisory Committee and recommended by them for adoption by the Executive Committee. The wording of the Declaration was unanimously approved of[151] … [A] letter was read from Mrs Simonton, Dynevor, Knock, enclosing a cheque for £22:0: 0: being the amount of a collection made by her for the Campaign Fund. The Secretary announced that further subscriptions sent in by Mrs Simonton brought the total of the collection to £23: 5 … It was proposed by Mrs Sinclair, (Strabane)[,] seconded by Mrs McCalmont, that each affiliated Association be asked to guarantee a sum of £20: 0: 0: to be called upon, as and when required, for Campaign and General Election purposes.

The Chairman suggested that no definite amount should be mentioned, but that each Association should be asked to promise as much as they could. After some discussion the proposal was carried with this amendment … Mrs King-Kerr had an

150 One hundred members were present at the meeting and there were thirty–five apologies for non–attendance.

151 Ulster Day was held on 28 September 1912. The Women's Declaration was similar to the Solemn League and Covenant organised by the UUC in opposition to home rule. The UWUC were responsible for both the wording and the setting up of stations throughout Ulster where women, who favoured the maintenance of the legislative union and were opposed to home rule, could sign the declaration.

interesting account of 'Speech Parties' which had been organized in connection with the East Belfast W.U.A. with a view to training speakers for Unionist meetings.

The next business on the agenda was a proposal by Mrs Talbot, that an office should be opened in London, in connection with the Ulster Women's Unionist Council.

Mrs Talbot said in view of the difficulties pointed out by the Advisory Committee, she wished to withdraw her proposal so far as she personally was concerned.

In response however, to the general wish of the meeting, and a request by the Chairman, Mrs Talbot gave an outline of her scheme and the reasons which led her to bring it forward.

The Chairman then read the following proposal from the Advisory Committee:- 'That Mrs Talbot's proposal to open a London office should be discussed by the Executive Committee to-day, but that a final decision on the question should be postponed until the next meeting of the Executive Committee, to give Members a full opportunity of considering this scheme in all its aspects.' [The Executive Committee read a letter and passed a resolution sent by Lady Londonderry,[152] dated 16 September 1912, which stated:]

My Dear Friends,

As Vice-President of the Ulster Women's Unionist Association I write this letter to be read at your meeting on Tuesday 17th., to say how very disappointed I am that owing to reasons of health I am not allowed to be with you on such an occasion and I would ask you to believe that it is only the imperative orders of my Doctor that has prevented me being present in Belfast today and also to take part in the services of 'Ulster Day'. I am asking Lady Dufferin to move a resolution in my name and I would earnestly ask all the members of the Advisory Committee of the Ulster Women's Unionist Associations present in the room at the reading of this letter to pass the resolution which I have put down and to continue working as hard as they have always done, since the formation of our great Association and to leave no stone unturned in their endeavours to further the Unionist Party's policy – and we are not working alone as we have the whole Unionist Party behind us as will be seen from the following quotation from Mr Bonar Law's letter to the electors of Mid-Lothian:– 'That the scheme of driving a population of more than one million people of Belfast

[152] Theresa, 6th Marchioness of Londonderry and a Vice President of UWUC.

[153] Established in New York in 1836 the Ancient Order of Hibernians (AOH) developed into the largest Irish American benevolent society. Its popularity was, however, limited in both Britain and Ireland until 1900. The order was both Catholic and broadly nationalist in outlook and operated under the slogan 'Faith and Fatherland'. The northern nationalist leader, Joseph Devlin, was the national president of the organisation from 1905–34 and turned it into a political machine of some significance. Membership of the order increased from 10,000 in 1905 to 60,000 in 1909. The order was especially popular in Ulster and Dublin and was seen by many as a rival to the Orange Order. The Ancient Order of Hibernians also had a Ladies' Auxiliary. Connolly, *Oxford Companion to Irish History*, p. 13.

and surrounding counties who are passionately attached to the Union and who look with horror on the transfer of their allegiance from the British House of Commons to a Parliament composed of men who are dominating the Ancient Order of Hibernians[153] and control the United Irish League[154] – and to drive these loyal citizens out of our community against their will, will be an action of criminal injustice of which the British people could never be guilty.' Even should the bill pass through the House of Commons, (which many doubt at present as the Coalition Government has shown great signs of disintegration lately in the divisions in the House of Commons and no doubt Ulster's firm attitude has caused searching of hearts among many supporters of the Government) we should then have over two years before us to convince England that under no circumstances whatever will we accept Home Rule and that we are unshaken in our antagonism to such a policy.[155] I would ask you in addition to passing this resolution to continue the excellent work which has been done by the Association, particulars of which no doubt will be given to you today, as I have heard on this side of the Irish Channel, the excellent effect our workers have produced wherever they have spoken, and distributed literature. As told you in our manifesto our one danger is that England is apathetic, but I think we now see signs of awakening! I shall hope to be with you early in January when I trust that we shall be able to have the annual meeting of our Association. The resolution which I have asked Lady Dufferin to move on my behalf is as follows:–

'Feeling as we do that the people of England will never support the Government in attempting to carry Home Rule without the consent of the country, we are confident at this juncture that the Ulster Women's Unionist Association will support the men of Ulster and the Unionist Party in their endeavours to frustrate the Government's plan of disintegrating the Empire. We in Ulster wish and intend to continue inside the Union and under the protection of the British Parliament at Westminster and we <u>refuse</u> to be driven forth by legislation which Ulster rightly declares has under present conditions no moral sanction whatever.'

I cannot tell you how sorry I am that these untoward circumstances should have prevented me taking my proper place among you all in Ulster at this crisis in our history …

[A report of a meeting of the Finance Committee held on 16 August 1912 is appended to the minutes] considering the question of making an Annual Subscription from the Members of the Executive Committee compulsory … while the Council are at present liable for an annual expenditure of, in or about Four hundred pounds (£400 –) the only fixed income available to meet this expenditure

[154] The United Irish League (UIL) was established in 1898 by William O'Brien to press for Irish land redistribution. The organisation played an important role in uniting nationalism in 1900 and thereafter became a constituency and fund–raising body which enjoyed a close association with the Ancient Order of Hibernians. The organisation was, however, in decline from 1916 onwards and its Dublin offices closed in 1920. Connolly, *Oxford Companion to Irish History*, p. 561.

[155] This situation was due to the Parliament Act of 1911 which removed the House of Lords' power of veto and replaced it with a two-year delaying power.

consists of the Affiliation Fees of three guineas each, paid by the various affiliated associations. As the affiliated associations at present number twenty seven, the income from this source would amount to £85: 1: 0 while the affiliation of South Derry W.U.A. and the three Donegal Associations would bring the total to £97:13:0 beyond this the Council is depending on voluntary contributions from Members and associations and its position from a Financial and business standpoint is therefore most unsound.

After a lengthy discussion it was decided to call the attention of the Executive Committee to this state of affairs at their next meeting and to request the Executive Committee to consider ways and means of providing a fixed income to meet the ascertained liabilities of the Council. The Committee considered that this might be done by making an Annual subscription from Members of the Executive Committee compulsory, but it was decided merely to place the matter before the Executive Committee and to make no definite recommendation for the present … [A report of a meeting of the Finance Committee held on 16 September 1912 is appended to the minutes, stating that the] credit balance at the Bank was £643 17 8 … [estimated expenses for active workers' expenses, rent, postage, stationary, telegrams, etc. were £600.] If no contributions are received from now until January the council will then have only £43: 17: 8: in hand.

The Finance Committee wish to draw the attention to the fact that only about one quarter of the Members of the Executive Committee have paid subscriptions for the year 1912.

When the question of subscriptions was left to the discretion of Members it was hoped there would be a more generous response, than has been the case.

As the Financial year is now almost at an end and as a list of subscriptions must be published in the Annual Report, the Committee hope that as many Members as possible will subscribe before the 1st December, 1912.

The Committee have much pleasure in reporting that Mrs Simonton has forwarded to the Treasurer, the sum of £23: 5: 0: which she has collected from friends of the Cause, also that Lady Dixon has kindly promised to send two workers to Scotland, and that Mrs James Moore has given a subscription of £5: 0: 0: to the Campaign Fund.

15 October 1912

The 31st meeting of the Executive Committee of the U.W.U.C. was held in the Committee Room, No. 4, Old Town Hall, Victoria Street, Belfast … at 2 p.m. … The Dowager Marchioness of Dufferin & Ava (in the chair)[156] … [The] Secretary read a list of amounts promised by various Associations to the General Election Guarantee Fund. A letter was also read from Mrs Dunbar-Buller, guaranteeing a

[156] Eighty–one members were present at this meeting and there were twenty–eight apologies for non–attendance.

sum of £100 (one hundred pounds) in the event of a General Election.

The Secretary read a number of resolutions of sympathy and support received from various Associations in England and Scotland; he was instructed to send a letter of thanks to each of the Associations mentioned … Miss Connor again called the attention of the Committee to the fact that it was desirable for the Council to have a fixed source of income to meet their known liabilities, and for this purpose the Finance Committee relied on the generous support and subscriptions from Members of the Executive Committee …

On a recommendation of the Advisory Committee it was unanimously decided that it would not be advisable to hold a public Demonstration in January …

A report was presented from the Active Workers' Committee in the form of replies to the arguments brought forward by Mrs Talbot, and which she had issued on a printed slip.

The report[,] amongst other things[,] expressed the opinion, 'That the Committee considers an Association of Ulsterwomen in London might advisably be formed, on broad, democratic lines to be affiliated in the same way as our other branches.'

'The committee feels that the time has now come to organize an Association of Unionist Ulster Women in London to be organised on the same lines as our existing Associations and affiliated to the Council in the ordinary way; and that this be a recommendation to the Executive Committee to instruct the Secretary to proceed at once with the organization of such an Association, and to take all steps necessary as he would in the organization of an Association in Ulster' … [and] 'That an Association of Unionist Ulsterwomen should be formed' … [This was] unanimously adopted.

Mrs Thomas Sinclair proposed that the work should not to confined to London alone, but that similar Associations should be organized where possible, in other important centres in England and Scotland.

This was seconded by Mrs Dunbar-Buller and passed unanimously

Mrs Sinclair (Strabane) suggested that the Committee should ask for Mr Talbot's help in organizing the London office, and that Lady Arthur Hill should also be approached on the matter.

This was supported by Mrs McMordie and Mrs Robertson … Members of the Executive Committee were asked to send in to the Secretary the names of any Ulsterwomen they knew of living in London and the neighbourhood.

The Secretary was instructed to inform the Marchioness of Londonderry of the decision of the Committee.

[A letter from Julia Talbot to Mr Hamill, dated 14 October 1912, is appended to the minutes, stating] I am more firmly convinced than ever of the necessity of an active, business-like London office and I think recent events there have gone a long way to prove my contention that such an office could easily pay its own way.

But to be really successful, I believe three things are necessary;

I It should be started at once.
II It should be worked by business-like women, who know and are known in London &
III there should be a greatly increased supply of active workers, ready to send over from Ulster.

19 November 1912

The 32nd meeting of the Executive Committee of the U.W.U.C. was held in the Committee Room No. 4, Old Town Hall, Victoria Street, Belfast ... Lady Anderson (in the chair)[157] ... The Bank Balance was stated to be £424: 12 : 4 ... the following associations have been affiliated to the Council:–

South Derry Women's Unionist Association.
North Donegal Women's Unionist Association.
South Donegal Women's Unionist Association.
West Donegal Women's Unionist Association ...

A number of letters were read which had been received from various associations in England and Scotland and Wales expressing appreciation of the work done by workers sent out by the Ulster Women's Unionist Council.

REPORT OF THE ADVISORY COMMITTEE ...

1 'That so far as Scotland is concerned the proposal to form an Association of Unionist Ulsterwomen in important centres be completely dropped.'
2 'That the Honorary Secretaries of Affiliated Associations should be strongly advised to exclude Newspaper Reporters from the business part of their Annual Meetings, as it is not desirable that the financial position of our Association should be made public, or the exact places in which our workers have been'.
3 'The Advisory Committee recommends that a telegram be sent to the Chairman of the meeting which is to be held to-night in the Wesleyan Westminster Hall, to protest against the Ne Temere Decree. The telegram should express appreciation of the work done by those who have organized the meeting, and should state the number of signatures obtained by the Ulsterwomen's Petition against Home Rule'.

The report and three recommendations were unanimously agreed to.
[A report of the Advisory Committee, dated 19 November 1912, is appended to the minutes, stating that] About the middle of October a request was received from a number of Ulsterwomen in Paisley who wished to be organized into an Association to be affiliated with the Ulster Women's Unionist Council.

The Advisory Committee instructed the Secretary to inform the West of Scotland, Women's Unionist Association that this request had been received and

157 Seventy–four members were present at the meeting and there were thirty–seven apologies for non–attendance.

that it was proposed to form such an Association in Paisley.

In reply a very strong letter was received from Lady Arthur, President of the West of Scotland, W.U.A. protesting against the formation of any Association in the West of Scotland, other than that already existing.

In view of Lady Arthur's letter the Advisory Committee thought it well to make further enquiries as to the views of existing Associations before proceeding with the formation of Women's Unionist Associations in any part of Gt. Britain ... The Advisory Committee now recommends that so far as Scotland is concerned, the scheme be completely dropped.

17 December 1912

The 33rd meeting of the Executive Committee of the Ulster Women's Unionist Council was held in the Committee Room, No. 4, Old Town Hall, Victoria Street, Belfast ... at 2 p.m. ... Mrs Thomas Sinclair (in the chair)[158] ... The Secretary reported that he had received a letter from Mr H. M. Gooch, Secretary of the Evangelical Alliance[159] acknowledging the telegram sent to the Ne Temere Protest meeting held on 19th November 1912, and stating the telegram had been laid before the meeting.

Some correspondence was read and dealt with including a number of letters of thanks for the services of workers.

FINANCE COMMITTEE REPORT

A report of the Finance Committee was submitted by the Hon Treasurer stating the bank Balance was £576: 6: 4. The report was agreed to.

ACTIVE WORKER'S REPORT

This report stated that three workers had been engaged in England and Scotland during December.

AFFILIATION REPORT

This report stated that East Donegal Women's Unionist Association had been affiliated to the Council bringing the total number of affiliated associations to 32.

ADVISORY COMMITTEE REPORT

The report of the Advisory Committee contained the suggested arrangements for the Annual Meeting on 16th January 1913. The report recommended that the Meeting should be held at 2.p.m. in the Minor Hall, Y.M.C.A. Wellington Place, Belfast and also that each of the Belfast Associations should be asked to send three

158 Sixty–eight members were present at this meeting and there were twenty–eight apologies for non–attendance.

159 This body has been described as providing not only 'pan–Protestant resistance to Home Rule but a pan–Evangelical campaign as well'. See David Hempton and Myrtle Hill, *Evangelical Protestantism in Ulster Society, 1740–1890* (London and New York, 1992), p. 175.

members to assist in finding seats for those attending and distributing voting papers etc.

Draft agenda for the meeting and Draft Annual Report were submitted by the Advisory Committee for approval and after detailed consideration were unanimously agreed to ...

The Sub-Committee appointed by the Advisory Committee to make arrangements were authorized to make any further necessary arrangements for the meeting … It was proposed by Mrs Robertson[,] seconded by Miss Cromie

'That the 32 Secretaries should receive copies of the reports of the various Committees monthly.'

Mrs Mitchell proposed as an Amendment

'That any Secretary wishing for a special report can have same on writing for it'[.]

On a vote being taken there voted

For the Amendment	47
Against	5
Majority for Amendment	42

The Chairman declared the Amendment carried. The Amendment was then put to the meeting as a substantive Motion.

In reply to a question The Secretary stated that he understood the men's organization were strongly opposed to any Financial Statement or report of Campaign work being printed and circulated.

The Motion was then put to the meeting when there voted for the Motion	4.
Against	36.
Majority Against	32.

The Chairman declared the Motion lost.

The Business concluded.

16 January 1913

A special Meeting of the Executive Committee was held … at 11-30 a.m. in the Committee Room, No. 4 Old Town Hall, Victoria Street, Belfast ... The Dowager Marchioness of Dufferin & Ava (in the chair)[160] … On the recommendation of the Sub-Committee to arrange for the Annual Meeting it was unanimously decided to insert the following paragraphs in the Annual Report:–[161]

Your Committee approved the following Declaration to be signed by Unionist Women of Ulster on Ulster Day, 28th September, 1912, in the following terms:–

[160] Ninety members were present at this meeting and there were sixteen apologies for non–attendance.
[161] For copies of UWUC annual reports from 1914–71 see PRONI, D/2688/1/9.

'We, whose names are underwritten, Women of Ulster and Loyal subjects of our gracious King, being firmly persuaded that Home Rule would be disastrous to our Country, desire to associate ourselves with the men of Ulster in their uncompromising opposition to the Home Rule Bill now before Parliament, whereby it is proposed to drive Ulster out of her cherished place in the Constitution of the United Kingdom and to place her under the domination and control of a Parliament in Ireland.

Praying that from this calamity God will save Ireland, we hereto subscribe or names.'

This declaration was signed by 234,046 women of Ulster, and the signed forms are now in the custody of the Ulster Unionist Council.[162]

WOMEN'S MEETING, 30TH SEPTEMBER, 1912

A Women's Meeting, to inaugurate the Autumn Campaign, was held in the Ulster Hall, Belfast, on 30th September, 1912.

The Dowager Marchioness of Dufferin & Ava presided. Half-an-hour before the time fixed for the meeting to begin that Hall and Minor Hall were both filled. The Assembly Hall was secured for an overflow meeting, and soon crowded to the doors. Thousands were unable to gain admission.

The meeting was organized by the four Belfast Associations, and the cost was defrayed by some working men's Clubs.

It is estimated that the combined gathering formed the largest women's meeting ever held in Ireland.

It was unanimously decided to recommend to the Annual Meeting of Council, to co-opt the following ladies as Members of Council:–

Mrs Herbert Ewart.
Mrs Packenham.
Mrs Geo. Preston.
Mrs D. D. Reid.
Mrs Walter Richardson.

It was decided by a large majority of those present that a list of the names and addresses of Members attending the Annual Meeting of Council, should both be published in the papers. The business concluded.

28 January 1913

The 34th meeting of the Executive Committee of the Ulster Women's Unionist Council, was held in the U.W.U.C. Committee Room, No 4 Old Town Hall,

162 Approximately 100 boxes containing signed copies of the UWUC Women's Declaration and the UUC Solemn League and Covenant are in PRONI, D/1327/3. Close to 16,000 more women signed the Women's Declaration than men signed the Solemn League and Covenant.

Victoria Street, Belfast ... at 11-30 a.m ... The Dowager Marchioness of Dufferin & Ava, (in the chair)[163] ... A letter from Mrs Corscaden, Vice-President of the Londonderry Women's Unionist Registration Association, asking if the Committee would present 400 badges to be worn by the Unionist workers at the Londonderry City Bye-Election, on January, 30th 1913, was read.

The Secretary reported that to save time he had on his own responsibility ordered 400 badges, same as sample submitted. The order would cost about 35/– or 40/–. It was unanimously resolved to present the badges to the Londonderry workers.

A telegram was read from Sir Edward Carson acknowledging the message of sympathy sent from the Annual Meeting of Council on Thursday, 16th January, 1913.[164]

A letter was read from Miss Burton, of Norwich, enclosing the Agenda for a Unionist Conference to be held in Norwich on Saturday, 8th February, 1913, and inviting the Committee to send the Organizing Secretary, to represent the Ulster Women's Unionist Council.

Some discussion took place in the course of which it was pointed out that the Secretary [Mr. J.M. Hamill] could at the same time interview the agents in East Anglia and Manchester, of the Joint Committee of the Unionist Associations of Ireland. It was unanimously decided that the Secretary should represent the Council at Norwich, on 8th February.

The Vice-President was requested to write personally to Miss Graham Hope, Organizing Secretary of the Women's Amalgamated Unionist & Tariff Reform Association, as she was to preside at the Conference, informing her that the Committee wished their Organizing Secretary to be present and to speak on the Home Rule question ... It was proposed by Mrs Mercier-Clements, seconded by Mrs John Thompson,

'That a list of ladies in Belfast willing to provide hospitality for country Members attending meetings of Committee and compelled to stay over night in Belfast, be prepared and kept in the office, and that ladies wishing to avail themselves of this arrangement be asked to apply to the Secretary.'

Passed unanimously.

The business concluded.

18 February 1913

The 35th meeting of the Executive Committee was held ... at 2 p.m. in the U.W.U.C. Committee Room, No. 4. Old Town Hall, Victoria Street, Belfast ... The Dowager Marchioness of Dufferin & Ava (in the chair)[165] ... The report of the

163 Eighty–three members were present at this meeting and there were fifty–three apologies for non–attendance.

164 The telegram from Edward Carson, dated 17 January 1913, is attached to the minutes and reads, 'I much appreciate the sympathy expressed by Ulster Women's Council in my present anxiety. Please thank them.' Carson's wife, Annette, was seriously ill at this time and died in April 1913.

165 Eighty–nine members were present at this meeting and there were thirty–nine apologies for non–attendance.

Finance Committee was read by Miss Connor, Hon. Treasurer, which showed the Bank balance on the No. 1 Account to be £1,003: 18: 3: and on the General Election No. 2. Account £308: 3: 11 ... The Secretary [Mr. J.M. Hamill] gave a detailed report of his visit to London, Kings Lynn, Norwich and Manchester. He recommended that the number of sets of Lantern Slides should be largely increased as he found a great demand for Lantern Lectures everywhere. He also reported that he had been asked to provide some Irish Notes for the Norfolk Chronicle, and to communicate with Mr. George R. Reid[166] and to ask if he would be willing to give any help in this matter.

After discussion the Secretary was authorised to supply notes after consultation with Mr. Reid ...

REPORT OF THE ADVISORY COMMITTEE

1 Recommendation of the names of The Countess of Belmore,[167]

The Lady O'Neill,[168]
Mrs McGeagh McCaw,

be added to the ex-officio members of the Council and Executive Committee.

2 Cards have been printed giving the address of the Office, that names of Office-Bearers, and some particulars as to the Organization, for circulation in England and Scotland.

3 As the Secretary reported that last year ladies had attended meeting of the Executive Committee who were not Members of the Committee, and as it is not possible at present to insure that no unauthorised person will attend meetings of the Committee, Members of the Committee are to be provided with cards of admission, to be shown at the door before entering any meeting of the Executive Committee.

4 A scheme for co-option of Members of Council and Members of Executive Committee on the lines proposed by MrsA. G. Finlay, and it is under

166 George R. Reid, a Belfast solicitor and Secretary of the Ulster Unionist Council's Committee of Businessmen. He advised Ulster unionists on the commercial problems involved in their anti–home rule campaign, for instance, on issues such as the non–payment of taxes. See Buckland, *Irish Unionism, 1885–1923.*

167 Anne Elizabeth Honoria, the 4th Countess of Belmore, second daughter of Capt. John Neilson Gladstone, MP. In 1861 she married Somerset Richard, the 4th Earl of Belmore, a JP in Cos. Fermanagh, Tyrone and Kent, a representative peer for 56 years and Under Secretary of State for the Home Department from 1866–67. He was also Governor of New South Wales from 1867–72 and a Lord Justice of Ireland on numerous occasions. The Countess of Belmore was widowed in 1913 and died in 1919. *Dod's Peerage*, pp 74–5.

168 Hon. Lady Sylvia O'Neill, later Lady Rathcavan, the daughter of Walter Sandeman of Morden House, Royston. In 1909 she married Hugh O'Neill, later Baron Rathcavan, an MP for Mid Antrim from 1915–22, Antrim County from 1922–50 and for the northern division of Antrim from 1950–52. He represented County Antrim in the Parliament of Northern Ireland from 1921–29 and was the first speaker of that parliament from 1921–29. He was also Pro–Vice Chancellor of The Queen's University of Belfast from 1922 and served as Under Secretary of State for India and Burma from 1939–40. *Dod's Peerage*, pp 657–8.

consideration by the Finance and Advisory Committees. Pending the result of this consideration it is strongly recommended that no further addition be made to the co-opted members of the Executive Committee.

1 April 1913

The 36th meeting of the Executive Committee of the U.W.U.C. was held … at 12-3.00 p.m. in the Council Chamber of the Old Town Hall, Victoria Street, Belfast … The Marchioness of Londonderry, Vice-President in the chair[169] … The following letters were read:–

From, Miss Bulkeley, Hon. Secretary, of the Women's Unionist Assoc. for the East & North of Scotland, expressing appreciation of the work done by Miss Clara A[.] Johnston.

From, Miss Muir McKean, Hon. Secretary, of the Women's Unionist Association of the West of Scotland, Paisley Branch, expressing appreciation of Mrs Murland's speech in Paisley on 19th February, 1913.

From, Mr. Matthew McMillan, Organizing Secretary of the Argyllshire Constitutional Association, giving a satisfactory report of the Lantern Lectures conducted by Mrs G. M. Shaw, and Miss Wilson.

From, Major Tombe, expressing appreciation of the work done by Miss Alice Gray, at the Kendal Bye-Election.

From, The Secretary of the Unionist Central Council of the Partick Division of Lanarkshire, expressing thanks for the work done by Mrs Malone in this Division.

From, Miss Agnes Smith, Hon. Secretary of the Eskdale Women's Unionist & Tariff Reform Association, enclosing Postal Order for £1:1: 0: as a mark of appreciation of the good work done by Mrs Wetherall during her stay in Langholme, Dumfries.

A telegram was also read from the Secretary of the British League for the Support of Ulster and the Union,[170] stating that the lady subscribing members would be welcomed in the League.

The Secretary also read a report of the work done be Mrs Wheeler in London and district, copy of which is attached to these minutes.

The report of the Finance Committee was read by Mrs Mercier-Clements on

169 Ninety–eight members were present at this meeting and there were forty–six apologies for non–attendance.

170 The British League for the Support of Ulster and the Union was a British organisation launched in March 1913. The driving force behind the league was Lord Willoughby de Broke. The organisation gained the support of over 200 members of both the House of Commons and the House of Lords. Branches were set up throughout Britain and members pledged to work by both constitutional and unconstitutional means in support of the unionist cause. See Buckland, *Irish Unionism, 1885–1923*, pp 336.

behalf of Miss Connor, Hon. Treasurer. The report showed a Bank Balance of £974: 13: 2: on 1st April, 1913 and a credit balance on the General Election No 2, account of £308: 3: 11: making a total credit balance on the two accounts of £1,282: 17: 1:

Mrs Mercier-Clements also read a short statement with reference to the 'Carson Fund' and a recommendation from the Advisory Committee that a collection should be made throughout the Affiliated Associations in aid of the fund[171] … On the motion of the Vice-President, seconded by the Countess of Kilmorey, the report, statement and recommendation were unanimously agreed to.

The report of the Active Workers' Committee showed a total of 23 workers sent to England and Scotland since the beginning of the year.

The following report was presented by the Affiliation Committee and unanimously agreed to:–

> 'The Lisburn Women's Unionist Association and the Antrim Women's Unionist Association have amalgamated into a new Association to be called 'The South Antrim Women's Unionist Association' which has been affiliated to the Ulster Women's Unionist Council.'

The next business on the agenda was 'To consider Mrs A. G. Finlay's scheme for co-option of Members of Council and Members of Executive Committee and to receive the reports of the Finance Committee and the Advisory Committee on the scheme.'

Mrs A. G. Finlay in explaining the scheme stated that the Ulster Unionist Council elected as members of the Council from time to time, gentlemen of approved standing. Those members paid an Annual Subscription of £3: 3: 0: (three guineas) and it had been found that the amount raised in this way paid the office expenses.

Mrs Robertson seconded the Motion … After discussion it was decided to make the following recommendation to the Council:– 'That ladies anxious to support the work of the Council be invited to do so by becoming Associates and paying an Annual Subscription of £2: 2: (two guineas); that details of the arrangements be referred to the Advisory Committee, including the appointment of a Sub-Committee to prepare a list of ladies who should be invited to become Associates' …

GENERAL REPORT OF MRS WHEELER'S TOUR.

DRAWING ROOM MEETINGS.

Mrs Arthur Jaffe, Kensington
Mrs Arthur Browne, Newport Essex
Miss Courtney, Kensington
Mrs David Reid, Norfolk Cresent.

171 The Carson Fund was an annual appeal, first launched in January 1912, to finance anti–home rule propaganda in Great Britain.

At all of these openings were obtained for other workers who will follow. Mr Hamill will arrange these.

WOMEN'S PROTESTANT UNION

On the Protestant Attitude (only)

Meeting at Head Office, Dennison House of Secretaries, 60
Meeting at Clarkenwell (Private House)
Meeting at Clapham Road. Y.W.C.A.[172]
Lantern Lecture, Tooting. (Broadwater Hall)
Meeting at Ilford (large Private about 70)
Meeting at Clapham (in local Y.W.C.A.)

I consider these most valuable as they included wives of Radicals and Non-Conformists who all seemed most interested and ready to help.

I also was asked to lunch with Lady Agnes Anderson, President of the Women's Protestant Union (Wife of Sir Robert Anderson whose book on Irish life is so well known)[.]

She will do what she can for us non-politically, and for this reason would prefer to write personally to any worker recommended by us. Also met Mrs Beeman, member of their Executive Committee, and Honorary Secretary Mrs Bell, also Organizing Secretary, and interested all.

PRIMROSE LEAGUE[173]

Public Meetings at Slough Town Hall	(500) Lantern Lecture
Eton Wick	(300) Lantern Lecture
Datchett	(300) Lantern Lecture
Guilford	(200) Working Men only

OTHER UNIONIST ASSOCIATIONS

Drawing Room Meeting	– Woking
Public Lantern Lecture	– Oatlands
Public Meeting Address	– Walton

PADDINGTON CONSERVATIVE CLUB

Public meeting working men only[.]

Arranged with Mrs Wilson, The Grange, Woking Village, to be corresponding Secretary for help in Protestant Associations with which she is associated …

WOMEN'S UNIONIST AND TARIFF REFORM ASSOCIATION

Asked to address workers at Head Office instead of Mr Boyd-Carpenter who

172 The Young Women's Christian Association.

173 The Primrose League was a popular Conservative association established in 1883 and named after Benjamin Disraeli's favourite flower. Membership of the league was open to both men and women. After 1918 many of the female branches of the Primrose League changed into local branches of the Women's Unionist Association. See J. H. Robb, *The Primrose League, 1883–1906* (New York, 1987).

disappointed. Wish to report that Miss Graham Hope gave every possible help, obtained invitation for me to Unionist Reception and introduced me to Members and Candidates. Also arranged for me to meet members of her Committee and to ask [for] their interest for the coming year. Have also received invitation to speak at Annual Conference and to appeal to their Secretaries. I am also grateful for the general hospitality shown in their Office. Total meetings 19[.]

INTERVIEWS

Mrs Bell, W.P.U.[174]
Lady Agnes Anderson, W.P.U.
Mr Walsh, Imperial Protestant Association.
Editor of the Protestant Observer, very useful for our work[.]
Lady Kinloch,[175] Vice Chair, W.A.U.T.R.A.

Miss Jeffreys, Hon. Secretary Bath. Arranged for her to be corresponding Secretary. She asked for duplicates of Norfolk notes to be sent [to] her for local papers.

Lady Betty Balfour.[176] Through Mrs Trimen[,] Woking. Asked to meet her to put her in possession of the facts re[.] Sweating[177] in Belfast which she was using to our disadvantage on Suffrage Platforms. Found she had been wrongly reported. Had not singled out Belfast only mentioned it as one of the many. Gave information desired and will continue correspondence.

INTERVIEWED MEMBERS AND CANDIDATES

Mr Proby, Saffron Walden.
Mrs Lloyd Graeme.
Mr Berhens.
Mr Hartley.
Mr Stainer.
Mrs Felix Cassel.

Captain Sandys and some others which we will hear of later through the Women's Unionist and Tariff Reform Association.

The general impression I form was that our Unionist friends are much more keenly interested than last year and that our Liberal opponents have now no doubt that

174 Women's Protestant Union.

175 Lady Ethel Mary Kinloch, the youngest daughter of Major James Hawkins. In 1906 she married Sir George, 3rd Baronet Kinloch, OBE and JP. Lady Kinloch was widowed in 1948. *Dod's Peerage*, p. 495.

176 Lady Betty Balfour (1858–1931), author, suffragist and keen supporter of the Church of Scotland. She was the daughter of the 8th Duke of Argyll and in 1879 married E. J. A. Balfour, brother of A. J. Balfour. *The Dictionary of National Biography, 1931–40* (Oxford, 1949), pp 34–5.

177 Term used to describe poor pay and conditions experienced by workers, particularly those in factory employment.

Ulster will hold out and that the question must receive serious consideration.

STATEMENT WITH REFERENCE TO THE CARSON FUND

By the request of the Finance Committee of the 'Carson Fund' Mrs Thomas Sinclair, Vice-Chairman, Miss Connor, Hon. Treasurer and Mrs Mercier-Clements, Assistant Hon. Treasurer, met Col. R. G. Sharman-Crawford and Mrs R. M. Liddell, in the office of the Ulster Women's Unionist Council, on Friday, 28th March, 1913.

Colonel Crawford explained the arrangements made for collecting money for the Carson Fund and asked how the U.W.U.C. would co-operate. After discussion it was agreed that the ladies present should recommend hearty co-operation and suggest to the Advisory Committee to advise the Executive Committee that Financial help should be given to the Carson Fund in the following way:-

'By a systematic collection in the various districts covered by the U.W.U.C. and Affiliated Associations. To facilitate this collection the Carson Fund Committee will supply the Ulster Women's Unionist Council with a list of all women who signed the Women's Declaration.

Small contributions are also very welcome and much needed.[']

REPORT OF THE ADVISORY COMMITTEE

... A request was received from the Women's Amalgamated Unionist & Tariff Reform Association, London, asking that Mrs Wheeler should be sent over to speak at the Annual Meeting of that Association on 27th May, 1913. The Advisory Committee asked Mrs Wheeler to accept the invitation and she has kindly consented to do so.

The Committee recommends that the Year Book for 1913 be printed containing a list of the Office-Bearers, Members of the Executive Committee, copy of the Annual Report, Constitution of the Council and a list of Affiliated Associations with the President and Secretaries.

REPORT OF THE FINANCE COMMITTEE ON MRS FINLAY'S SCHEME FOR CO-OPTION

1 From a financial point of view the scheme would be an advantage to the Council as a means of securing a fixed income.
2 That if adopted the subscription should be £2: 2: 0: (two guineas) per annum.
3 That a list of ladies to be approached and invited to allow their names to go forward for co-option, be selection by a small Committee.

(Signed) Maria Allen, 19th February, 1913.

REPORT OF ADVISORY COMMITTEE ON MRS FINLAY'S SCHEME

The Advisory Committee recommends to the Executive Committee that if the scheme proposed by Mrs Finlay be adopted, ladies coming within its provisions should be called 'Associates' not co-opted Members.

15 April 1913

The 37th meeting of the Executive Committee was held ... at 2 p.m. in the Council Chamber of the Old Town Hall, Victoria Street, Belfast ... The Marchioness of Londonderry, President in the Chair[178] ... Before the business of the meeting was entered upon the President said she was sure all present would wish to join in expressing their sympathy with Sir Edward Carson and she therefore proposed on their behalf to send the following telegram:–

'The Executive Committee of the Ulster Women's Unionist Council deeply deplores your sad bereavement; we trust your own health continues good and tender sincere sympathy' ... The following letters were read:–

From, The Duchess of Abercorn[,] Vice-President, expressing her very best thanks for being elected Vice-President. A letter was also read from the Duchess of Abercorn apologizing for her inability to attend meetings of the Committee for some time.[179]

From, The Rev. J.W. Timson expressing appreciation of the work done by Mrs Stach in East Cambridgeshire ... The Financial Statement ... showed a Bank Balance in the No 1 Account of £988. 17. 7 and in the No 2 Account £308. 3. 11 making a total of £1,297. 1. 6.

It was proposed by Miss Connor [,] seconded by Mrs R. H. Wallace[180] and passed unanimously 'That the report of the Finance Committee and the arrangements made for the Carson Fund Collection be approved of and passed' ... The President informed the Committee that with its approval she would be glad to get an account of the work done by the Council inserted in the 'People', a Sunday Newspaper.

The President also expressed her willingness to summon a meeting of Ulsterwomen in London in the Summer to be addressed by some members of the Council with a view to helping the work of the Council in England.

The business concluded.

178 Theresa, 6th Marchioness of Londonderry took over the presidency of the UWUC in 1913. She retained this position until a few months before her death in 1919. Seventy–seven members were present at this meeting and there were thirty–six apologies for non–attendance.

179 These letters are attached to the minutes. A letter of thanks from Sir Edward Carson to the Hon. Secretary of the Ulster Women's Unionist Council, dated 25 April 1913, is also included, stating, 'I received the kind message of the Executive Committee of the Ulster Women's Unionist Council for which I am grateful, and shall be much obliged if you will convey my sincere thanks for their sympathy and kind thoughts in my present trouble.'

180 Caroline Wallace, the daughter of J. B. Twigg of Cookstown, Co. Tyrone. In 1895 she married the Rt. Hon. Robert Hugh Wallace, a barrister, Privy Councillor and a Deputy Lieutenant for Co. Down. *Thom's Irish Who's Who*, p. 254.

REPORT OF FINANCE COMMITTEE

The Finance Committee met on Thursday 19th April 1913, at 3-30 p.m. in the Ulster Women's Unionist Council, Committee Room, No 4, Old Town Hall, Belfast.

The first business was the arrangements for the carrying out the collection in aid of the Carson Fund. A letter was read from Mr R Dawson Bates, Secretary of the Ulster Unionist Council, enclosing a number of suggestions for the organization of collections. Mr Bates also sent a sample of the cards which the Ulster Unionist Council was prepared to supply for the use of collectors.

Objection was made to the cards on the ground that they stated the collections were to be returned to Lord Dunleath at the Unionist Council. It was decided to ask the President to approach the Unionist Council with a view of getting cards provided with the name and address of the Hon Treasurer of the Ulster Women's Unionist Council, instead of Lord Dunleath's name, as Colonel Sharman Crawford had stated that the Ulster Unionist Council would be prepared to supply cards for the collection.

An appeal was drafted, to be signed by the President, Vice-Presidents and other officials of the Council, copy of which is attached to this report.

It was decided that the appeal should be printed on one page of the papers and on the opposite page, Sir Edward Carson's appeal.

The Secretary was instructed to have receipt books printed with the Hon Treasurer's signature lithographed in gac-simile and a space provided for the countersigning by collectors …

Dear Madam,

On the opposite page you will see an appeal from Sir Edward Carson which has already appeared in the Press for funds to carry on the Anti-Home Rule Campaign. We feel that we cannot add anything to that appeal except to say that if each of the 234,999 women who signed the Women's Declaration would give but one shilling we should collect a sum of over £11,500 …

APPEAL BY SIR EDWARD CARSON

Unionist Headquarters,
Old Town Hall,
Belfast

As the present year will, undoubtedly, prove to be the most critical in the campaign against Home Rule, I earnestly call upon every loyal Ulster man and woman to contribute to the Defence Fund liberally and in accordance with their means.

I gratefully acknowledge the splendid response made to last year's appeal, and I am now confident of a still more generous one. I specially hope that those who can only afford a small subscription will not fail to send it in. We shall thus secure a result worthy of Unionist Ulster.

The victorious campaign, already in active operation throughout the United Kingdom, must be carried out without abatement, and I therefore do not hesitate to make this appeal, knowing as I do that there is no sacrifice which Ulster loyalists are not prepared to make in order to defeat the most degrading and humiliating conspiracy which now aims at the destruction of their civil and religious liberties.

EDWARD CARSON

ADVISORY COMMITTEE REPORT

A telegram has been sent to Sir Edward Carson expressing the sympathy of the Council at the death of Lady Carson ... A letter be sent to all ladies invited to become Associates has been drafted by the President. It is recommended that this letter be printed and signed by the President and the Vice-Presidents and that a copy be sent to all ladies invited to become Associates. It is also recommended that each member of the Executive Committee be asked to be responsible for getting at least one lady to become an Associate of the Council.

BRITISH LEAGUE FOR THE SUPPORT OF ULSTER AND THE UNION

The Secretary has been instructed to write to the Secretary of this League asking him to provide cards for our workers to distribute and to send to any friends in different Constituencies in which we have worked.

20 May 1913

The 38th meeting of the Executive Committee of the Ulster Women's Unionist Council was held ... at 2 p.m. in the Old Town Hall, Victoria Street, Belfast ... The Marchioness of Londonderry, President of the Council in the Chair[181] ... The report of the Advisory Committee stated that in accordance with the resolution passed at the meeting of the Council on 15th April 1913, a circular inviting ladies to become Associates of the Council was drafted and copies sent to each member of the Executive Committee. That 80 ladies had accepted the invitation and had become Associates and that the total subscribed by them was £202. 4. 0. The Secretary then read a list of Associations up to date.

The report contained the following recommendation:–

No 1 That the following words be added to paragraph 4 of the Constitution:–

'Ladies who are anxious to support the work of the Council, and whose names are approved of by the Executive Committee may become Associate Members of the Council on payments of an Annual Subscription of two guineas, and such ladies need not necessarily be residents in, or natives of Ulster. Associates shall not as such

[181] Ninety–one members were present at this meeting and there were forty–five apologies for non–attendance.

be eligible as Office-Bearers or members of the Executive Committee, who shall be chosen only out of ordinary members of the Council, as approved under paragraph 8'.

No 2. 'That instead of printing a list of the Executive Committee in the Year Book the full list of members for the Council including Associates, should be printed and members of the Executive committee indicated by an asterisk.'

The report was unanimously adopted.
Mrs Mercier-Clements had given notice of the following Motion:- 'That as one or two cases have been before the Executive Committee in which the names of ladies who were members of the Committee last year were through misunderstanding not sent forward by their own Association as Members of the Council and such ladies are not therefore eligible for co-option as members of the Executive Committee and as it is desirable that the Council should have all possible advice and assistance in this most critical year, it be decided to invite these ladies to attend meetings of the Executive Committee during the year 1913. But that this action be not taken as a precedent for any future year and that no ladies shall come within its terms except those whose case had already been considered prior to the passing of this resolution.'

Mrs Mercier-Clements stated that since she had handed in her Notice of Motion a meeting of Council had been summoned and would be held that after-noon; she would therefore with the permission of the Committee slightly alter the sense of her Motion and would move 'That Miss Tracey and Mrs Wetherall be co-opted members of the Executive Committee provisionally on their being co-opted members of Council at the meeting of the Ulster Women's Unionist Council in the after-noon.' Mrs Mercier-Clements stated that if this motion were adopted it would save a month's delay and would enable Miss Tracey and Mrs Wetherall to attend the next meeting of the Executive Committee.

This motion was seconded by Mrs Huey and passed unanimously … The President stated that as most members of the Committee were probably aware First Aid classes and work were being carried on in several of the Affiliated Associations with the approval and at the wish of the Ulster Leaders [Sir Edward Carson and Sir James Craig], that for some time the organization and correspondence in connection with this movement had been performed by Mrs G. H. Wheeler privately but that the work had now grown too great for any private individual. She would therefore propose that the Secretary of the Ulster Women's Unionist Council be authorised to take over this work from Mrs Wheeler and to carry it on. Passed unanimously.

The business concluded.

17 June 1913

The 39th meeting of the Executive Committee of the Ulster Women's Unionist Council was held … at 2 p.m. in the U.W.U.C. Committee Room, No 4 Old Town

Hall, Victoria Street, Belfast ... The Dowager Marchioness of Dufferin & Ava, (in the chair)[182] ... [An] application had been received from the Typists for an increase of wages. After discussion it was proposed by Mrs R. T. Martin[,] seconded by Lady Ewart that Miss E. Hagan's wages be increased to £1 per week and Miss S Hagan's wages to 17/6 per week. Passed unanimously ... A letter dated 24th May was read from Mr Riddell thanking the Committee for the help given by the Ulster Women workers at the Altrincham Bye-election.

A letter dated 28th May was read from Mr Todman[,] Agent for the Frome division of Somerset thanking the Council for the work done by Miss Grange in that division.

A letter dated 28th May was read from Miss Graham Hope thanking the Committee for allowing Mrs G. H. Wheeler to address the Annual Meetings of the Women's Amalgamated Unionist & Tariff Reform Association.

A letter dated 3rd June was read from Miss Ridge of Weston-Super-Mare expressing appreciation of the address delivered by Miss Bushe at a Drawing Room meeting.

A letter was read from Miss Bushe in which a cheque for £16 was enclosed being the amount of 2 subscriptions and a collection given after one of Miss Bushe's meetings in London.

A joint recommendation was received from the Active Worker's Committee and the Advisory Committee

'That a Literary Sub-Committee be appointed containing a representative from each of the four Belfast Associations. It should be the duty of this Sub-Committee to watch both Unionist and Nationalist newspapers and when suitable matter appeared to send out to selected addresses in England and Scotland large numbers of the issue in question. That the Sub-Committee should be responsible for getting all necessary assistance in the work of sending papers but that the papers and Postage should be paid for out of the Central Funds'.

The Finance Committee recommended that a sum of not more than £20 be expended on a three month trial of the scheme.

Mrs A. G. Finlay at the request of the Chairman explained the proposed work of the Sub-Committee and stated the copy of the Witness containing a report of the debate in the General Assembly on the Memorial against Home Rule had been posted to every Minister in Scotland and that to enable this to be done Miss Connor had given a donation of £25.

Proposed by Mrs Mercier-Clements[,] seconded by Lady Anderson that the scheme be approved of and that a sum of £50 be given in addition to the £20 recommended by the Finance Committee and that the Sub-Committee should submit a statement of accounts and a report of their work at the next meeting of the Executive Committee.

Passed unanimously.

[182] Seventy members were present at this meeting and there were forty–six apologies for non–attendance.

A joint recommendation was also received from the Active Worker's Committee and the Advisory Committee.

> 'That the Secretary should go over to England before the end of June and visit as many of the different Offices and Agents as possible in order to get arrangements made for the Autumn Campaign.'

The recommendation was unanimously agreed to. The report of the Advisory Committee stated that the total number of Associates up to 16th June 1913 was 135 and that the total amount contributed by these ladies to the Funds of the Council was £328. 15. 0.

The report also contained the following recommendations:–

1 That there should be no meetings of the Executive Committee in July or August except in the case of emergency but that the necessary business be transacted by the Advisory Committee.

2 That the Office be closed for holidays from 11th to 25th August.

The report and recommendations were unanimously agreed to.

The business concluded.

16 September 1913

The 40th meeting of the Executive Committee of the Ulster Women's Unionist Council was held … at 2 p.m. in the U.W.U.C. Committee Room, No 4, Old Town Hall, Belfast … The Dowager Marchioness of Dufferin & Ava (in the Chair)[183] … The Secretary gave a report of his visit to England arranged at the last meeting of the Committee.

PROVISIONAL GOVERNMENT

The Vice-President said that all those present had probably seen Mr Bates['] letter to Mr Hamill with regard to the representation of women on the Provisional Government,[184] that the details of the scheme had not yet been received from the Ulster Unionist Council, and she would therefore suggest that discussion should be postponed until the Committee had fuller information. The Vice-President further said that she hoped Members would remember that the Ulster Women's Unionist Council was formed with one single object, and that no other question would be allowed to interfere with the work of the Council in opposing Home Rule[185] … a

[183] Ninety–eight members were present at the meeting and there were forty–one apologies for non–attendance.

[184] The provisional government of Ulster was set up on 23 September 1913 by the Ulster Unionist Council.

[185] This is a cloaked reference to women's suffrage. There was considerable discussion and dissension over the proposal to allow women to sit on the provisional government of Ulster. The UWUC was wary of splitting the organisation over the contentious issue of votes for women and as a result did not discuss either the motivation or the implications of the UUC's decision. In comparison many suffragists throughout Ireland heralded the UUC's decison to allow women to sit on the Provisional Government in Ulster as the first step towards securing votes for women from the Imperial Parliament. See Urquhart, *Women in Ulster Politics*, pp 23–8.

letter was read from Colonel Sharman Crawford, Hon Treasurer of the Carson Fund asking how soon it would be possible to have a return of the collection made by the Ulster Women's Unionist Council. It was decided to request all affiliated Associations to send in their return by 1st October if possible and to write [to] Colonel Sharman Crawford accordingly.

The report also contained a recommendation that a sum of £400 (four hundred pounds) be transferred from the No 1 account to the No 2 General Election account. A statement was submitted showing the probable cost of a General Election Campaign [a] copy of which is attached to these Minutes.

The report and recommendation were unanimously adopted … The report of the Advisory Committee which was approved of stated that the total number of Associates was then 175 and the amount contributed to the Funds of the Council by these ladies [was] £412. 15. 0. … Roughly speaking, a General Election Campaign lasts about a month. If the Ulster Women's Unionist Council is to supply the number of workers asked for by the Agents of the Unionist Associations in England, at least 80 workers will be required and probably another 20 will be needed for Scotland, making the total of 100 workers. Having regard for the increased cost of accommodation at Election times and including travelling expenses, the cost per worker per week can hardly be less than £4: thus each worker for the whole month will cost £16: and the staff of 100 workers will there-fore cost £1,600.

To meet this there is at present in the General Election Fund a little over £400; and the addition of £400: now proposed would bring this amount up to £800, about half the minimum amount required.

Report of the Literature Sub-Committee.

The Literature Sub-Committee was formed by the Executive at its last meeting on May 19th, 1913, and consists of one member from each of the four Parliamentary divisions of Belfast, who act as 'Heads', and who have the power to get as many helpers as they require to aid them in their work.

On June, 13th, 4127 copies of the 'Witness' containing the account of the Home Rule Debate and vote in the General Assembly of the Presbyterian Church were sent to Scotland, one to every Protestant clergyman. The cost of this was very kindly defrayed by Miss Connor, who most generously sent £25 for this purpose.

In connection with the Leicester bye-election, Mr. Dawson Bates procured for us from the Leicester Unionist Agent a list of 255 names of electors, to whom copies of the 'Ulster Echo' were sent on three successive dates, making 765 copies in all; the Editor of the 'Echo' having by our request written special articles on the Ulster question for these three dates.

Mr. Wood, the Unionist Agent for Scotland, having sent us a list of voters in the West of Scotland to whom he wanted papers sent, 480 copies of 'Irish Freedom' were forwarded to them.

As your Sub-Committee thought they were working in a rather haphazard way, they felt they must have some definite plan of action, therefore they decided to write to every Unionist Election agent in England whose district was not already covered by one of [the] Branches, and to ask him for a list of fair-minded opponents, working-men's Clubs, and Unionist workers to whom newspapers might be sent with advantage. Mr. Hamill lent us the dupilcator from the office, and 237 copies of a circular letter to this effect were made and sent out. Quite ... [a] considerable ... number of replies have been received, containing lists of addresses, but as we cannot possibly cope with them all on account of our limited funds, we have decided only to take up those constituencies that have been marked by the Ulster Unionist Council and the Union Defence League 'For Work'. We shall send both Unionist and Nationalist Papers to these addresses when we think they contain facts or articles that would be of use across the Channel. Attached to this Report are copies of slips one of which is fastened to each paper sent out according to whether it is Nationalist or Unionist.[186]

Bye-elections will receive special attention when they occur. Private applications for newspapers will be willingly dealt with if the applicants will defray the expense.

In order to prevent overlapping no papers will be sent to those constituencies which are being worked by any of the Branches of the U.W.U.C. As the Literature Sub-Committee learns that only 21 of the 32 Branches are linked up with constituencies in England and Scotland, it would strongly urge upon the remaining 11 that they should link themselves up with constituencies across the Channel, and thus take a share in spreading information in defence of Ulster's position. If they would do so, it would set more of the Sub-Committee's funds at liberty for special work.

21 October 1913

The 41st meeting of the Executive Committee was held ... at 2 p.m. in the Old Town Hall, Victoria Street, Belfast ... The Dowager Marchioness of Dufferin & Ava in the chair)[187] ... The following letters were ... read:–

Letter from Mr. Louis A. Ewart, of Birmingham, stating that Mrs R. H. Finlay's speeches in Liverpool 'had done a tremendous amount of good',

A letter from Miss Hogg, Hon. Secretary of the Battersea Women's Unionist & Tariff Reform Association, thanking the Committee for sending Miss Leatham, Miss Kingsborough and Miss Hodges to work in Battersea, and stating that they had done excellent work.

A letter was read from Mr. George Hewitt, Agent for Mid-Norfolk, reporting very favourably on the work done by the Misses McConnell[,] Miss Webb, and Miss Forde.

186 These slips were printed either with the message 'With the Compliments of the Ulster Women's Unionist Council, Old Town Hall, Belfast' or 'With the Compliments of the Ulster Women's Unionist Council, To show you what Home Rulers really think and say in Ireland. Compare Mr. Redmond's professions in England, Old Town Hall, Belfast'.

187 One hundred and one members were present at the meeting and there were forty–five apologies for non–attendance.

A similar letter [was read] from Mr. Askew, agent of the Ipswich Conservative Association, with regard to the work done by Miss Armstrong, Miss Kennedy, Mrs Malone, Miss McKelvey, and Miss Park.

The report of the Advisory Committee dealt entirely with the question of 1st Aid and Ambulance Organization.

The Vice-President read a letter which she had written to the Medical Board [of the Ulster Volunteer Force],[188] (copy of which is attached to these minutes)[.] She also read the reply received from the Secretaries of the Medical Board, and a formal request from the Board that three ladies be nominated for co-option as members of the Medical Board, and that the ladies of the Ulster Women's Unionist Council interested in nursing would formulate and submit for consideration of the Medical Board, a draft scheme for the carrying out of the training and control of the various nursing corps of the Ulster Volunteer Army.

The Vice-President further read a draft scheme of organization (copy of which is attached to these minutes) which was unanimously approved of, and ordered to be submitted to the Medical Board.

The following names were suggested by the Advisory Committee for co-option to the Medical Board:–

Lady Hermione Blackwood.
Mrs Robert Campbell.[189]
Mrs Gamble.
Mrs G. H. Wheeler.

Mrs McMordie stated that a number of the members of the Committee felt that the Executive Committee had not [the] power to make these nominations but that the matter must be referred to the Council, and she further moved that the nominations be referred to the Council.

The Vice-President pointed out that great delay would be caused if the nominations should be deferred until the Council meeting in January. Mrs Mercier-Clements seconded Mrs McMordie's proposal and pointed out that a special meeting of the Council could be summoned within a few days and so prevent any delay.

Mrs Riddell supported the proposal.

On a vote being taken the majority of those present voted against referring the nominations to the Council and the Vice-President therefore declared the motion lost.

188 The Ulster Volunteer Force, often referred to as the UVF, was established in January 1913. The UVF co–ordinated the paramilitary activities of Ulster unionists which began in some areas in 1911–12. Such activities were brought under the control of the unionist leadership by the creation of the 90,000 strong UVF. Many women were also keen to enrol in the nursing and first aid classes that were organised under the auspices of the UVF's Medical Board. The UVF formed the 36th Ulster Division in World War I and was revived in July 1920. The UVF was later largely incorporated into the Ulster Special Constabulary. Connolly, *Oxford Companion to Irish History*, pp 563–4.

189 Possibly Alice, daughter of Henry Ferguson who, in 1893, married Robert Garrett Campbell, CBE a Belfast flaxspinner. *Thom's Irish Who's Who*, p. 31.

Mrs Mercier-Clements stated that as the Executive Committee had taken the full responsibility for making the nominations at once she proposed,

Lady Hermione Blackwood,
Mrs Robert Campbell &
Mrs G. H. Wheeler,

to be nominated as members of the Medical Board, as she wished it clearly understood that they thoroughly approved of these ladies, as members of the Board.

The proposal was seconded by the Countess of Kilmorey, and passed unanimously.

Mrs R. H. Macaulay on behalf of the Literary Sub-Committee asked that a return might be obtained from the various affiliated Associations of the places to which Newspapers and Leaflets were being sent and an estimate of the average numbers of papers etc[.], posted per week. The business concluded.

[A copy of the letter from Hariot, the Marchioness of Dufferin and Ava, the Vice-President of the UWUC, to the Secretary of the Medical Council of the Ulster Volunteer Force is attached to the minutes, stating:]

Clandeboye,
Ireland.
October 16th 1913

Sir,

We are very anxious to call the attention of the Medical Committee to the question of the organization of a nursing service in Ulster.

In England, Scotland and Wales, a splendid scheme has been evolved under the auspices of the Red Cross, whereby there is hardly a village that does not possess its Voluntary Aid Detachment,[190] the members of which are all trained in first aid and home nursing, and can be relied upon to give efficient and willing help if called upon for active service. It is much to be desired that a similar scheme should ultimately to extended to all parts of Ireland, but we in Ulster feel that in view of the possible crisis in our affairs it is a matter of special urgency that some organization should be set on foot here without further loss of time.

There are at this moment hundreds of women eager and willing to be of service if the need arises, but without organization and without preliminary training in first aid and nursing they cannot hope to be of much use. Here and there efforts are being made to get up classes in these subjects, but so far there is no system and no unity of action. It is essential if these efforts are to be effective that there should be a central authority established and a settled plan of action drawn up.

It must be remembered that the two courses given by the St. John's Ambulance cover a period of at least three months so that a considerable period must in any

[190] Voluntary Aid Detachments [VADS] provided nursing support and performed domestic work under the auspices of the Red Cross during World War I.

case elapse before there are enough women qualified to become members of voluntary aid detachments.

In England the Red Cross works with the Territorial Force, but as we have no Territorial Army and are in rather peculiar circumstances, the Red Cross authorities will not at present consider the question of enrolling us as members of their Association.

The rules of the St. John's Ambulance do not suit our present requirements in every respect, therefore we ask that your Medical Council should at once draw up a scheme based on the lines of these two societies but modified in certain particulars to suit our present needs. We would like to suggest also that it would be advisable that a sub-committee be appointed immediately to deal with the subject of nursing organization. The Sub-Committee to consist of Matrons and trained nurses, as well as of Medical men. We should be grateful if the Medical Council would issue, as soon as possible, some general instructions for the guidance of local organizers, and would state what the minimum standard of training, required of Volunteers will be.

[A reply to this letter, addressed to the Executive Committee of the UWUC, is also attached to the minutes. It states]

The Medical Board of the Ulster Volunteer Force has decided to co-opt three ladies as members of the Board and hereby requests the Ulster Women's Unionist Council to nominate three ladies to fill the vacancies.

The Medical Board has further to request that the members of the Women's Unionist Council who are interested in Nursing may be good enough to formulate and submit for consideration of the Board a draft scheme for the carrying out of the training and control of the various nursing corps of the Ulster Volunteer Army.

As it is important that this work should be proceeded with at once we should be glad if the Council would regard the matter as urgent.

[The requested report is attached and states]

A uniform be settled for the 'Vadets'.

Advisable that the St. John's Ambulance text books be used but that trained nurses should be permitted to give the course on home nursing.

Advisable that examinations and doctors fees be covered.

Advisable that the examinations should be more practical than technical.

All local Secretaries to enter into communication with the County Secretary.

A medical and nursing inspector to inspect all V.A. Detachments and their work.

All members of the V.A.D. to meet at least 12 times in the year to practice and to attend further lectures.

In every County a Depot should be opened for storing gifts of equipment contributed by private individuals.

There should be in connection with every V.A.D. a body of men trained under the St. John's Ambulance.

Suggested that a body of fully trained nurses be called upon to volunteer. These nurses to be attached to various V.A.D. when and where required.

Suggested that a Red Cross fund be inaugurated.
A central store of equipment to be established, but each V.A.D. to collect a certain amount of equipment for its own use. Beds, bedding, cooking utensils, etc., to be guaranteed by its own local people. Quartermaster to keep a list of these.

All this scheme follows that of the Red Cross which is found to work well.

Ulster Women's Unionist Council meeting,
Ulster Hall, 18 January 1912.
HP/99 ULSTER MUSEUM

ULSTER WOMEN'S UNIONIST COUNCIL EXECUTIVE COMMITTEE MINUTES 1913–40[191]

[191] This minute book is held by PRONI under reference number D/1098/1/2.

18 November 1913

The 42nd meeting of the Executive Committee was held … at 2 p.m. in the Old Town Hall, Victoria Street, Belfast … Her Grace, the Duchess of Abercorn, (in the chair)[192] … Letter read from the Secretary of the Mid-Lanark Women's Unionist Association enclosing resolution of support and sympathy passed at the Annual Meeting of that Association, held on 1st November, 1913.

Letter from Miss Graham Hope,[193] was read stating that the Executive Committee of the Women's Amalgamated Unionist & Tariff Reform Association and the Primrose League Grand Council were jointly pushing forward a scheme for providing hospitality for Ulster women and children, inaugurated by Mr. Harold Smith, M.P. and asking that a letter be sent to Branch Secretaries in the name of the Ulster Women's Unionist Council welcoming the offer of hospitality, and asking that each copy of the letter should be signed by the Secretary. It was decided that the letter should be sent as requested and that it be left to the Advisory Committee to draft it.

A letter was read by Miss Clegg, stating that the Ladies' Committee of the Irish Unionist Alliance had offered 10 seats at the Bonar Law Demonstration on 28th November, to members of the Ulster Women's Unionist Council. Reported that the Advisory Committee recommend that a deputation be sent from the Ulster Women's Unionist Council and that the President, Vice-Presidents, Vice-Chairmen and the Hon. Treasurer and Hon. Assistant Treasurer be asked to form the deputation. That if any of these ladies refuse, tickets should be offered to the Provincial representatives who had attended best at meetings of the Committee.

Letter read from West Belfast Anti-Home Rule Association, enclosing the following resolution:–

'That the very best thanks of the Executive Committee of the West Belfast Anti-Home Rule Association be given to the West Belfast Branch of the Ulster Women's Unionist Council for all the assistance they have rendered us since the inauguration of our Association and especially to Miss Whitaker and the ladies who assisted her in the arduous task of bringing up Claimants to the Revision Court'…

Letter read from Capt. W. B. Spender,[194] A.Q.M.G.[,] U.V.F. asking that a lady be appointed to take charge of the Post House system in Ulster and suggesting the name of Mrs Ainsworth Barr. The Secretary intimated that Mrs Barr was willing to take up this work and her appointment was therefore confirmed.

192 One hundred and ten members were present at this meeting and there were forty–eight apologies for non–attendance.

193 Miss Graham Hope was the Organising Secretary of the Women's Amalgamated Unionist and Tariff Reform Association.

194 Captain Wilfrid Bliss Spender, re–raised and commanded the UVF in 1920 and was Permanent Secretary to the Northern Ireland Ministry for Finance and head of the Northern Ireland Civil Service from 1925–44. He died in 1960. Foster, *Modern Ireland*, p. 558.

Letter was read from the Mid-Devon Women's Unionist & Tariff Reform Association, thanking the Committee for sending Miss Alice Gray and Miss Tracey.

Letter read from the Secretary of the West Wilts[hire] Federation of the Women's Unionist & Tariff Reform Association, thanking the Committee for sending Mrs Sinclair.

A list of meetings to be addressed by Miss Austen Park[195] on the Ulster question was submitted and the Secretary reported that a letter of thanks had been sent to Miss Park for her work …

Read letter from Mr. H. Vernon Wilkins, agent for the Unionist Associations of Ireland for the London district, thanking the Committee for the valuable assistance rendered by the workers sent from here to the Reading Bye-Election.

Letter was read from Mr. W. F. Forrester, Secretary of the Scottish Women's Protestant Union, thanking Mrs Wheeler for the meetings she had taken on behalf of the Association.

Letter was read from Miss Agnes B. White, Secretary of the Bathgate Women's Unionist Association, stating that Mrs Wheeler's meeting there before the Linlithgow election had been very helpful.

Read letter of thanks from Miss Moutray Read for Mrs Wheeler's speech at the meeting in Fulham, on 23rd October, and asking that the Empire Habitation 259,[196] be officially thanked for their help in organizing the meeting …

Medical Board. The Minutes of the Advisory Committee with reference to the Medical Board [of the UVF] were read. The minutes included the following questions which Mrs Wheeler had been instructed to put before the Medical Board:–

1 How do the Medical Board wish the Ulster Women's Unionist Council to co-operate[?]
2 Point out that there is so much work to be done already for the Ulster Women's Unionist Council that the Council cannot allow its Secretary to undertake the whole Secretarial work of the Medical Board.
3 Point out that in the event of the Medical Board using the office or Secretary of the Ulster Women's Unionist Council, the former must bear any extra expense involved.
4 A sub-committee should be appointed by the Medical Board consisting mainly of ladies, to be responsible for the organization of all nursing work
(a) Can the Medical Board appoint ladies who are not members of the Board to be members of such a Sub-Committee?
(b) If not, can the Board co-opt additional ladies who might then be put on the Sub-Committee?

The following reply was received from the Medical Board:–

To the Ulster Women's Unionist Council.

[195] Miss Austen Park was a member of the Women's Amalgamated Unionist and Tariff Reform Association.

[196] This was a branch of the Conservative organisation, the Primrose League.

MrsWheeler having placed before the Medical Board several points from your Council we are directed to reply as follows:–

RE[.] OFFICE AND SECRETARY

As the Medical Board has applied for a separate office wherein to carry on its own work the question of office accommodation does not arise; and as Mr. Hamill has now resigned his position as Honorary Secretary to the Board it will not be necessary to discuss the details brought before the Board by MrsWheeler …

CO-OPERATION

The Medical Board desires us to express an earnest hope that the members of the Women's Unionist Council and the members of the various Women's Unionist Associations throughout the Province will co-operate in the work of organising first aid classes in every district with the least possible delay, and where possible obtaining equipment and supplies for each medical unit.

NURSING SUB-COMMITTEE

As regards a sub-committee to deal with Nursing the Medical Board – which includes three qualified ladies nominated by your Council – will itself supervise the carrying out of the Organisation Scheme it has already adopted.[197]

Having read the minutes and reply the Secretary [Mr John M. Hamill] asked [for] permission to make a personal statement as follows:–

1 'Although I have resigned on this occasion in order that there may not be the slightest ground for friction and grievance on my part of the Ulster Women's Unionist Council against the Medical Board, I wish it clearly understood that I do not admit the Right of any person or Committee to control my private actions or to interfere in any way with the use I choose to make of my private time.[']

2 'For the sake both of this Committee and of myself I wish to point out at once the only possible deduction to be drawn from this incident. Work on behalf of the Unionist Cause is rapidly increasing and is daily assuming new forms, and at any time I may be asked to help another office or another organization. Up till now I was under the impression that the object of bringing all the offices to one building was that they might co-operate and work into each other's hands. Now if I get a request for help I feel I must refuse; and that the only reason for refusal is that the Committee of the Ulster Women's Unionist Council is unwilling that I should do any Unionist work except its own.'[198]

The Vice-President made an appeal for earnest and hearty co-operation between

[197] This letter is dated 18 November 1913.

[198] Considerable tension had been caused by John M. Hamill, the paid Organising Secretary of the UWUC, also acting as Honorary Secretary to the Medical Board of the UVF. He resigned from the latter position.

the Ulster Women's Unionist Council and the Medical Board[199] …

LITERARY SUB-COMMITTEE

Report for November

During this month the Literary Sub-Committee has been giving its attention chiefly to the bye-elections. For Reading we had no addresses in time but the Ulster Unionist Council assured us that would not matter very much, so much work was being done there, and we all know the result.

To Linlithgow we sent 144 copies of 'Ulster's Appeal' and the Witness with the account of the Business Men's meeting. The same papers went to Keighley to the numbers of 38 and 172 respectively. We also sent 512 copies of Irish Freedom to South Lanark and Wick Burgs and 253 copies of a special Number of the Witness to the former place, – the Ulster Unionist Council sending to the latter one.

Banbridge Women's Unionist Association kindly sent its list of Linlithgow addresses to the Committee for comparison with theirs so that no overlapping should occur and it was found that in no case were the addresses in duplicate.

The Committee was much gratified to receive through Mr. Hamill, the sum of 5/– from a lady for their work. Recognition of their work in this practical form is very encouraging.

16 December 1913

The 43rd meeting of the Executive Committee was held … at 2 p.m. in the Old Town Hall, Victoria Street, Belfast … Lady Ewart (in the chair)[200] … [Letters of thanks were read] for the work done by speakers and canvassers[201] … Read a letter from Miss G. Russell, Hon. Secretary of the Newmains Branch of Mid-Lanark Women's Unionist Association conveying the resolution of sympathy with the loyalists of Ulster at a meeting held on 12th December, addressed by Mrs Shaw-Hamilton … Read the following message from the Medical Board, Ulster Volunteer Force: – 'That the Ulster Women's Unionist Council be asked to co-operate in arranging working parties after January 1st, to make supply stores for the Ulster Volunteer Corps. Those who are willing to send their names … to the Secretaries of the Medical Board.

199 A letter is attached to the minutes addressed to Lady Dufferin from Florence Henderson, Belfast, a local Honorary Secretary of the St. John's Ambulance Association and former Honorary Secretary of the UWUC. Dated 18 November 1913 the letter stated that lecturers of the association were not paid and that 'at the present time 58 Classes are either going on, or being organised, and requests for the formation of others are coming in almost daily, so that there should be a large number of Volunteers to join the Ambulance and Nursing Units of the Ulster Volunteer Force, if accepted, as it is hoped they will be, by the Medical Committee of the Military Board.'

200 One hundred and seven members were present at this meeting and there were thirty–seven apologies for non–attendance.

201 UWUC speakers and canvassers had been working in the following areas: Torquay, Mid–Devon, Peeblesshire, West Renfrewshire, the West of Scotland and addressed meetings of the Primrose League in Carlisle, Northumberland, Durham, Cumberland and Westmoreland.

These working parties should be asked to co-operate in making bandages according to directions, hemming sheets, making pyjama suits and in other ways.

Lists are being prepared which can be had on application from the Hon. Secretaries of the Medical Board.'

Mrs Wheeler on behalf of the Medical Board urged that an effort should be made in all affiliated Associations to prepare medical stores without delay[202] …

LITERATURE SUB-COMMITTEE'S REPORT

The Literature Sub-Committee has been very busy this month with the bye-elections in Wick and South Lanark. 960 copies of November's 'Irish Freedom' were sent to these two places to addresses sent to us by Mr. Wood. These were followed by 960 packets of Unionist Literature, and these again by 960 copies of December's 'Irish Freedom' making 2,880 in all.

As there was a suspicion that all our papers did not get safely through the post office in Belfast, Mrs Macauley suggested [that] after the papers had been put into stamped wrappers, that they should be made into parcels and posted to Unionist friends in England who would post them separately from their own towns to their destinations. It was decided to adopt this scheme for safety. Mrs Macauley kindly bore the cost of posting the first set of parcels, and we were helped with the last set we sent out by a gentleman who was crossing to Scotland and took a large parcel with him to post on his arrival there, thus saving expense. If any lady crossing the Channel after the first of January, would do us the same kind of service, we should be greatly obliged.

20 January 1914

A special meeting of the Executive Committee was held [to elect members of the U.W.U.C.'s Advisory Committee, Affiliation Committee, Active Workers' Committee, Literary Sub-Committee and Finance Committee for 1914] … in the Minor Hall of the Y.M.C.A.[,] Wellington Place, Belfast … The Marchioness of Londonderry, President, in the chair.[203]

17 February 1914

The 44th meeting of the Executive Committee was held … at 2 p.m. in the Old Town Hall, Victoria Street, Belfast … The Dowager Marchioness of Dufferin and Ava, Vice-President, (in the chair)[204] … [Resolutions of sympathy were passed on the death of Charles C. Connor and the Right Honourable Thomas Sinclair, who] took a deep interest in the work of the Ulster Women's Unionist Council and all

202 A letter dated 30 November 1913, regarding the payments of fees to lecturers of the St. John's Ambulance Association, is attached to the minutes.

203 A list of the members present at this meeting is not included in the minutes.

204 One hundred and ten members were present at this meeting and there were forty–two apologies for non–attendance.

that tended to its success. From the moment when the formation of the Council was first suggested down to the last days of his life his great experience, wise forethought, and sound common sense, were freely at the disposal of the Council and all connected with it … Read letter from the Agent of Widnes Division, Conservative Association, conveying a message of sympathy from the Whiston Branch of the Ladies' Conservative and Unionist Association … Mrs McMordie … gave a detailed statement of the financial position of the council and made a special appeal for funds to carry on campaign work … it was decided to send a circular to each member of the Committee who had not yet paid her subscription fee …

The Secretary reported that he had received a very disappointing response to an appeal made to workers and he hoped members of the Committee would urge on all workers in their Associations the great need of an immediate campaign in England and Scotland.

Read a letter from the President to the same effect, and stating that she was sending a subscription of £50 (fifty pounds) through the North Down Women's Unionist Association for the Campaign Fund …

LITERATURE SUB-COMMITTEE

During the month of January 3,184 newspapers and packets of leaflets [were sent] to England, owing to the courtesy of Unionists crossing to England and Scotland none of these were sent through the local post office.

Special attention was given to the Bye-Elections of North West Durham and South Bucks. We are this month concentrating our efforts on the coming Bye-Elections.

17 March 1914

The 45th meeting of the Executive Committee was held … at 2 p.m. in the Old Town Hall, Victoria Street, Belfast … Lady Anderson (in the chair)[205] … Read letter from Lady Ewart suggesting that a letter be sent to the Editor of 'The Times' thanking him for the support given by his papers to the Ulster Cause and congratulating him on the price of the paper having been lowered. The Secretary was instructed to write accordingly[206] … [The Executive Committee unanimously decided] That an effort be made to arrange that in the various places where the British Women's Covenant was being signed openings should be found for Ulster workers to explain the meaning of the Covenant and the Home Rule Question.[207]

205 One hundred and nineteen members were present at this meeting and there were forty–five apologies for non–attendance.

206 Letters were also read conveying thanks for the work done by women unionist canvassers and speakers in Tring in West Herts., Kirkintilloch in the West of Scotland, Port Glasgow and Mid–Gloucester. In addition to this, a collection was made from those present at the meeting to contribute to the funds of the Literature Sub–Committee.

207 This was launched in March 1914, as a British equivalent to the Ulster Women's Declaration signed in Ulster on 28 September 1912.

[Letters of thanks for the resolutions of sympathy passed by the Executive Committee on the deaths of Charles Connor and the Right Honourable Thomas Sinclair are attached to the minutes. The letter, from Mrs Sinclair, dated 19 February 1914, states] My husband was very deeply interested in the work of the Ulster Women's Unionist Council. He was so convinced that the Unionist Cause should be supported not only by the energies, abilities, and self-sacrifice of the men but also by that of the women of Ulster.

When the formation of the Council was first mooted he saw the good the women of Ulster could do. The knowledge that our Cause was bringing together in singleness of purpose men and women who were ready to sacrifice much that makes life pleasant, who were prepared to go out of our Province in order to lay before those who were ignorant the true facts of our Unionist feeling, was to him a real joy. He felt how right and just was this Cause which had so unanimous a support. He recognised the great moral effect the interest, sympathy, and support of their womankind would have on the Unionists of Ulster. He valued and admired that way in which the women endeavour, in their sphere, to fit themselves to be of use in the struggle which may yet, please God, even at this eleventh hour be avoided …

[A letter from the West of Scotland Women's Unionist Association is also attached to the minutes, stating] … it is desired that the Council should know the work of the Lady Canvassers has been of the greatest value, and while thanking the Council for the services of these ladies who have worked so well in the West of Scotland, the Executive desires to urge that further help is very necessary and at the request of the Scottish Unionist Association, they would desire to apply for all assistance possible in this way, for, by the method adopted of sending those ladies to canvas doubtfuls or Radicals who never attend meetings, voters are reached and influenced[208] …

LITERATURE SUB-COMMITTEE

February has been a very busy month for your Sub-Committee, owing to four bye-elections having taken place[209] … The total amount of Literature dispatched during February was, 1371 newspapers, and 3,383, packets containing 33,144 leaflets. The Executive will scarcely be able to realise the amount of time and labour involved in handling this large quantity … If the work of this Sub-Committee is to continue … a further sum will have to be voted for this purpose. We must therefore, now make a very special appeal to the Executive for funds, otherwise our work must stop at once as our account is somewhat overdrawn.

Our best thanks are due to the Lurgan Branch for their very generous gift of £5. Such practical appreciation is most encouraging. We would hope that other Branches would follow their example.

If the Executive values the work done by their Committee, and wishes it to

[208] Three UWUC members, Miss Gregg, Mrs Mercier–Clements and Mrs Shaw Hamilton had recently returned from canvassing in the West of Scotland.

[209] These by–elections occurred in South Bucks, South West Bethnal Green, Poplar and Leith Burghs.

continue it will be necessary to make provision at this meeting for its continuance.

Had it not been for the generous supply of literature given free of cost by the [Ulster] Unionist Council it would have been utterly impossible to have accomplished, with the funds at our disposal what has been done. The principal items of expenditure had been for postage.

21 April 1914

The 46th meeting of the Executive Committee was held … at 2 p.m. in the Old Town Hall, Victoria Street, Belfast … The Marchioness of Londonderry, President, (in the chair)[210] … The President … emphasised the great need for immediate campaign work in England, on the ground that 'Prevention is better than Cure.' There were many who could do Ambulance and Signalling work at home and the President urged on the Members that they should do everything possible to send all those who could go for work in England or Scotland … The President appealed to Members of the Committee to exercise great care in any appeals for help made to friends in England as it was most important that the impression should not be allowed to become broadcast that the resources of Ulster were becoming exhausted.[211]

19 May 1914

The 47th meeting of the Executive Committee was held … at 2 p.m. in the Old Town Hall, Victoria Street, Belfast ... The Dowager Marchioness of Dufferin & Ava (in the Chair)[212] … Read [a] letter from the Hon[.] Secretary, Mid-Lanark Women's Unionist Association (Wishaw Branch) to Mrs Mercier-Clements enclosing £2 for the Carson Defence Fund.

Read [a] letter from Mrs Mercier-Clements suggesting that Miss Goring-Thomas, Secretary of the Women's Amalgamated Unionist & Tariff Reform Association, Miss Bulkeley, Secretary of the Women's Unionist Association for the North and East of Scotland and Miss Gow, Assistant Secretary of the West of Scotland Women's Unionist Association be invited to come to Ulster at Whitsuntide to see the work of the Ulster Volunteer Force and of the different women's Associations. Decided to invite all three ladies … Decided to pay over the money in hands to

210 One hundred and thirty members were present at this meeting and there were thirty–six apologies for non–attendance. At the start of this meeting a resolution of sympathy was passed on the death of the Lord Mayor of Belfast, Mr R. J. McMordie, MP. He had been MP for East Belfast and five times Lord Mayor of Belfast between 1910–14. He was married to Julia McMordie, a vice chairman of the UWUC. *Thom's Irish Who's Who*, p. 154.

211 The resources of the UWUC were certainly under pressure at this time as a result of their extensive literature and propaganda campaign.

212 One hundred and four members were present at this meeting and there were forty–one apologies for non–attendance. The minutes note that a letter of appreciation for the work conducted by women unionist workers in North Oxford was read at the start of this meeting, but no further information is given.

the Trustees of the Carson Defence Fund as soon as it reached the sum of £1000 (one thousand pounds)[.]

Report of the Active Worker's Committee read by the Secretary showed a total of 56 workers in England and Scotland since the last meeting of the Committee.

[It was unanimously passed] That the sum of £40 (forty pounds) per month for three months be paid to the Literature Sub-Committee out of the General Election Fund ... [and] That Miss Hagan's wages be increased to £1 (one pound) per week.[213]

STATEMENT FROM LITERATURE SUB-COMMITTEE

In reply to the decision of the Advisory Committee that the Literature Sub-Committee should make arrangements for an extensive campaign based on the probability of a General Election, and of the request of the Finance Committee for an estimate of the money that would be required, the Sub-Committee beg to furnish the following statement, which has been drawn up very carefully, for the consideration of the two Committees asking for it ... your Sub-Committee would strongly recommend that such a Campaign, to be of real value, should be undertaken at once, and carried on vigorously till a General Election begins when it would cease, except, possibly, in the case of a very few exceptional constituencies, as, during the excitement of a General Election, people are not inclined to read or study newspapers or leaflets. This, we would say in passing, is the view strongly held by the Office of the Ulster Unionist Council whose help has been of such immense service to us.

Any scheme for a Literature Campaign resolves itself into a question of funds ... Between June 1st, 1913, and March 13th, 1914, literature has been sent to 14,902 electors in 65 constituencies in England and Scotland at a total cost of £95. During the four busiest months of that time, from November 14th, till March 13th, 4749 newspapers and 5368 packets of Literature were sent out at a cost of £58-19-10.

The question now arises do the Advisory and Finance Committees wish additional constituencies undertaken?

Many suitable and useful pamphlets have been brought under the notice of your Sub-Committee but they had to be rejected with reluctance owing to their cost ... to send a penny pamphlet to 1000 electors costs £8-14-8. This will explain why your Committee has judged it best to adhere to the literature supplied free by the Ulster Unionist Council.

In conclusion if an extensive Election Campaign is desired, it would be necessary for the Sub-Committee to meet much more frequently than they have done, and the Expense would be much greater than hitherto. To keep up what is already being done will require at least £6 per week, so that an increase of work would entail a proportionately increased expenditure.[214]

213 Miss Hagan was a junior typist in the UWUC office in the Old Town Hall, Belfast.

214 Appended to the minutes is a list of the 65 English and Scotch constituencies 'which have been worked' by members of the UWUC.

15 June 1914

The 48th meeting of the Executive Committee was held … at 12-30 p.m. in the Old Town Hall, Victoria Street, Belfast … The Marchioness of Londonderry, President, (in the chair)[215] … [The President read a letter which she had received from Sir Edward Carson, dated 11 June 1914 and stating] Thank you for your letter enclosing the Memorandum for submission to me from the Ulster Women's Unionist Council. I can well understand the difference of opinion having arisen owing to the persistent conduct of the Government in refusing to hold out any hopes of our being allowed to have an expression of opinion on the subject of Home Rule by the electors of the United Kingdom. At the same time I think it would be a mistake to depart from the policy hitherto prevailing of trying to influence the constituencies in Great Britain and I am still devoting a great deal of my time to that object. The Women's Council have already collected a most handsome contribution to the Defence Funds and I believe that hospital and other arrangements in which they are so interested are very far advanced, and I have no doubt that further money will be forthcoming for such a laudable object, when it is required. I am therefore of [the] opinion that the monies referred to in the memorandum should be devoted to influencing[,] in the way hitherto adopted[,] the English constituencies …
[It passed unanimously that] the monies referred to in the Memorandum should be devoted to influencing in the way hitherto adopted the English Constituencies.

14 July 1914

The 49th meeting of the Executive Committee was held[216] … at 2 p.m. in the Old Town Hall, Victoria Street, Belfast … The Marchioness of Londonderry, President, (in the chair)[217] … [The council received a donation of £25 from the Women's Amalgamated Unionist and Tariff Reform Association] to be used in whatever way the Committee thought best.

19 January 1915

A Special Meeting of the Executive Committee of the Ulster Women's Unionist Council was held … immediately after the Annual Meeting in the Minor Hall of the Y.M.C.A., Wellington Place, Belfast … The chair was taken by the President, the

215 One hundred and six members were present at this meeting and there were forty–four apologies for non–attendance. A letter of appreciation was read for work conducted by Miss K. Grange in Gloucestershire, enclosing £5 'for the funds of the Ulster Women's Unionist Council.'

216 This was the last meeting of the UWUC's Executive Committee to be held before the outbreak of World War I. Unionists suspended their anti–home rule campaign for the duration of the war and as a result all political work was put on hold. The UWUC's Executive Committee met three times in 1915, twice in 1916, and once in 1918 before peace was declared. The Executive Committee did not meet during 1917.

217 Ninety–three members were present at this meeting and there were thirty–seven apologies for non–attendance.

218 Numbers of members present at this meeting are not included in the minutes.

Marchioness of Londonderry[.][218] [Members were appointed to the Advisory, Active Workers' Affiliation and Finance Committees of the UWUC for the year of 1915].

11 February 1915

A Special Meeting of the Executive Committee of the Ulster Women's Unionist Council was held ... in the Old Town Hall, Belfast ... The Dowager Marchioness of Dufferin & Ava (Vice-President) in the chair[219] ... [The Executive Committee passed a resolution of sympathy on the death of the Marquis of Londonderry, stating] our sense of the great loss sustained by Ulster and the Unionist cause.

By the people of Ulster his memory will ever be cherished as a sturdy champion of their rights, and a trusted leader in their long struggle against Home Rule.[220]

27 April 1915

A meeting of the Executive Committee of the Ulster Women's Unionist Council was held ... at 2 p.m. in the Old Town Hall, Victoria Street, Belfast ... The Hon Lady Kennedy[221] (in the chair)[222] ... [The Executive Committee discussed the following resolution] That this Association should ascertain in their districts what Temperance Refreshment Rooms exist, and use their influence to help improvement where needed ... [but it was decided] That while heartily sympathising with the spirit of the Resolution, we regret that as an Association, we cannot carry out its proposals ... The next business on the agenda was to consider a request from the Labour Exchange and Unemployment Insurance, Divisional Office for Ireland, for co-operation in the Registration of Women for War Service ... and to take such steps or make such arrangements as may be considered advisable.

After considerable discussion it was ... passed 'That individual Members of the Council and its Affiliated Associations be recommended to assist in carrying out the scheme to the best of their ability, but as a Council we cannot take the scheme up officially.'

219 Fifty–two members were present at this meeting and there were sixty–three apologies for non–attendance.

220 Charles Henry Vane Tempest Stewart, 6th Marquis of Londonderry and husband of the UWUC President, Theresa Londonderry. See *Thom's Irish Who's Who*, p. 139.

221 The Hon. Bertha Ward, daughter of the 5th Viscount of Bangor. In 1883 she married Sir Robert Kennedy, a Deputy Lieutenant, JP and High Sheriff for Co. Down who held numerous diplomatic appointments including Attaché at Madrid from 1874–76, Acting Diplomatic Agent in Bulgaria from 1882–84, Acting Chargé d'Affaires in Romania from 1886–88, Chargé d'Affaires at Montenegro from 1893–97 and Minister Resident in Uruguay from 1897. *Dod's Peerage*, pp 48–9; *Thom's Irish Who's Who*, p. 123.

222 Eighty–six members were present at this meeting and there were forty–six apologies for non–attendance.

The business concluded.

8 February 1916

A Special meeting of the Executive Committee of the Ulster Women's Unionist Council was held … in the Old Town Hall, Belfast … The Hon. Lady Kennedy (in the Chair)[223] … Lady Kennedy explained that the Lord Mayor of Belfast[224] having received an intimation that Women's Associations throughout Ireland were being asked to help in recruiting came specially to the Advisory Committee on Tuesday, 1st inst. to ask for the help of the U.W.U.C.[225] … Read the following letter from the President – the Dowager Marchioness of Londonderry, and the Duchess of Abercorn, Vice-President:–

… It is common knowledge that the wastage in every battalion at the front amounts to 100 percent per annum, and as we have large divisions in the field, and the losses caused by casualties of every description must be replenished, it is absolutely necessary that every one of us should do our best to find more men, so as to hasten the end of this terrible war. I am sure we, viz: myself and the Vice-Presidents of this great organization, will not appeal in vain to our splendid body of workers, when we ask each member, each in her own district, to place herself at the disposal of the recruiting officers, to assist in every possible way. We are confident that the same all-conquering spirit that has always inspired the women of Ulster, particularly when it is a question of the honour of their Province, will again enable them to achieve this object and will crown their efforts with success. [The following resolution was recommended for adoption] 'That this meeting of the Ulster Women's Unionist Council desires to assure the Lord Mayor of Belfast that the Members of the Council and its Affiliated Associations have since the outbreak of the War done everything in their power to aid the Empire in the great struggle in which it is engaged and have in particular done their utmost to secure recruits for the Ulster Division and the Imperial Forces generally. The Council realises the serious need for continued and increased efforts to ensure the speedy and successful termination of the War and will impress upon the individual members of their affiliated associations the urgent necessity for bringing every available man to the colours and the desirability of taking such further steps in their respective districts as may be calculated to obtain this object' … To recommend the following Resolution to the Council for adoption –

'We the members of the Ulster Women's Unionist Council representing a quarter of a million loyal women of Ulster desire to express our deep dissatisfaction at the

223 Eighty members were present at this meeting and there were sixty–one apologies for non–attendance.

224 The Lord Mayor of Belfast at this time was Sir Crawford McCullagh.

225 The Advisory Committee approved of this suggestion and called a special meeting of the UWUC Executive and Council accordingly.

exclusion of Ireland from the Compulsory Service Act.[226] We protest against the refusal of the Government to join our people with their fellow citizens of Great Britain in a common bond of service to the Empire knowing as we do the readiness of Loyal Ulster already proved on many occasions to undergo and suffer whatever may be necessary to bring victory to our armies over the forces of tyranny and barbarism'.

5 December 1916

A Special Meeting of the Executive Committee of the Ulster Women's Unionist Council was held in the Old Town Hall, Belfast … [at] 12 noon … The Dowager Marchioness of Dufferin & Ava (in the chair)[227] … [The Constitution of the Council was amended] to meet changed conditions after the War; The President had consulted Sir Edward Carson who was on a visit to Wynyard Park,[228] and that the changes proposed were approved and recommended by the President and the Rt. Hon. Sir Edward Carson K.C., M.P. [The changes enabled the UWUC] To take action as may from time to time in the opinion of the Ulster Unionist Council be necessary in the interest of the Imperial Province of Ulster in relation to the questions of trade after the war, the employment and settlement of Ulstermen who have fought for their country, and generally, and all other matters arising out of the war which may tend to the benefit of Ulster and the Empire … [The constitutional changes were passed and it was agreed that] … a message of confidence and support be sent to Sir Edward Carson from the Meeting.[229]

18 June 1918

A Special Meeting of the Executive Committee of the Ulster Women's Unionist Council was held … in the Old Town Hall, Belfast … The Marchioness of Dufferin & Ava, Vice-President (in the chair)[230] … The first business was to receive reports from the Advisory and Finance Committees with reference to steps taken to assist in the Registration of Women Voters under the Representation of the People Act

[226] This is a reference to the Military Service Act of January 1916 which imposed conscription on single men aged between 18 and 41. Those who were exempt from conscription included ministers of religion, conscientious objectors, the medically unfit, men who were employed in essential war industries and the Irish. It was considered too contentious to introduce conscription to Ireland. In late April 1916 a second Military Service Act extended conscription to married men.

[227] Seventy–five members were present at this meeting and there were forty–eight apologies for non–attendance.

[228] Wynyard Park was the Marquis of Londonderry's seat near Billingham in County Durham.

[229] A letter of thanks from Carson is appended to the minutes. The letter, dated 14 December 1916, thanked the UWUC 'for their good wishes that I may be successful in my efforts to secure a more vigorous prosecution of the war.
I am much encouraged by the loyal support of my friends in the North of Ireland, and shall be glad if you will convey to them my warmest thanks'.

[230] Sixty–three members were present at this meeting and there were forty–seven apologies for non–attendance.

1918[231] … the Hon. Treasurer be authorised to make such payments, not exceeding in all £5000 as may be required for the purpose of the scheme in connection with [the] Registration of Women Voters … and that the General Election Fund be drawn upon for the purpose of the above payments … With regard to the Registration of Women Voters in Belfast the Secretary pointed out a House to House canvass would be impossible in the short time available, and in view of the great changes in the Constituencies, and stated that subject to the approval of the Committee he had arranged to open a special office in the Old Town Hall in charge of an experienced Registration Official for the purpose of giving information, and assisting Women Voters or Claimants in taking the necessary steps. This arrangement was unanimously approved of … [A letter was sent to each Honorary Secretary of associations affiliated to the UWUC stating] With a view to helping in securing the Registration of every possible Unionist Voter in your Constituency, and particularly of safeguarding the interests of women Electors, it is proposed to make a Grant from the Central Funds for this purpose of paying Inspectors to go round the Constituency and see that every eligible woman has already been registered, or to assist those who have not yet done so in filling up their claim forms.

The lists of Electors are to be published on 15th June and the last date for claims or objections to the list will be 5th July.

Will you kindly put this suggestion before the Unionist Registration Agent in your Constituency, and if he is favourable and willing to facilitate in carrying out the scheme, you might then try to secure the services of a number of Canvassers or Inspectors, preferably women, but if suitable women are not available, then men, who are willing to undertake the work … These workers would of course be paid where necessary and in all cases would receive their necessary out-of-pocket expenses for travelling etc.

On hearing from you that you can secure the necessary workers, and having an estimate of the probable sum required for expenses the matter will have immediate attention. It is expected that in no case will the total expenses exceed £50.

I should like to impress upon you the importance of this work not only for its own sake but also as a means of demonstrating the practical usefulness of our women's Associations, and their ability to be of service to the Cause; and would request you to give it your prompt attention …

[An Assistant Secretary was] appointed to assist Mr. Hamill … [The Executive Committee also decided] 'to ask for an interview with Sir Edward Carson when he is here shortly in Ireland, and to ask him to define our status with regard to the Unionist Party in Ulster, and to give us his advice as to whether we should undertake this re-organisation or not. If he approves, we will then proceed' … Lady Dufferin then suggested that she should consult Sir Edward Carson as to whether he would meet the whole Advisory Committee or a small deputation … and the Vice-President's suggestion was unanimously agreed to.

[231] This legislation gave the vote to all women aged thirty and over, who were on the local government voting register or who were married to registered men.

11 October 1918

A Meeting of the Executive Committee was held in the Old Town Hall[,] Belfast … The Dowager Marchioness of Dufferin & Ava in the Chair[232] … [The financial position of the organisation was discussed as an excess of expenditure over income of £159: 15: 0 was reported.] This Excess must be met by subscription from members, increased contributions from affiliated associations and subscriptions from associates.

Since the outbreak of the war[233] associations have not been asked to pay their subscriptions although a very few have continued to do so … In 1916 only 14 Associations out of 31 paid their Affiliation fee[.] In 1917 only 9 paid and in 1918 up to the present 5 have paid … [It was decided] that Affiliated Associations be required to pay Affiliation Fees in arrears … it was decided that [a] statement of [the] financial position of the Council be sent to the Affiliated Associations …
[A resolution was read from the Standing Committee of the Ulster Unionist Council in response to the resolution passed by the UWUC on 11 September 1918 referring to the co-option of women onto the Ulster Unionist Council, stating that] as a temporary measure to grant to the Ulster Women's Unionist Council the same representation as that proposed to be given to the [Unionist] Clubs, namely 12, and that the whole question of representation of Special bodies to the Council be reconsidered after the next general election … That the Ulster Unionist Council be requested in revising its constitutions, to provide for the inclusion of representatives elected by the Ulster Women's Unionist Council in the same way as the Orange Order[234] and the Unionist Clubs …

SUGGESTED PROGRAMME FOR BRANCHES OF THE U.W.U.C., 1918–1919

1 To see that Branch Association is in full nominal working order i.e. appointment of officials, 8 representatives to Council, etc.
2 To undertake as first work in connection with local Parliamentary Division Committee the Canvass of all Women in the Constituency, and to see they are

[232] Eighty–four members were present at this meeting and there were forty apologies for non–attendance. At this meeting Miss Alice Gray, Adelaide Place, Newcastle Co. Down, was appointed Assistant Secretary. The salary for this position was £125 per annum

[233] World War I broke out on 4 August 1914.

[234] The Orange Order was a Protestant society dedicated to the memory of King William II and his victory at the Battle of the Boyne. The order was established in 1795 but was suppressed under the 1825 Unlawful Societies Act. Orangeism survived at a local level and, led by William Johnston, grew in popularity from the late 1860s onwards. The Orange Order flourished with the first home rule crisis of 1886 and with the subsequent crises of 1892–93 and 1912–14. The order was represented on the Ulster Unionist Council from 1905. See Connolly, *Oxford Companion to Irish History*, p. 415; Hereward Senior, *Orangeism in Ireland and Britain, 1795–1836* (London, 1966). A female auxiliary of the Orange Order, the Association of Loyal Orangewomen of Ireland, was established in Cavan in December 1887. This body was revived in December 1911 and by 1919 twenty–five female branches of the women's association had been established in Ireland and branches were also set up in Canada and America.

all on the 1919 register ... When doing this distribute 'Win the War Literature,' and other suitable Unionist leaflets.

3 To hold an annual meeting in each Division, and at this to have a speaker on some subject which will educate Women for their responsibilities as voters, or as Imperialists.

4 The local Secretary in each place with her Committee must decide what sort of work best suits her Division. It is realised that Town and Country have different objects of interest to pursue ...The Executive Committee of the Ulster Women's Unionist Council desire to again place upon record their firm conviction that the only effective method of securing equality of service and sacrifice as well as obtaining from all parts of Ireland a proper proportion of recruits for His Majesty's Forces, is an immediate and resolute enforcement of compulsory military service in this country.

5 November 1918

A Meeting of the Executive Committee of the Ulster Women's Unionist Council was held in the Old Town Hall, Belfast ... The Dowager Marchioness of Dufferin and Ava in the Chair[235] [Lady Anderson, the Countess of Erne and Mrs Saunderson tendered their resignations as members of the UWUC. The Committee decided to hold the Annual Meeting in Belfast on 13 January 1919].

17 December 1918

A Meeting of the Executive Committee was held in the Old Town Hall, Belfast ... Lady Carson in the Chair[236] ... The Secretary reported that Branches had been formed in the new constituencies of Cromac, Victoria, Duncairn, Shankill, Woodvale and Falls, and would shortly be formed in Pottinger and Ormeau. A meeting would be held that night to form St. Anne's.[237] Tyrone had been re-formed in accordance with the new Divisions and Mid Down was in [the] process of formation ... A suggestion made by Lady Dufferin was unanimously approved of :–

That the Ulster Unionist Council be asked to send two representatives to the Annual Meeting. It was afterwards decided to increase the number to four.

235 Fifty–two members were present at this meeting and there were–twenty eight apologies for non–attendance.

236 Ruby Frewen, the daughter of Colonel Stephen Frewen of Somerset, became Sir Edward Carson's second wife on 17 September 1914. They had one son, Edward, who was born in 1920. She was widowed on 22 October 1935. Lady Carson was a Vice President of the UWUC from 1914 until her death in 1966. *Thom's Irish Who's Who*, p. 33.
Twenty–five members were present at this meeting and there were thirty–three apologies for non–attendance.

237 These were new parliamentary constituencies in Belfast formed as a result of the Redistribution of Seats Act of 1918.

25 February 1919

A meeting of the Executive Committee was held … in the Old Town Hall, Belfast … The Dowager Marchioness of Dufferin and Ava (Vice-President) in the Chair[238] … The Chairman said she thought the Committee would like to send a vote of appreciation to Miss Rosabelle Sinclair[239] in recognition of the good work she had done in France … and of the Ulster Hospital Unit. This was passed unanimously … The question of co-option was then discussed. It was felt that co-option should be used sparingly … Mrs Mercier-Clements proposed that a small temporary sub-Committee should be appointed to submit a programme of work and to define the future policy of the Council.[240]

18 March 1919

The Executive Committee met … in the Old Town Hall, Belfast … The Dowager Marchioness of Dufferin and Ava (Vice-President) in the Chair[241] … The Chairman read the following Resolution, which was passed in silence, all the members standing:–

That we, the members of the Executive Committee of the Ulster Women's Unionist Council, have heard with deep regret of the death of out former President the Dowager Marchioness of Londonderry. By her constant and unflagging interest in Ulster, and her untiring energy, she largely promoted the welfare of the Council and the success of its work. We beg to offer our deepest sympathy to the members of her family in the great loss which they have sustained … The Secretary was instructed to order a wreath for the late Lady Londonderry, and to represent the Council at the funeral …

The Committee was pleased to learn that Miss Rosabelle Sinclair had received a decoration from the French Government, and the Secretary was instructed to forward its congratulations …

SUGGESTION COMMITTEE.

REPORT…

1 That our library in the Old Town Hall be considerably enlarged, and that the Executive [Committee] should send a very strong recommendation to each

238 Forty–one members were present at this meeting and there were thirty–seven apologies for non–attendance.

239 Rosabelle Sinclair of Strabane was Commandant of the Ulster Volunteer Force Nursing Corps in N. Tyrone and during World War I she managed the Ulster Volunteer Force Hospital in Pau, France. The hospital was provided by the French authorities but was financed by the UWUC from 1915–17. In April 1916 the hospital moved to Lyons and then moved closer to the front line at the request of the French authorities. The hospital was subsequently re–organised and its association with the UWUC came to an end.

240 This committee was named the Suggestion Committee.

241 Forty–three members were present at this meeting and there were twenty–five apologies for non–attendance.

Branch to start a lending library on similar lines; where necessary funds to be given for this purpose from [UWUC] headquarters ... authorization to be given to each Hon. Treasurer to use any funds at her disposal, to buy books. The committee would even carry this further and think that each sub-Branch in each Association should have a library of its own.

2 That classes for speakers and workers be formed (a) to train speakers, (b) when trained, to address meetings to instruct Unionist women in the use of the franchise, qualifications of the voter, Imperial responsibility, etc. Meetings for young people should be organized so that they may be imbued with the right ideas before going out in the world. The Branches to be called upon to organize similar training classes and meetings. The speakers, when trained, should be sent to address meetings all over Ulster. A sub-Committee should be appointed to work out the details of all these arrangements.

3 That all the Branches should be asked to find suitable Unionist women candidates for Urban District Councils, County Councils, etc., and to support their candidature by every possible means.

4 That a grant be given to each Hon. Branch Secretary, to be used in conjunction with the men's Association for the purpose of registration.

5 The Committee recommends that, having regard to the number of Orange Lodges for women now being formed, these lodges should be given official representation on the Council.

6 That members of Parliament, or other prominent speakers, be invited to address each meeting of the Council and Executive Committee on matters of current interest.

7 That each Branch be asked to report work done at least twice per annum to the Executive Committee. In this way ideas will be circulated, and different parts of Ulster will learn what others are doing. For the same reason, the Committee suggests that each Branch should receive an annual visit from Headquarters.

8 That leaflets be prepared and circulated on:–

(a) Rules of voting at Elections.
(b) The Industrial Situation.
(c) Finance and Economy.
(d) The Report of the Industrial Commission.

9 In the course of discussion, the Committee foresaw the likelihood of money being required for subsidizing various forms of anti-Socialist and Industrial Propaganda. It is obvious that more particulars cannot be given at the moment, but they earnestly recommend that a fund, not exceeding three hundred pounds, be set aside for Industrial Propaganda, to be distributed at the discretion of the Finance Committee.

The Suggestion Committee, in presenting this Report to the Executive Committee, for adoption, feels that the subjects upon which they have touched are full of possibilities of usefulness and, if taken up heartily and unanimously, will be of great future benefit to the Province of Ulster.

8 April 1919

The Executive Committee met … in the Old Town Hall, Belfast … The Duchess of Abercorn (President) in the Chair[242] … [The Suggestion Committee of the UWUC successfully proposed] That a monthly newspaper would be of more use than a library, or would be of help in addition to the library.

That papers like the 'National Review', 'The Round Table', 'The Nineteenth Century', 'The Fortnightly Review', and the 'Spectator' might be circulated.

That the leaflets proposed in the first report should be embodied in the proposed newspaper.

That Associations applying for assistance in Registration, and furnishing satisfactory accounts, should be assisted up to £25 per annum.

6 May 1919

The Executive Committee met … in the Old Town Hall … The Duchess of Abercorn (President) in the Chair[243] … The President mentioned that the proposed newspaper had the full approval of Sir Edward Carson.

Mrs McMordie proposed and Lady Kennedy seconded that the suggestion Committee be re-elected as a Newspaper and Report Committee to carry out the project and be responsible for the publication of the newspaper … This was passed unanimously, the Suggestion Committee being thanked for its services.

The Report of a meeting of Hon. Secretaries was read. It had been decided at this meeting to revive the Active Workers Classes subject [to] the approval of the Executive.

3 June 1919

The Executive Committee met on 3rd June 1919, in the Old Town Hall … The Dowager Marchioness of Dufferin and Ava (Vice-President) in the Chair[244] … The question of members' subscription was discussed and it was decided to leave the minimum annual subscription to be settled locally by each Branch …

NEWSPAPER COMMITTEE
REPORT …

A special number will be ready for the 12th July, and the regular monthly

[242] Forty–eight members were present at this meeting and there were twenty–seven apologies for non–attendance.

[243] Forty–one members were present at this meeting and there were twenty–four apologies for non–attendance.

[244] Thirty–three members were present at this meeting and there were thirty apologies for non–attendance.

publication will begin in September.

The Branches are asked to send in reports for the July number not later than Monday 9th June.

1 July 1919

The Executive Committee met in the Old Town Hall … The Dowager Marchioness of Dufferin and Ava (in the Chair)[245] … The Chairman … proposed that the Committee should send a message congratulating His Majesty the King on the signature of Peace, which was passed with acclamation.

Mrs Lowry proposed and Mrs MacGregor Greer seconded that a Thanksgiving Meeting should be held in the Ulster Hall. This was passed unanimously, and it was decided to ask the Bishop, the Moderator, and the Vice-President of the Methodist Conference to address the meeting. It was hoped that Lady Dufferin would preside. Special music to be provided and a collection to be taken up to defray expenses. A sub-Committee was appointed to make the arrangements, to consist of the Chairmen and Hon. Secretaries of the Belfast Branches. It was decided to hold the meeting during the week commencing 20th July.

The Secretary reported that since the last meeting of the Executive, a meeting of the Belfast Secretaries had been held to make arrangements for the distribution of the 'Ulsterwoman'; that orders had been received for 11,076 copies of the Special [12th July, 1919] number. An advertisement had been published drawing attention to the necessity for Registration … In accordance with the Suggestion Committee's first report, the Branches had been requested to receive a visit from Headquarters. The request had met with a hefty response, and the Assistant Secretary had already visited Greenisland, Coleraine and Larne. She would go to Duncairn that night and other visits were in the course of arrangement … [It was proposed] That speakers of other political organizations be not invited to or allowed to speak at our meetings. This was passed by a large majority …

REPORT OF NEWSPAPER COMMITTEE

1 July 1919 …

The work of the Committee has been chiefly in discussing the articles submitted for the paper. There will be a special 12th July number ready for distribution to the Secretaries on 5th July, and after that the paper will be published monthly beginning on the 15th September. The special number will contain contributions from Sir Edward Carson, the 3rd Duchess of Abercorn, Lady Dufferin and others. Other articles will be on politics, Women's Orange Lodges, domestic management (Cookery, poultry, gardening, etc). There will also be a short story and a poem.

With regard to future numbers, it is hoped that members of the Executive who are able to obtain articles from writers of their acquaintance will do so, and submit

[245] Thirty–eight members were present at this meeting and there were twenty–three apologies for non–attendance.

them to the Committee. The Committee will also be glad to have suggestions and criticisms from members of the Executive ... Local Secretaries must arrange for the distribution of the papers to subscribers and newsagents in their own areas. The quantities ordered will be sent to local centres from the printers' office.

3 September 1919

The Executive Committee met ... in the Old Town Hall ... Hon. Lady Kennedy (in the Chair for the first part of the proceedings until the arrival of the Dowager Marchioness of Dufferin and Ava who conducted the rest of the meeting)[246] ... The Right Hon. Sir Edward Carson K.C., M.P. was present during the first part of the meeting and addressed the members. Before he left, Lady Dufferin thanked him for coming to the meeting and proposed a vote of confidence in his leadership which was passed with acclamation ... A correspondence between Mr Bates and the Secretary was read, dealing with the Watch Committee, the Ulster Unionist Council having requested that a representative of the Ulster Women's Unionist Council should be appointed to sit on this Committee ... Mrs McMordie be asked to represent the Council on the Watch Committee.

Miss F. H. Whitaker proposed that [the] Women's Orange Order should have representation on the Council, and it was decided to recommend this to the next meeting of the Council.

The Committee decided to print 10,000 copies of Sir Edward Carson's speech to the Ulster Unionist Council, the previous day, in pamphlet form, for distribution in Great Britain, America and the Colonies.

It was decided to have an instruction class to train speakers and canvassers, and Mrs Wheeler undertook to arrange this ...

NEWSPAPER COMMITTEE
REPORT ...

Mr George Reid [had been appointed] ... with sole responsibility ... for sub-editing and making up for the Press ... All matter to be passed by the Committee who must take full responsibility for the policy and contents of the paper ... The paper will be issued about the 15th of each month. It will be magazine size and will consist of eight pages. There will be articles on subjects of varied interests including Parliamentary Notes, First instalment of and [an] article on demobilzed Soldiers by Sir James Craig, Poetry, Poultry, Household Notes, Notes for the South, etc.

Cost of Publication (roughly)	£38
Sales (roughly)	£36
Advts (Commission to be deducted)	£7

[246] Sixty–seven members were present at this meeting and there were twenty–six apologies for non–attendance.

WORK DONE.
REPORT

Owing to the holiday season there have not been as many meetings as usual. During July the following places were visited from Headquarters:–

Duncairn and Greencastle
A meeting was held last night at Ballyclare.

During the next few weeks the following Branches will be visited:–

East Cavan	Fermanagh
South Derry	Pottinger[.]

7 October 1919

The Executive Committee met in the Old Town Hall ... The Duchess of Abercorn (in the Chair)[247] ... The Hon. Treasurer explained to the Committee that owing to greatly increased expenditure, there was a danger of the current account getting very low, and she asked all those members who had not already subscribed to do so as soon as possible ... Letters were read from Mrs Mercier-Clements and from the Secretary of the Unionist Clubs of Ireland. The latter stated that the question of women being allowed to join the Clubs had been discussed and asked for the opinion of the Committee. The Secretary was instructed to reply that if a definite offer was made it would be considered by the Committee, and to suggest that a certain number of women might attend as delegates ... The Secretary reported that five meetings had been held in different Branches during September, including visits from Headquarters, and that six had already been arranged for October; that Mrs Wheeler was holding weekly classes to train speakers and canvassers; two classes had already been held and the work would be continued till Christmas ... Each affiliated association be asked to give active assistance in propaganda work, by linking up with a constituency in Great Britain.

The Secretary stated that the office had been trying to get in touch with some constituencies having small majorities; arrangements would have been complete but for the Railway Strike ... After some discussion the Secretary was instructed to write to all Branch Secretaries asking them to make arrangements for linking with Great Britain and for propaganda; to send copies of 'The Ulsterwoman' to all Associates of the Council, and to write to the Women's Branch of the National Unionist Association to enquire [of] its policy as to the Union.

Miss Murray-Ker asked for advice as to how the Women's Orange Order could be worked without interfering with existing Unionist Associations. Miss Connor and Miss Whitaker explained that the dues were so small they would scarcely interfere with subscriptions to other funds and that sometimes the establishment of a Lodge

247 Forty–eight members were present at this meeting and there were seventeen apologies for non–attendance.

aroused interest where an Association was not very active.

4 November 1919

The Executive Committee met in the Old Town Hall … [The] Duchess of Abercorn (in the Chair)[248] … The Hon. Treasurer reported that since the last meeting, she had received over £30 subscriptions and two donations of £50 each from Cromac Women's Unionist Association and South Derry Women's Unionist Association … Mrs Shaw reported that she had succeeded in arranging a link between North Down and Newbury (Berks[hire]) … The Secretary reported that different agents had been written to with no result … members undertook to write to … constituencies where they have personal acquaintances … Read a report of meetings in North Down, and a report from Mrs Wheeler of her class. The report suggested that every Association should be asked to appoint a representative to look after vacant houses and removals with a view to securing the houses for Unionists. The Secretary was instructed to inform the Secretaries of affiliated Associations of this and ask for their co-operation. The class also offered to assist at local Municipal elections. The Secretary suggested that the elections were looked after by the Unionist Municipal Association, and that as local elections were not always run on strictly party lines, it would be better not to be officially identified with them. It was decided that the Secretary should inform the class that if any members wished to offer themselves, he would communicate unofficially with the Unionist Municipal Association …

[The UWUC was asked to send representatives to a preliminary meeting] of women's organisations in the city which will be held under the auspices of the [Women's Political] League … The object of the meeting which will be private is the formation of a Women's Advisory Council on Housing, which will afford a means for bringing the opinion of women on the question before the City Council and the public … A deputation was received by the Committee which stated that a deadlock having arisen in the Corporation regarding housing it was proposed to confer with representatives of various women's Associations, this Committee possibly to become a women's Advisory Board similar to the one in London which was recognised by the Government.

The deputation having withdrawn, it was … passed unanimously 'That the Ulster Women's Unionist Council take no part in the meeting, in view of the fact that the deputation stated that everything must be done in the name of the Women's Political League, also having regard to the other organisations which had been invited to attend.'[249]

[248] Thirty–nine members were present at this meeting and there were twenty–two apologies for non–attendance.

[249] No further details are given.

2 December 1919

The Executive Committee met … in the Old Town Hall … Hon. Lady Kennedy, in the Chair until the arrival of the Dowager Marchioness of Dufferin and Ava, who presided during the rest of the meeting[250] … Read a letter from the President (Duchess of Abercorn) relating her interviews with leading Unionists in London, with a view to facilitate communications with agents in England … Read a letter from Lord Glenarthur[251] to Mrs Shaw-Hamilton on the subject of work in Scotland.

A Statement of the financial position of the 'Ulsterwoman' was read[252] … The Secretary reported that efforts had been made from unofficial sources to obtain names and addresses of voters in Great Britain. Mrs Macaulay reported that she had been able to obtain a link for Cromac with the Wells division of Somerset. Nine meetings were arranged for November and so far, five for December.

6 January 1920

The Executive Committee met … in the Old Town Hall … [the] Dowager Marchioness of Dufferin and Ava (in the Chair)[253] … Mrs MacGregor Greer (Chairman of [the] Newspaper Committee) spoke on the preparations for the January number of 'The Ulsterwoman' and asked for criticisms, and a discussion followed, during which many useful suggestions were made.

The Secretary reported that 13 meetings had been held during December, which had been addressed by Mrs Mercier-Clements, Mrs Harding, Miss F. H. Whitaker, Miss Speers, and Mrs Shaw-Hamilton. Up to date, 6 meetings had been arranged for January. Since the last Executive a number of influential Unionists in Great Britain had been written to by the Office, but only 5 answers had been received so far. A report was also read of Mrs Wheeler's Class for Speakers and Canvassers.

3 February 1920

The Executive Committee met … in the Old Town Hall … The Dowager Marchioness of Dufferin and Ava (in the Chair)[254] … The Secretary reported that since the last meeting the Workers' Class had been addressed by Mr McGuffin,[255]

250 Forty–four members were present at this meeting and there were twenty apologies for non–attendance.

251 Lord James Cecil, 2nd Baron Glenarthur (1883–1942). *Dod's Peerage*, p. 358.

252 The statement stated that 'Excess of receipts over expenditure [was] £50–0–0' and that the 'Estimated cost of [the] Oct[.] and Nov[.] nos. [was] £50–0–0'.

253 Thirty members were present at this meeting and there were twenty–three apologies for non–attendance.

254 Forty–five members were present at this meeting and there were twenty–four apologies for non–attendance.

255 Samuel McGuffin, draper and President of Belfast (no. 12) Branch of the Amalgamated Society of Engineers. In 1921 he was elected MP for N. Belfast in the Parliament of Northern Ireland. *Thom's Irish Who's Who*, p. 152.

that Mrs Wheeler's Instruction Class had resumed its weekly meetings and that meetings had been held in Cookstown, Armagh, Comber, Whiteabbey and Carrickfergus. Further meetings were arranged in Strandtown, Portrush, Woodvale, South Antrim, Newtowncrumlin and Clough (Co. Antrim) ... It was decided to ask each Division of Belfast to nominate a representative to act on the Literature Committee.

2 March 1920

The Executive Committee met on Tuesday, 3rd Feb in the Old Town Hall ... The Dowager Marchioness of Dufferin and Ava (in the Chair)[256] ... Reports were read of the weekly class for Canvassers and Speakers, and the Secretary reported that the office had been in correspondence with a number of English Unionists, who had nearly all undertaken to distribute literature (a large quantity of which had been sent) but that it still seemed impossible to get links with constituencies. 53 American clubs had been undertaken by different Branches.[257] Meetings had been held during February at Portrush, Newtowncrumlin, Clough (Co. Antrim) and Carrickfergus, and so far one had been arranged for March [1920] at Portstewart.

A sub-Committee consisting of Mrs Allworthy, Mrs Macaulay, and Mrs McClung was appointed to meet representatives of the Women's Orange Order to arrange the representation on the Council.

30 March 1920

The Executive Committee met in the Old Town Hall ... [the] Duchess of Abercorn (President) in the Chair[258] ... A letter was read from Miss Clarke asking that the Unionist Candidates in the forthcoming Poor Law Elections should receive official and financial support from the Council ... [It was] passed unanimously:–

'That the Unionist candidates should receive support, and assistance equal to the amount raised by Miss Clarke's Committee, £1 for £1, the total amount granted not to exceed £100. The Finance Committee to be instructed to vote it from the Election Fund.'

The Hon[.] Secretaries of the Belfast Branches were appointed as a Committee to confer with Miss Clarke's Committee ... Reports were read of the last two classes held by Mrs Wheeler, before closing for the summer. The Secretary reported that meetings had been held in Portstewart and Woodvale, and two had been arranged for April for Coleraine and Greenisland. ... Letters were read from Mrs Shaw-Hamilton and Mrs Talbot resigning their membership of the Council owing to the exclusion of the three counties. The President undertook to write to them to ask

[256] Fifty–eight members were present at this meeting and there were twenty–three apologies for non–attendance.

[257] Under this scheme Women's Unionist Associations affiliated to the UWUC sent propagandist leaflets and Ulster newspapers to pro–unionist organisations in America.

[258] Forty–six members were present at this meeting and there were sixteen apologies for non–attendance.

them to re-consider their resignations. Lady Mabel Annesley[259] said she felt that she too would be constrained to resign if no protest was made by the Council, and the proceedings terminated.[260]

23 April 1920

The Executive Committee met in the Old Town Hall … [the] Duchess of Abercorn (President) in the Chair[261] … Arising out of the Minutes the President said that she had received replies from Mrs Talbot and Mrs Shaw-Hamilton who had courteously stated they were unable to reconsider their resignations … A letter was read from the Assistant Secretary resigning her position for personal and domestic reasons.[262] The President said that since this letter had been received, some Members of the Committee had interviewed Miss Gray, and an arrangement had been arrived at whereby Miss Gray's salary would be reduced to £100 per annum, Miss Gray [would] not to be required to attend so early in the office or to come in if domestic circumstances prevented. Miss Lewis, in the employment of the Ulster Unionist Council to be appointed Typist and Office Assistant while retaining her position in the Ulster Unionist Council, at a salary of £50 per annum. This was unanimously agreed to … as it was considered wiser not to bring in a stranger.

The Secretary reported that the Sub-Committee had met the ladies who were going forward for election at the Board of Guardians, and that a letter had been received from the Belfast Unionist Municipal Association stating that they were willing to adopt these Candidates officially but could take no financial responsibility in connection with the elections.

Mrs Allworthy (Chairwoman of [the] Literature Committee) reported that this Committee had made arrangements to meet every Wednesday morning at 11 o'clock for the present to send the local Newspapers to America etc[.], and requested the Committee to send in their daily papers when finished with.

The Secretary reported that the sub-Committee appointed to meet the representatives of the Association of Loyal Orange Women in Ireland had met and recommended that the following paragraphs be added to the Constitution:–
Paragraph 4 – The Council shall consist of –

(b) Three representatives from each District Lodge in Ulster, of the Association of

259 Lady Mabel Annesley (1881–1959), artist and member of the Belfast Art Society and Society of Wood Engravers. She exhibited her work in Belfast, Dublin, London and Manchester. She resigned from the UWUC in 1920. *Dod's Peerage*, p. 23.

260 These resignations and tensions were provoked by the Government of Ireland Bill introduced to the House of Commons on 25 February 1920. This bill envisaged a six–county parliament and devolved administration for Ulster and not nine county exclusion from home rule as had been originally hoped. The counties of Cavan, Donegal and Monaghan were, therefore, excluded from this bill which passed into law on 23 December 1920.

261 Forty–six members were present at this meeting and there were twenty–five apologies for non–attendance.

262 Miss Alice Gray held the paid position of UWUC Assistant Secretary from October 1918. The salary for this position was £125.

Loyal Orangewomen of Ireland, and of such District Lodges as may hereafter be formed, such representatives to be approved of by the Grand Lodge of the Association.

Paragraph 8 – The Executive committee shall consist of the following –

(b) Representatives of the Association of Loyal Orangewomen of Ireland to be nominated by the Grand Lodge of the Association, out of, and in the proportion of two for every three representatives of the Association of the Council.

The Committee decided to add the following words to the first paragraph – 'And to be already members of the Women's Unionist Association for the constituency in which they respectively reside'.

The Secretary also reported that since the last Executive Meetings had been held in Woodvale, Coleraine and Greenisland. A further meeting had been arranged in Islandmagee … The following Recommendation from the Finance Committee was adopted by the Committee for recommendation to the Council:–

'That a minimum subscription of 10/– be fixed for each member of the Council, which may be paid by the Member herself direct or by the Association which she represents at her option'.

1 June 1920

'The Executive Committee met in the Old Town Hall … Mrs McMordie (in the Chair)[263] … Mrs Allwothy made the following report: – That 5 meetings of the Literature Committee had been held – 208 papers had been sent to women's Clubs in America. It was decided to hold the meetings in June but not in July or August. An appeal for more papers was made.

The Secretary reported that 7 ladies had come forward as Candidates for the Board of Guardian elections. Of these, 4 had undertaken to pay their own expenses, and he did not think the expenses of the other 3 would be very heavy.

Resignations were received from:–

Lady Rode; Lady Bangor,[264] Lady Mabel Annesley; East Cavan Women's Unionist Assn.[,] and Co. Monaghan Branch W.[omen's] U.[nionist] Association.[265]

The Secretary was instructed to forward these to the President and ask her to

263 Forty–seven members were present at this meeting and there were seven apologies for non–attendance.

264 Agnes Elizabeth, the third daughter of Dacre Hamilton, Deputy Lieutenant of Cornacassa, Co. Monaghan. In 1905 she married Maxwell Richard Crosbie Ward, 6th Viscount Bangor, OBE and representative peer for Ireland from 1913. He was also a member of the Northern Ireland Senate from 1921, Parliamentary Secretary to the Prime Minister of Northern Ireland in 1921 and Speaker of the Northern Ireland Senate from 1930. *Dod's Peerage*, pp 48–9.

265 This was due to the Ulster Unionist Council's acceptance the Government of Ireland Bill on 20 March 1920. See footnote 260 above.

write personally to the signatories to see if they would reconsider their decision ... The Secretary reported that 3 Meetings had been held in East Antrim and one in Victoria.

Mrs MacGregor Greer explained her position as to the exclusion of the 3 counties. Mrs Sidmonton also spoke ... The Secretary reported that £5 had been received from Woodvale Branch and £10 from St Anne's.[266]

6 July 1920

The Executive Committee met in the Old Town Hall ... Mrs McMordie (in the Chair)[267] ... [A resolution of sympathy was passed on the death of Mrs Mercier-Clements, Honorary Assistant Treasurer of the U.W.U.C., who] took a leading part in the formation of the Council in 1910, and her great enthusiasm and organising ability contributed largely to the rapid growth and strengthening of the Council and its Affiliated Associations.

Afterwards, she worked indefatigably in many campaigns in England and Scotland, to further Unionist principles and to uphold the cause of Loyal Ulster. Her persuasive eloquence and whole-hearted sincerity for the Cause which she advocated won a large measure of support at English and Scotch elections.

Her services were never grudged to the Council and its Committees, and her regular attendance at our Meetings, her wide outlook and far-seeing vision, she assisted greatly in controlling and developing the policy of the Council.

Her great energy and zeal for public service found many other outlets, and particularly during the recent War, she worked unceasingly in aid of numerous patriotic movements.

Her death had caused a gap in our ranks which it will be hard to fill. She will be sorely missed by her many friends, and greatly regretted by all loyal Ulster men and women. ... Mrs Allworthy[268] reported that four Meetings of the Literature Committee had been held at which over 200 Newspapers had been sent to Women's Clubs in America ... That several members had responded to the appeal for papers, and she hoped that when the Committee met again in September, it would not be necessary to make a further appeal.

Letters of resignation from Hon. Zoe Maxwell and members of West Cavan were read ... [It] was unanimously carried as a recommendation to the Council: -

'That the representation on the Ulster Women's Unionist Council and on the Executive Committee of the Council from each Affiliated Association be increased by 2 Members on each, making 10 instead of 8 on the Council, and 5 instead of 3 on the Executive Committee of the Council' ... the question of the approaching revision of the registration [was discussed], as this leaves much to be desired ... As

266 Both of these branches were situated in Belfast.

267 Forty–four members were present at this meeting and there were fourteen apologies for non–attendance.

268 Mrs Allworthy was chair of the UWUC Literature Committee.

a result of the discussion the Secretary was instructed to write immediately to all Branch Secretaries requesting them to see that the registration was looked after during the coming weeks.

The Secretary reported that a Meeting had been held in Shankill at which the speaker was the late Mrs Mercier-Clements.

Donations had been received from North Down	£10
Donaghadee	5
Comber	15
(previous donation) Bangor	25
Total	£55

The Secretary read the Trading Account prepared by the Accountants in connection with the 'Ulsterwoman' which showed a loss of about £140 to the Ulster Women's Unionist Council; also a Report of the Orders for the paper which were received in [the] Office, and which showed a decrease during the nine months of about 1266 copies.

A discussion took place as the advisability of keeping on the paper … On a vote, (by a show of hands) it was decided by a large majority to discontinue the paper after publication of the August number.

7 September 1920

The Executive Committee met in the Old Town Hall … The Dowager Marchioness of Dufferin & Ava (in the Chair)[269] … It was decided to print for distribution in England and abroad 10,000 copies of Father Lawless's letter condemnation [of] murders etc, also Cardinal Logue's pronouncement.[270]

The Secretary reported the Balances in [the] Bank at the present time, and it was decided to place £2,000 on Deposit Receipt.

5 October 1920

The Executive Committee met in the Old Town Hall … The Dowager Marchioness of Dufferin & Ava (in the Chair)[271] … The Secretary reported that after the last meeting it had been suggested that an account of the evictions of Protestants in the R.C. districts of Belfast should be printed as a leaflet, that he had submitted all the leaflets to the Duchess and had now received them from her

269 Thirty–one members were present at this meeting and there were seventeen apologies for non–attendance.

270 The Lawless letter condemned the violence directed towards British government officials, policemen and soldiers in the south and west of Ireland. No condemnation was received from the Roman Catholic Church until District Inspector Swanzy was murdered in Lisburn. This event was followed by sectarian riots in Belfast and Lisburn and prompted Cardinal Michael Logue (1840–1924), to issue a statement condemning these activities.

271 Forty members were present at this meeting and there were nine apologies for non–attendance.

approved of, and hoped that they would shortly be printed and ready for distribution … Mrs R. K. Gilliland called the attention of the Committee to the Sinn Fein campaign at present being conducted in London, and particularly to the meetings that were being held in Hyde Park and elsewhere, some of which she herself had attended.

The Viscountess of Massereene & Ferrard[272] said that a similar state of affairs existed on the Clyde, and that there were regular recruiting stations for Sinn Fein.[273]

Mrs Carson reported that an Association called the 'Ulster Economic Association' had held several meetings in the Coleraine district appealing to Farmers to support Sinn Fein and particularly urging upon them that if they did so they would relieve themselves from the heavy taxation which was a consequence of the present Union with England.

It was proposed by Mrs Gilliland [and] seconded by Mrs Harding that the attention of the Ulster Unionist Council should be called to the various meetings, and a recommendation sent to them to take steps to counteract the different campaigns.

Mrs McMordie suggested that the recommendation should be conveyed by a Deputation and 8 women were appointed accordingly. Proposed by Mrs Gilliland [and] Seconded by Lady Kennedy [–]

That the French Priest's letter which appeared in the 'Newsletter' of 4th inst, 'MacSwiney's Mortal Sin' be published for distribution.

The proceedings terminated.

2 November 1920

The Executive Committee met in the Old Town Hall … Mrs McMordie (in the Chair)[274] … The Secretary reported that 10,000 copies of the Leaflet with reference to Boycott and Evictions had been printed and are now ready for distribution … Mrs Sidmonton said the Literature Committee had come to consist of about three active members who received no support from the other members of the Executive Committee and they felt that they could not carry on without additional support.

[272] Jean Barbara, Viscountess of Massereene and Ferrard, the eldest surviving daughter of Sir John Stirling Ainsworth, MP. In 1905 she married Algernon William John Clotworthy Skeffington, 12th Viscount of Massereene and Ferrard, a JP and HM Lieutenant in Co. Antrim, Parliamentary Secretary to the Prime Minister of Northern Ireland and a member of the Northern Ireland Senate, 1921–29. The Viscountess of Massereene and Ferrard died in 1937. *Dod's Peerage*, pp 585–6; *Thom's Irish Who's Who*, p. 161.

[273] Sinn Féin had been launched by Arthur Griffith (1871–1922) in 1906. By 1918 a politically transformed Sinn Féin was the dominant Irish nationalist party having defeated the Irish Parliamentary Party in a number of by–elections and then in the general election of 1918. For details see D. G. Boyce (ed.), *The Revolution in Ireland, 1879–1923* (Dublin, 1988).

[274] Forty–five members were present at this meeting and there were eighteen apologies for non–attendance.

Mrs Chichester[275] said the Committee should make up its mind either to carry on active propaganda work or to dissolve, that it was almost too late now but a great deal might still be done if proper steps were taken. She read a letter from a friend in America testifying to the value of the Newspapers and literature sent out there combating the Sinn Fein campaign.

The Secretary was instructed to write to the Loyal Coalition[,] 24 Mt. Vernon Street, Boston, Mass. to endeavour to arrange a scheme of co-operation for propaganda work in the United States.

Mrs McMordie reported that the Deputation arranged at the previous meeting had seen Mr Bates that day and had put the views of the Committee before him. Mr Bates assured the Deputation that the Ulster Unionist Council was fully alive to the situation but that the great difficulty in the way at present is to obtain the necessary funds. That at least £100,000 would be required for a proper anti-Sinn Fein campaign in England and Scotland and that in the present conditions of trade in Ulster it would be hopeless to appeal for such a sum.[276]

After further discussion it was … [agreed] that the Committee should offer to contribute the sum of £200 from the funds of the Council to pay the expenses of four Speakers in London for one month. Two to be working-men and two clergymen … Mrs Harding suggested that a Professional Elocutionist be engaged to train Speakers.

Mrs McMordie said that if a sufficient number of workers would guarantee to attend the classes and afterwards to give their services as Speakers, she was sure the matter could be arranged and would certainly be considered.

Mrs McMordie said that it had been suggested that the Meetings of the Council and the Executive Committee should be opened with Prayer … the President be requested to ask the Lord Primate to write a short form of Prayer suitable for the occasion … A letter was read from Pottinger Women's Association promising £10 to the funds of the Council.

7 December 1920

The Executive Committee met in the Old Town Hall … Mrs McMordie (in the

275 Born in Kilrea in 1882, and privately educated, Dehra Chichester married Lt. Colonel Robert Spenser Chichester, a unionist MP in 1901. Widowed in 1921 she later married Admiral W.H. Parker in 1928, but was widowed for a second time in 1943. She was a Vice Chairman of the UWUC from 1918–30 and was elected to the Northern Ireland Parliament in 1921 as a unionist representative of Londonderry City and County. She retained her seat until her resignation in 1929. On the death of her son–in–law, Captain Chichester Clark, she was re–elected in 1933 as a unionist member for South Derry. Dehra Chichester was Parliamentary Secretary to the Minister of Education from 1937–44 and Minister for Health and Local Government from 1949–57. From 1948–49 she was Chairman of the Northern Ireland Health Services Board. She also served as a JP, a rural district councillor in Magerafelt and as the Chairman of Magherafelt Board of Guardians. She was made a Dame of the British Empire and died in 1963. See Urquhart, *Women in Ulster Politics; Thom's Irish Who's Who*, p. 36.

276 This was a result of the end of the post–war boom.

Chair)[277] … Mrs Chichester be requested to interview Sir James Craig and Captain C.C. Craig when in London, and ascertain more fully their views on campaign work in England at present.[278]

Attention was called to the numerous exaggerated and unfounded statements with reference to the Irish Question at present appearing in the Press, more particularly in English newspapers. The [Executive Committee] … appointed a sub-Committee to collect and where possible answer such statements …

A letter was read dated 5th November 1920 from the Hon. Sec. of the Belfast Women's Advisory Council, stating that the Constitution of the Council had been enlarged to include other social work in the City and asking the Ulster Women's Unionist Council to reconsider their decision on 5th November 1919 regarding representation.

It was unanimously decided to adhere to the decision already come to and the Secretary was instructed to reply accordingly.

A letter was read from Lady Muriel Close resigning her position as President of South Armagh Women's Unionist Assocn.

The Secretary reported that for sometime past owing to the small number of Unionists in South Armagh, the Association had not been at all active.

Mrs W.J. Allen confirmed the Secretary's report and stated that she is at present trying to get something done in the district by the Orange Order.

Lady Muriel Close's resignation was then accepted with regret.

A letter was read from the President suggesting that in view of the present political situation and that probably at an early date a meeting of the Council would be required to confer with the men's council, the Annual Meeting should be adjourned for the present. The suggestion was unanimously adopted.

4 January 1921

The Executive Committee met in the Old Town Hall…Mrs McMordie (in the chair)[279] … [Mrs Chichester] informed the Committee that she had received a letter from the President expressing the opinion that in view of the wishes of the Parliamentary Party, the question of sending Speakers to England should be deferred in the meantime.

The Minutes of the two Meetings of the 'Vigilance Committee'[280] held on the 10th and 17th December were read … It was unanimously decided … to change the name of the Committee to [the] 'Propaganda Committee'.

The Secretary was instructed to write to Mr Wm. Coote[281] M.P. to ask if there is

277 Forty–five members were present at this meeting and there were ten apologies for non–attendance.

278 Due to Colonel Chichester's illness, Mrs Dehra Chichester was unable to go to London.

279 Forty members were present at the meeting and there were ten apologies for non–attendance.

280 This committee scoured the press assessing how the Irish political situation was being portrayed.

281 William Coote (b. 1863), MP for S. Tyrone from 1916 and MP for Fermanagh and Tyrone in the Parliament of Northern Ireland from 1921. He was a JP and County Councillor for Co. Tyrone. *Thom's Irish Who's Who*, p. 46.

in any way in which the Council can co-operate in the proposed Anti-Sinn Fein campaign about to be launched by the Grand Orange Lodge of England.

The recommendation of the Committee with reference to the strengthening and support of the 'Literature Committee' was approved of and it was decided to ask each Belfast Association to provide three helpers for the Literature Committee.
It was also decided to send a selection of Leaflets to each Affiliated Association and ask that they be distributed in England, Scotland, The Dominions and the United States.

As some objections were raised to the continuation of Propaganda work outside Ireland in view of the necessity for Educational work at home to prepare Voters for the coming Elections to the Ulster Parliament, the Chairman asked for a vote on the question, which resulted as follows:–

For the continuation of Propaganda Work	31
Against	3

The Chairman announced that the decision of the Committee was clearly in favour of continuing the work.

Proposed by Mrs Allen [and] Seconded by Mrs Macgregor Greer

'To consider the forthcoming elections for the Ulster Parliament, and to make such arrangements as may be deemed advisable'.

Various methods of Educational work at home were then discussed, and amongst other things it was suggested that Cinema Films or Lantern Slides explaining the system of Proportional Representation and the method of voting should be shown round the country, and the Secretary was instructed to make inquiries as to the possibility of getting such films or slides and their possible cost.

25 January 1921

The Executive Committee met in the Old Town Hall ... The Duchess of Abercorn (in the Chair)[282] ... The President ... addressed the Members and pointed out that a serious crisis had been reached in the affairs of the Council, and a decision must come to either take up and carry on definite work or to dissolve. Her Grace emphasised the necessity for securing proper representation on the men's Unionist Associations throughout the country, and urged representatives of local Associations to take this matter up strongly.

With regard to women coming forward as candidates for Parliament,[283] the President expressed the opinion that the time was not ripe for this, and the essential thing in the first Parliament was to preserve the safety of the Unionist cause, that much organisation and construction work would be necessary for which perhaps women had not the necessary experience, and except in the case of outstanding qualifications, men candidates were preferable.

282 Sixty members were present at this meeting and there were ten apologies for non–attendance.
283 This is a reference to the newly established Parliament of Northern Ireland.

The President then outlined the following scheme of work to be undertaken by the Council:–

A Central Committee to be formed in Belfast with a separate Treasurer. Each County to appoint representatives to work with this Committee, and a scheme of organisation to be prepared which would reach every individual voter within the Parliamentary area; that Mr Hiley (Agent for Sir Ed. Carson in Duncairn Division) who is an expert in organisation had promised to attend at the Old Town Hall at 3 p.m. that afternoon, and that all who intended to work should come to hear his system of organisation explained …

It was unanimously decided to send a Resolution to the Ulster Unionist Council offering assistance in the election campaign, and pointing out the necessity of official co-operation between the men's and women's Associations.

On the suggestion of Mrs Chichester it was also decided to call the attention of the Ulster Unionist Council to the desirability of giving the Ulster Women's Unionist Council due representation on the Standing Committee [of the Ulster Unionist Council]; and the President, Mrs McMordie and the Secretary were authorised to draw up the Resolution.

Mrs W. J. Allen asked the Secretary to report to the Executive Committee on the existing state of the Organisations of the U.W.U.A. in the Constituencies of the six counties, and stated that she had put this question on the Agenda for the purpose of calling attention to the lack of organisation in South Armagh. The Secretary explained that South Armagh had always been a difficult constituency as the few Unionists in the district were very scattered and were afraid to hold meetings or otherwise draw attention to themselves, that owing to the resignation of Lady Muriel Close[284] and the absence of Mrs Richardson in England, there is now no one in South Armagh to take the lead, but that as the Constituency would now be merged with North and Mid Armagh which were strongly Unionist, he hoped that the Unionists in South Armagh would be helped to organise.

Mrs Sidmonton asked if the Secretary had any information about Cinema Films or Lantern Slides on the subject of Proportional Representation. The Secretary explained that the cost of films would be abortive; that he had obtained specimen slides from the P. R. Society of Ireland[285] which were not suitable. That Mrs Wheeler had kindly undertaken to write a short lecture to be illustrated by slides which could be easily manufactured for the purpose.

284 Lady Muriel Albany Close, the eldest daughter of the 5th Earl of Castlestuart. In 1891 she married Maxwell Archibald Close, a JP, Sheriff and Deputy Lieutenant of Co. Armagh. *Thom's Irish Who's Who*, p. 40.

285 The PR Society of Ireland was active during the 1920s and promoted the use of the proportional representation (PR) electoral system as the fairest voting system allowing for the representation of a wide range of interests. Only the Northern Ireland local election of 1921 and the Northern Ireland general elections of 1921 and 1925 were conducted using the PR system. PR was abolished for local elections in Northern Ireland in 1922 and for general elections there in 1929.

1 March 1921

The Executive Committee met in the Old Town Hall ... Mrs McMordie (in the Chair)[286] ... The Secretary reported that he had arranged with Councillor Gordon to conduct a class for the instruction of workers in Proportional Representation, that Councillor Gordon wished the class to be confined as far as possible to those who were prepared to undertake the instruction of others on the subject.

The Secretary also reported that Mrs Wheeler has now prepared the outlines of a Lecture to be illustrated by Lantern Slides, that the Lecture is not confined to the subject of Proportional Representation but deals with the entire Political situation, and that as a result of Councillor Gordon's class it is hoped to secure a few ladies who will undertake to go round the country districts and deliver this Lecture and give instructions of Proportional Representation.

The Secretary asked for the instructions of the Committee as to payment [for] ladies undertaking this work and suggested that it might be necessary to pay a small fee in addition to the actual out-of-pocket expenses. The payment of a fee was approved of ... [and it was decided that] each individual case be considered by the Finance Committee having regard to the ability of the particular Association in question to pay ... Letters were read from the Lurgan and Portadown Branches W.U.A. asking for grants towards the expenses of revision and electoral work, and were referred to the Finance Committee.

The following Resolution from South Antrim W.U.A. was read:–

That 'This Meeting of the S.A.W.U.A. is of opinion that the time has arrived when Women's Unionist Associations in Ulster should cease to exist and that in future Ulster Unionist Associations should include men and women' ... A letter was read from the Belfast Women's Advisory Council asking the Committee to give consideration 'to the urgent need for the inclusion of women among the candidates for the coming election to the Northern [Ireland] Parliament ... such inclusion is especially needed in view of the nature of the problems with which the new Parliament will have to deal. These must include Poor Law reform, which will necessitate re-organisation of the system of Medical Relief, some form of provision for necessitous widows with children, and drastic reform of the laws affecting the unmarried mother and her child. Temperance and Education Reform must also be dealt with at an early date.

In all these questions the assistance of competent women is especially necessary' ... The Secretary was instructed to reply stating that the matter has already been under consideration.

5 April 1921

The Executive Committee met in the Old Town Hall on Tuesday 5th April, 1921

[286] Thirty–eight members were present at this meeting and there were eighteen apologies for non–attendance.

... [the] Hon. Lady Kennedy (in the Chair)[287] ... The Secretary reported that Councillor Gordon's class on P.R. had been held twice a week since 8th March with very satisfactory results ... The Secretary reported that Miss Gregg expected to arrive in Belfast on the 6th inst[.] and would be ready to take up Lantern work almost immediately, and gave an outline of the Lecture prepared by Mrs Wheeler.

A further letter was read from the Belfast Women's Citizen Union urging the vital necessity for the nomination of women candidates at the coming elections.[288] The Secretary was instructed to reply stating that the letter had been laid before the Committee.

Mrs Murland asked if it was correct to say that any woman wishing to stand as [a] Unionist candidate for Parliament must obtain the sanction of the Ulster Women's Unionist Council.

The Secretary pointed out that at the Annual meeting held in February last, the Duchess of Abercorn had expressed the opinion that women should not offer themselves as candidates but that she had said nothing to indicate that where a woman was invited by the Electors generally to become a candidate she was to refuse the offer.

Mrs Montgomery called attention to the fact that in County Derry Mrs Spencer Chichester, O.B.E. had been unanimously selected as one of the Unionist candidates ... [It was] enthusiastically passed

'That the hearty congratulations and best wishes of the Executive Committee of the Ulster Women's Unionist Council be tendered to Mrs Spencer Chichester O.B.E., J.P. on her selection as one of the Unionist candidates for the City and County of Derry' ...

Mrs Morrison, (Secretary of the Women's Branch, Labour Unionist Association)[289] gave some information about the position of Labour in Ulster and the Ulster workers Trades Union ... The Secretary read a letter from the 'Empire Movement' Union Jack Committee, inviting members to the annual Empire Day Service on 22nd May, and requested members wishing to attend to notify him in good time and he would try to have seats reserved for them.

·

3 May 1921

The Executive Committee met in the Old Town Hall ... Lady Craig (in the

[287] Fifty–six members were present at this meeting and there were twenty apologies for non–attendance.

[288] This letter from E. S. Montgomery, dated 5 April 1921, stated that 'The Committee feels the overwhelming need for such a nomination in view of such legislation as Education, Moral Reform, and Safeguards for Child Life which undoubtedly will be dealt with by the new Parliament.'

[289] The Ulster Unionist Labour Association was formally established in June 1918 with the aim of combining trade unionism with unionism. The association sought to mobilise working–class voters. Sir Edward Carson was the first President of the organisation. However, the association failed to mobilise significant working–class support or increase working–class influence in the Ulster Unionist Party. See Patrick Buckland, *Irish Unionism: Two. Ulster Unionism.*

Chair)[290] ... The Secretary reported that Councillor Gordon's class on Proportional Representation was now closed ... and [it was] passed by acclamation:

'That the hearty congratulations and best wishes of the Executive Committee of the Ulster Women's Unionist Council be tendered to Mrs Julia McMordie, C.B.E., J.P. on her selection as one of the Unionist Candidates for South Belfast'.

The Secretary reported that since Miss Gregg's arrival, she had held meetings in Dundrum, Holywood, Portadown, Six Roads Ends, Dunmurry, Dundonald and Armagh, and that several other applications for her services had been received, and urged on the members the necessity for immediate applications so that dates could be arranged ... The Secretary reported that he had sent out letters to all Branch Secretaries drawing their attention to the need of providing refreshments for workers on election day, and asking for a report of any special work that was being done by the Associations, that he had received replies from 16 branches which he read ... The Secretary was instructed to write to the Branch Secretaries and make it clear that the matter of providing refreshments etc. should not be done in the name of the Branch Association but should be made to appear as a voluntary effort on the part of private individuals. Also that meetings should not be announced as being in support of candidates but as meetings of instructions in P.R., lectures etc.

21 June 1921

The Executive Committee met in the Old Town Hall ... The Duchess of Abercorn (in the Chair)[291] ... The President said she would like to thank each member of the Council and Executive, and through them, all the women who so willingly helped to make the Election such a splendid success, and suggested that the hearty congratulations of the U.W.U.C. should be sent to Sir James Craig, and to Mrs Chichester and Mrs McMordie on their election as members of the Northern Parliament[292] ... The President spoke as to the Address which it was decided should be presented to H.M. the Queen, and explained that although it was being presented as from the U.W.U.C., it must not appear that it was from a Political Organisation, that it had been signed by herself, Lady Craig, The Lady Mayoress, Mrs Chichester and Mrs McMordie; that as the deputation presenting the address was limited to three whose names had to be sent at once, she had given the names of herself, Lady Craig and Mrs McMordie. A copy of the Address was read and unanimously approved of ... The president spoke on the subject of [electoral] Registration, and the importance of having every eligible person to put on the Register ... Mrs MacGregor Greer spoke on the importance of women being given appointments in the different departments of the Northern Parliament ... a vote of sympathy be

290 Sixty–five members were present at this meeting and there were eleven apologies for non–attendance.

291 Sixty–four members were present at this meeting and there were fourteen apologies for non–attendance.

292 This election was held on 24 May 1921. The result was a victory for Ulster unionists, who had expected to win 32 seats, but all 40 unionist candidates were returned, along with 6 Sinn Féin and 6 nationalist candidates, to fill the 52 seats in the Northern Ireland House of Commons.

tendered to the family of Miss Francis H. Whitaker who had been a member of the U.W.U.C. from its foundation and took an active part in every movement which had for its object the welfare of the loyal population of the Province[.]

20 September 1921

The Executive Committee met in the Old Town Hall … Mrs James McCalmont (in the Chair)[293] … A letter was read from the President in which she referred to the matter brought before the members at the last meeting as to the inclusion of women in the different departments of the Northern Parliament and stating that she had been approached as to the advisability of sending a Manifesto to Sir James Craig embodying these views, that as it was thought best that such a Manifesto should come through the Association she had asked the Vice Presidents and Office Bearers to sign same as time seemed of importance, but that as it was pointed out the Executive Committee might misconstrue their action, nothing further was done as she felt it her duty to ask the members to discuss the matter, and giving her views … It was decided that a short letter should be sent to Sir James Craig … to bring before the Government the importance of the services women can and are anxious to render to their country, especially in such matters as Education, Care of Children, Local Government, Agriculture and Labour.

We ask, therefore, that our desire to be included in the above named Departments be seriously considered, either as Advisory Committees, or Women to consult with Ministers and Officials, or as Women Officials … Copies were also directed to be sent to Mrs Chichester and Mrs McMordie.[294]

The President in her letter also referred to the advisability of keeping on the Association as at present constituted owing to the altered conditions of politics since the War, and suggested that a sub-Committee be appointed to go into the matter … The Secretary was instructed to write to the various Railway Companies to see if it would be possible for them to issue Vouchers to the Members.

4 October 1921

The Executive Committee met in the Old Town Hall … Lady Craig (in the Chair)[295] … A letter was read from Sir James Craig asking if the Ulster Women's Unionist Council would supply two flags to be flown permanently from the flagstaff on the Ulster Division [War] Memorial to be erected at Thiepval [France].

It was decided that a Flag Fund be opened not only to supply the first two flags but to renew them from time to time … The Secretary was instructed to write to

293 Sixty–two members were present at this meeting and there were nineteen apologies for non–attendance

294 The two women members of the Parliament of Northern Ireland who were also active members and office bearers in the UWUC.

295 Sixty–one members were present at this meeting and there were eighteen apologies for non–attendance.

all the Branch Associations informing them ... Mrs Huey reported that a friend of hers in Battersea had complained of the active anti-Ulster Propaganda being carried on there by Lady Bonham Carter[296] and others, and suggested that speakers should be sent over to counteract this. Mrs Huey was asked to find out from her friend if meetings would be properly organised. [If] Hospitality [would be] provided and other details of this kind ... [A sub-committee of eight Executive Committee members was drawn up to consider the future of the U.W.U.C.] It was decided that the sub-Committee should submit its draft report to each of the Affiliated Associations and get their views before presenting its final report to the Executive ... [A letter from the Duchess of Abercorn is attached to the minutes, dated 16 September 1921, stating] I am deeply impressed with the necessity of the inclusion of suitable Ulsterwomen in the newly formed [Government] Depts. In England they have been found invaluable in Education, Health and Agriculture Depts., and believing as I do that these Depts. in Ulster will make great advances in the welfare of the people of the 6 counties, I do trust women will be able to assist in their great work ... I shall be only too pleased to help in any way that is approved of.
The second question I want discussed is are we justified in the entirely altered condition of politics since the war, in running an expensive office, summoning Executive meetings, when so far as I can see, we have no tangible work or results to show. Under the existing constitution we are much handicapped, and it has occurred to some of our members that it might be for the best to consider seriously the winding up of the present Association,[297] but I personally should deeply regret the breaking up of our Council, Executive, and Branches, where we have a fine, solid body of loyal women working – I suggest therefore that the Executive appoint a small sub-Committee to thoroughly go into the matter –

First of what work we can hope to do for the Cause under the present conditions and if that does not prove fruitful to:

Secondly go into the question of winding it up, and I suggest that to keep the Organised Branches going that some kind of Club might be formed, which would start on a wider base than at present, and would bring town and country Branches more together, and be more workable and useful than we seem to be at the present –

296 (Helen) Violet Bonham–Carter (1887–1969), Baroness Asquith of Yarnbury, the only daughter of H. H. Asquith. In 1915 she married Sir Maurice Bonham-Carter. She was President of the Women's Liberal Unionist Federation from 1923–25 and from 1939–45 and President of the Liberal Party Organisation from 1945–47. She stood unsuccessfully for election in 1945 and 1951. Violet Bonham–Carter also served as Governor of the BBC from 1940–46, was Vice–Chair of the United Europe Movement in 1945 and President of the Royal Institute of International Affairs, 1946–49. *The Dictionary of National Biography: The Concise Dictionary, Part II*, p. 283.

297 A letter is attached to the minutes from C. W. Wallace of Myra Castle, Downpatrick, resigning from the Executive Committee of the UWUC stating 'I can see no good in the continuation of these meetings.'

1 November 1921

The Executive Committee met in the Old Town Hall … Lady Craig (in the Chair)[298] … [A letter, dated 6 October 1921, was read from] Sir James Craig [who] expressed his thanks for the message sent to him giving his views on the question of employment of women in the different departments of the Northern Parliament. With regard to the resolution emphasising the importance of the services women can and are anxious to render at this juncture in the affairs of Northern Ireland, I can assure you that the matter is one which will engage the anxious consideration of my Colleagues and myself. We are all well aware of the immense assistance the Women of Ulster have been to the Government and to their late Leader,[299] through long years of strain and anxiety, and you may rest fully assured that when the opportunity presents itself, the fullest co-operation and assistance will be requisitioned from your Council.

With regard to appointments in our Local Civil Service, we have already the names of a large number of women on our Register, but owing to the non-transference of the various services from Dublin occasioned by the 'truce' between the British Government and Sinn Fein,[300] we are unable to do more than absorb a few of the Local Applicants in the meantime …

[A report of the sub-committee established to consider the future of the UWUC stated]

1 That in the opinion of the Committee it is desirable in the interests of efficient working and for the promotion of the Unionist Cause, that separate Women's Unionist Associations be continued in all Constituencies, but that a scheme of close affiliation with the Men's or Parliamentary Associations be adopted for the purpose of election work.

2 That the Ulster Unionist Council be asked to appoint representatives to meet representatives from the Ulster Women's Unionist Council to decide the best means of affiliation.

3 That as the importance of the Imperial Union was never greater than at present, the name 'Unionist' be retained by the Council and all its Affiliated Associations.

4 That as a measure of economy, Mr Hamill be asked to carry on the work of the council at his own office, and at an increased salary of say £200 per annum, thereby saving the cost of rent and staff at the Old Town Hall.

5 That Committee meetings continue to be held at the Old Town Hall, but that the Executive Committee meet only quarterly instead of monthly, except where special business makes more frequent meetings necessary.

298 Fifty–nine members were present at this meeting and there were seventeen apologies for non–attendance.

299 This is a reference to Sir Edward Carson. James Craig had taken over as Ulster unionist leader in January 1921.

300 A truce between the British government and the Irish Republican Army (IRA) was agreed on 9 July 1921. Negotiations between Britain and Ireland began on 11 October 1921 and resulted in the Anglo–Irish Treaty signed on 6 December 1921. The treaty gave dominion status to the 26 counties of Ireland which were thereafter to be known as the Irish Free State.

6 That these recommendations, if adopted by the Executive Committee, be submitted to a Special Meeting of [the] Council to be called in November, and any special changes in the Constitution and the objects of the Council be considered and submitted at the same date ... Miss Connor read a list of Subscriptions which had been received in connection with the Ulster Division War Memorial Flag amounting to £24 ... and it was finally decided to purchase two flags ... The Committee had been informed that it would be necessary to renew these flags three or four times in the year.

6 December 1921

A Special Meeting of the Executive Committee was held ... in the Old Town Hall. ... The Duchess of Abercorn (in the Chair)[301] ... The Committee proceeded to consider the draft revised Constitution as prepared by the Sub-Committee[302] ... A Deputation from the Loyalist Relief Fund attended and asked for the support of the ladies in the effort which was being made to provide for the families of men who were killed or injured in the recent disturbances in the City. A hearty response was made ... and a sum of Twenty guineas be given as an immediate donation out of the funds of the Council.[303]

3 January 1922

The Executive Committee met in the Old Town Hall ... [the] Duchess of Abercorn (in the Chair)[304] ... A letter was read from the Secretary, Ulster Unionist Council stating that he hoped to have a meeting of the Standing Committee in the first or second week in January and that it was intended to get a Sub-Committee appointed to confer with the Ulster Women's Unionist Council in regard to representation.

Arising out of this letter representatives of the various Associations reported on the conditions in their districts with regard to the representation of women on the Parliamentary Associations ... it was suggested that after the Annual meeting the [Annual] Report should be sent to as many English and Scotch newspapers as possible ... Miss Connor reported that up to date she had received £103.18.0 for the Flag Fund ... the amount already raised would more than suffice to keep the supply of flags for a good many years, and that if the fund could be raised to about £250 the income would be sufficient to provide flags without touching [the] capital.

301 Sixty–seven members were present at this meeting and there were fifteen apologies for non–attendance.

302 See Appendix II.

303 There had been sectarian riots in Belfast. The Loyalist Relief Fund aimed to provide financial assistance to the loyalist widows, orphans and victims of sectarian violence.

304 Fifty–five members were present at this meeting and there were twenty–one apologies for non–attendance.

4 April 1922

The Executive Committee met in the Old Town Hall ... [the] Hon. Lady Kennedy (in the Chair)[305] ... The Secretary reported that as instructed he had sent a copy of the Annual Report to the Press Association, Central News, Spectator, Morning Post and other newspapers, but had received no replies ... A letter was read from the President expressing regret at her absence from the meeting and enclosing a letter from the Prime Minister, Sir James Craig Bart.[,] M.P. of which the following is a copy ... My dear Duchess

... I desire to put you in possession of all the facts regarding my plans for an extensive propaganda throughout Great Britain, Ulster and the Colonies. You and your friends will readily recognise how useless it would have been to have started such a campaign until the House of Lords had finally dealt with the Free State Bill;[306] and also how futile it is to count upon the success attending any sporadic efforts on a small scale – they only touch the fringe of the matter and cause ultimate disappointment. I have felt all along that it would be more satisfactory in the end to reserve our united strength, and when the psychological moment came we would launch forth with such weight and influence that we could carry the Ulster cause with overwhelming force to triumph ... I propose to begin with a comprehensive appeal for funds, and have already arranged a meeting with the leading Ulster business men next Monday, when I am assured that sufficient financial support will be forthcoming to see us through.

My plans are to begin with a personal deputation from Ulster to the Chairman and Office-Bearers of every Unionist Association in England, Scotland and Wales, probably consisting of: –

(1) A Member of:–

- (a) The Imperial Parliament, or our own Senate or House of Commons
- (b) The Ulster Labour Unionist Association
- (c) The Ulster Women's Unionist Council
- (d) The Loyal Orange Institution of Ireland
- (e) The 3 Protestant Churches
- (f) The Business Men's Association.

(2) The work to be entirely voluntary throughout – travelling and subsistence allowance to be paid.

(3) There will be some 600 Constituencies to be approached – dividing them into groups of 15, 40 such deputations could do the work in about a fortnight.

(4) They would be charged with the duty of filling in their time by holding such

[305] Sixty members were present at this meeting and there were twenty–five apologies for non–attendance.

[306] The Irish Free State (Constitution) Bill was passing through parliament at this time. The Irish Free State was formally established on 6 December 1922.

meetings as could be arranged, by speaking individually to the principal workers in the Constituency, and by ensuring that their visit and the terms of their appeal for help were made widely known in the local Press.

(5) They would be instructed rather to appeal for help generally than to make attacks on any sitting Member. I feel that to launch a campaign against those now backing the Treaty[307] might cause grave embarrassment and alienate all help in the future if the same persons were returned at the next General Election … if we make a general appeal for Ulster and ask the Chairman and his Committee to insist that the Candidate, whoever he may be, pledges himself to no coercion, and to alteration of the Boundaries[308] by agreement only, we will have trodden upon no one's corns, and will have prevented the accusation that we are endeavouring to smash up the Unionist Party. I believe a moderate, though vigorous and effective campaign along the lines I indicate will bear the best fruit.

The first step will only be a beginning to be followed by similar deputations on the same large scale to every Candidate when nominated, and the offer of assistance from the various delegations here to help where help can be usefully given, and also to be followed by mass meetings in the various great centres such as we used to hold in the old days …

The Secretary explained that it would be necessary to take immediate steps to find ladies willing to volunteer for work as Canvassers and Speakers in England and Scotland, and having obtained the workers to train them; that classes would have to be arranged in suitable centres and leaflets or other literature provided to enable the workers to make up their subject … we assure Sir James Craig of our wholehearted support for his scheme, and pledge ourselves to do all in our power to assist in bringing our Cause before the people of England, Scotland and Wales … That we particularly desire to impress upon Sir James Craig the importance of securing the support of the Press of England and Scotland … Miss Connor reported that she had received up to date the amount of £175. 8. 0 for the Thiepval Flag Fund … [It was] passed[:]

'That we desire to record our horror at the outrages which have been perpetrated in Belfast and Ulster, and express our heartfelt sympathy with the victims and their families. That it is our earnest desire to assist by any means in our power in restoring peace and mutual good-will amongst all classes of the community.'[309]

£962. 13. 5 had been 'received from the different Associations for the Loyalist Relief Fund'[.]

307 The Anglo–Irish Treaty of 6 December 1921. The treaty was accepted by Dáil Éireann on 7 January 1922. The majority of voters in the June 1922 Irish Free State elections also endorsed acceptance of the treaty.

308 This is a reference to the boundary between Northern Ireland and the Irish Free State. Plans for a Boundary Commission were instituted under the terms of the Anglo–Irish Treaty of 1921.

309 Serious sectarian violence was occurring in Northern Ireland, particularly in Belfast, at this time.

20 June 1922

A special Meeting of the Executive Committee was held on Tuesday, 20th June 1922 … [Edith] The [7th] Marchioness of Londonderry (in the Chair)[310] … Lady Londonderry explained that the meeting had been specially called to consider, and if approved of, to support a scheme for the organisation of an Ulster Women's Volunteer Association to give assistance to the Northern Government in case of emergency.[311] That this organisation would be mainly concerned with the selection, registration and allotment of suitable women personnel for the different work for which the various Government Departments concerned may ask [for] its services. That all women employed in the Special Constabulary would serve in a Women's Branch of the Royal Ulster Special Constabulary of which she had been appointed Hon. Commandant, and that this Department would bear full responsibility for the supervision and proper control of its members. That all members would receive rates of pay according to scales laid down by the Government; that it was intended to enrol as many members from Ulster as possible, but it would be necessary to enrol a certain number of fully trained women from England to fill certain positions. That in order to carry out this scheme it would also be necessary to appoint County Organisers for the different Counties.

After discussion it was … passed unanimously

'That we heartily approve of the proposed scheme and promise to support it by every means in our power'.

It was decided to appoint a sub-Committee to help Lady Londonderry to carry out the scheme[.]

21 June 1922

Report of [the] Sub-Committee appointed by the Executive Committee of the Ulster Women's Unionist Council … As the sanction of the Cabinet of Northern

310 Edith Helen Vane–Tempest Stewart was the daughter of Henry (later Viscount) Chaplin. She married Charles, the 7th Marquis of Londonderry in 1899. The 7th Marquis was a unionist MP for Maidstone from 1906–15, Minister for Education in the first Northern Ireland Parliament from 1921–25 and leader of the Northern Ireland Senate from 1921–26. However, after this date he returned to British politics and was appointed Secretary of State for Air from 1931–35. In 1935 he was appointed Lord Privy Seal and leader of the House of Lords but only retained these positions until November 1935. The 7th Marchioness was a Vice President of the UWUC from 1919–59. She established and led the Women's Legion during World War I and was granted a DBE for this work in 1917. She also served as a JP from 1926. She died on 23 April 1959. See Urquhart, *Women in Ulster Politics; Dod's Peerage*, p. 540. Sixty–one members were present at this meeting and there were twenty–two apologies for non–attendance.

311 The Ulster Women's Volunteer Association was established in 1922 with the aim of enlisting and training a body of women who would be prepared to assist the Northern Ireland government in any emergency situation. Women were trained to work as telephonists, telegraphists, nurses, cooks, policewomen, searchers and were prepared to staff government departments, St. John's Ambulance and the Red Cross Association. Edith Londonderry was appointed as the head of the association. See Urquhart, *Women in Ulster Politics*, p. 83.

Ireland had been received for the registering of all loyal women in Ulster who would be prepared to help the Government in case of a crisis, a Scheme for the working of the Ulster Women's [Volunteer] Association was drawn up and submitted to the Minister for Home Affairs for his approval.[312]

Recruiting was started, but the work was considerably hampered by the fact that the Government approval for the Scheme was only obtained in the month of August, when the Summer holidays had begun ... The Ulster Women's [Volunteer] Association is a non-political organisation under Government auspices, and if the need for its services arises, it will immediately pass under Government control, therefore, it must be kept separate and distinct from any political association, and the Ulster Women's Unionist Council has no control or responsibility, but has been asked to help and advise in furthering the Scheme as one which is considered to be for the good government and prosperity of Ulster ... No part of the funds of the Ulster Women's Unionist Council has been used for the work of the Ulster Women's [Volunteer] Association. The small expenses incurred in carrying out the Scheme of enrolment are met by a grant from the Ministry of Home Affairs.

It should be pointed out that the registering of recruits cannot be allowed to drag on indefinitely, and the Government has therefore intimated that this work must be completed and the Association to that extent wound up at the earliest possible date.

Lady Londonderry expressed her warm appreciation of the assistance and co-operation which she has already received from the Ulster Women's Unionist Council, its Affiliated Associations and individual members, which has mainly contributed to the success of the Scheme.

4 July 1922

The Quarterly meeting of the Executive Committee was held ... The Marchioness of Londonderry (in the Chair)[313] ... The Secretary reported that the first meeting in connection with the Propaganda work had been held and was addressed by Sir Robert Kennedy, Lord Hugh Cecil[314] and Mr H. de F. Montgomery,[315] but that owing to the turn in events nothing further had been done ... Lady Londonderry stated that since the Special Meeting of the Committee it had been pointed out to her that a Government service [the Ulster Women's Volunteer Association] should not be carried out in the offices of a political Association and that other offices outside would be provided for her Committee. At the same time she herself was

312 Richard Dawson Bates.

313 Sixty–two members were present at this meeting and there were fourteen apologies for non–attendance.

314 Lord Hugh Cecil, Baron Quickwood (1869–1956), the youngest son of the 3rd Marquess of Salisbury. He was a Conservative MP for Greenwich from 1895–1906, a burgess for Oxford University from 1910–37 and provost of Eton from 1936–44. *Dod's Peerage*, p. 164.

315 Hugh de Fellenberg Montgomery (b. 1870), Deputy Lieutenant, JP and High Sheriff for Co. Tyrone and a JP and Deputy Lieutenant for Co. Fermanagh. He was a member of the Northern Ireland Senate from 1922. *Thom's Irish Who's Who*, p. 168.

most anxious that the U.W.U. Council should keep in close touch with her work and should really have the credit of it ... The Secretary reported that the Sub-Committee appointed had met the Representatives of the Ulster Trades Defence Association on the 21st June, when it was explained that owing to the Treaty nothing had been done in the way of a counter boycott, but in view of the economic pressure and the increased activity by the Sinn Feiners, ending in the campaign of incendiarism, it had been decided to take some step in the matter and to stop the importation of Southern goods into the Six Counties and asking for the co-operation of our members as it was only by the united efforts of the women that this plan could be carried through ... Mrs McMordie, on behalf of the Committee, said she was sure the women would do all in their power to help in this way ... The Secretary stated that it had been found necessary to change the plans which had been made in regard to Refugees,[316] and Branch Associations were now asked to send their Representatives to the Old Town Hall on the days selected by them, and that a room would be provided for interviews etc[.], and arrangements made with the Railway officials to send any Refugees direct to the O.[ld] T.[own] Hall.

The following letter was read from the Secretary, Ulster Unionist Labour Association ... [stating] 'That we endeavour to secure for our various Branches having women Members direct representation on the Ulster Women's Unionist Council'[.]

10 October 1922

The Quarterly meeting of the Executive Committee was held ... in the Old Town Hall ... The Duchess of Abercorn (in the Chair)[317] ... The Secretary reported that ... the arrival of Refugees seemed to have almost ceased ... passed unanimously

'That the Council take part in the Loyalist Relief Fund Bazaar and provide a Stall to be known as the Ulster Women's Unionist Council Stall' ... Some discussion took place as to the various matters in connection with Lady Londonderry's Scheme (Ulster Women's [Volunteer] Association), but the President ruled that these matters did not come within the powers of the Committee and could only be dealt with by Lady Londonderry or her own Committee.

19 October 1922

A Meeting of the County Organisers [of the Ulster Women's Volunteer Association] was held on Thursday 19th October 1922, in the Old Town Hall ... The Marchioness of Londonderry (in the Chair)[318] ... A Report was submitted of the

316 This is a reference to Protestants who were leaving the Irish Free State and migrating to Northern Ireland.

317 Sixty–two members were present at this meeting and there were nineteen apologies for non–attendance.

318 Eight members were present at this meeting, representing Ulster Women Unionist Associations affiliated to the UWUC in Antrim, Armagh, Belfast, Down, Fermanagh and Londonderry.

number of Recruits to date. (230)[.]

Mrs Ainsworth Barr read some letters she had received from her helpers, and stated that the general idea was that there was no immediate necessity for enrolling, but that as soon as an emergency arose there would be plenty of recruits. It was decided to write a circular letter to these ladies stating that in an emergency those who have already enrolled will be called up first and all the important positions filled by them ... Other ladies also spoke of the difficulties arising regarding enrolling V.A.D.'s [Voluntary Aid Detachments] as the County Directors had not yet received instructions ... Miss Johnston reported that she had held 33 meetings, but had not enrolled any member for 'General duties'. It was considered advisable that this should be done wherever possible.

The question of rates of Pay for 'General Duties', Cooks etc[.], was discussed, and it was decided to send a copy of proposed wages to each County Organiser.[319]

The provision of telegraphists and Telephonists was discussed, and Lady Londonderry promised to see the Minister for Home Affairs on the matter.

2 March 1923

The Quarterly meeting of the Executive Committee was held ... in the Old Town Hall ... Mrs McMordie (in the Chair)[320] ... Mrs McMordie stated that owing to the appointment of his Grace the Duke of Abercorn[321] as Governor of Northern Ireland, the Duchess of Abercorn felt bound to resign her position as President of the Council, as she could no longer hold that position[322] ... [Five representatives of the Ulster Labour Association were to be given representation on the UWUC and] this recommendation be submitted to the Council for adoption ... The Secretary read a letter from Mr [A. W.] Hungerford[323] giving details of the work done by the Members of the Deputation in England and Scotland ... [which] was beyond all praise. In fact we could not have done without them. In London, where I remained all the time, their work was invaluable, and I have received similar reports from all the centres. They never wearied or tired. No trouble was great for them to undertake provided the cause of Ulster could be furthered and the concise[,] lucid, and forcible way in which they presented that case frequently turned opponents into friends ... Their services given so freely and patriotically could not be improved upon.

319 The rates of pay were based on the rates that had been in force for the General Service Voluntary Aid Detachments and Queen Mary's Army Auxiliary Corps during World War I.

320 Sixty–three members were present at this meeting and there were nine apologies for non–attendance.

321 The 3rd Duke of Abercorn served as Governor of Northern Ireland from 1922–45.

322 The Duchess of Abercorn was replaced by Lady Cecil Craig.

323 Sir Wilson Hungerford, official and later chief unionist agent in Northern Ireland. He was a member of the Ulster Unionist Council from 1912 and streamlined the organisation's finances as well as improving its administrative structure. He was also Secretary of the Ulster Unionist Labour Association from its establishment in June 1918. Jonathan Bardon, *A History of Ulster* (Belfast, 1992), p. 498.

5 June 1923

The Quarterly meeting of the Executive Committee was held … in the Old Town Hall … [the] Hon. Lady Kennedy (in the Chair)[324] … The secretary explained that Lady Craig hoped to be able to lay a programme of winter work before the next meeting of the Committee, and … a Committee to confer with Lady Craig on preparing a programme of work … [was established.]

2 October 1923

The Quarterly Meeting of the Executive Committee was held … in the Old Town Hall … Lady Craig (in the Chair)[325] … Mrs Montgomery explained that during the last General Election[326] she had visited England as one of the Ulster Deputation and had found that a lack of sympathy and an unwillingness to help in several cases where a personal acquaintance with responsible officials and organisations might have smoothed matters over, and urged that all members of the Committee who visit England should make an effort to get into personal touch with the Primrose League[327] and other similar organisations … Lady Craig suggested that the Committee might meet once a year say in Derry and Fermanagh instead of in Belfast as this might stimulate interest in the country districts. After discussion it was decided that the matter be brought up at the Annual Meeting.

20 November 1923

A Special Meeting of the Executive Committee was held … in the Old Town Hall … Lady Craig (in the chair)[328] … The President said that the meeting had been summoned to consider the Scheme of Organisation … The President also announced that the Ulster Unionist Council had again been asked to send workers and speakers to Great Britain for the Election, and expressed the hope that as many as possible would help in this work.[329]

22 October 1923

A meeting of the Sub-Committee was held … Lady Craig (in the Chair)[330] … Lady Craig read the draft Scheme …

[324] Fifty–four members were present at this meeting and there were twenty–three apologies for non–attendance.

[325] Sixty–seven members were present at this meeting and there were twenty–three apologies for non–attendance.

[326] The last general election in the United Kingdom had been held on 15 November 1922.

[327] This Conservative Party organisation, established in November 1883, admitted both men and women as members.

[328] Forty–seven members were present at this meeting and there were twenty–nine apologies for non–attendance.

[329] A general election in the United Kingdom was due to take place on 6 December 1923.

[330] Eighteen members were present at this meeting and there were five apologies for non–attendance.

ULSTER WOMEN'S UNIONIST COUNCIL
SCHEME

1 If women are to learn to use the vote and fulfil the responsibilities placed upon them, they must be educated in Political Thought. At present some of them do not realise their need of education, nor have they any desire for it, and therefore, they will not seek education unless it is made palatable and attractive.

2 The following is recommended as a Scheme of reorganisation ... A small group or area, whether townland, parish, Polling district or street, should be taken as the Unit of Organisation.

If possible, a small Committee should be formed in each such Unit ... The next step should be the formation of a Divisional or Area Committee, consisting of at least one member from each of the primary units comprised on that particular Division or Area. These Divisional or Area Committees should then send representatives to the Central Body of that particular Association, and that Central Body in its turn sends representatives to the Ulster Women's Unionist Council, thereby forming a connected chain from the Organisation at Headquarters down to the most remote or scattered districts throughout the Six Counties.

It should be the duty of the workers in the primary units to organise a thorough canvass of their own area, as at election times, and try to get each Protestant woman in the locality to become a member. It is desirable that a small annual subscription should be charged, in return for which the member should receive a card with her name inscribed which should entitle her to special rights on entry to meetings organised by the Ulster Women's Unionist Association in her locality. Women would thus realise that there are privileges attached to membership, and that they would receive value for their contributions.

When a substantial membership has been worked up, meetings would appear to be the best means of keeping the women together, and if these meetings are to be well attended, they will require to be made socially as well as politically interesting. Of course a personal canvass should be made in the first instance to secure a good attendance.

4 These meetings might consist of :–

(a) A Concert with a short address in the middle.
(b) A Lecture on one of the Colonies, the Empire, or any Educative subject, illustrated by Lantern slides or Cinematograph.
(c) In small places even a monthly Sewing Party at which someone would read an interesting article or articles, and competitions might be organised in Needlework, Knitting or Baking etc. Local members should be encouraged to take part in the smaller meetings.
(d) Little debates might be arranged, or a paper read or criticised.
(e) Interchange of visits from Speakers between the strongly Unionist parts of the

country and the Borders would help. This would not merely provide temporary interest in the meetings, but should in time lead to closer touch with all parts of the Province, a better appreciation of each others difficulties, and a firmer bond in the Common Cause.

(f) The services of a Concert Party or Parties might be availed of in country districts where the people are not blasé as a result of Picture Houses etc …

(g) Other members might be able to persuade their friends in Schools, Colleges or Technical Institutes to give Lectures in the country districts during the winter.

5 A Sub-Committee has been appointed to prepare a small Handbook containing:–

(a) The Constitution of the Ulster Women's Unionist Council.
(b) Hints on Organisation.
(c) Hints on Registration, etc., etc.

6 That the experiment be tried of holding two of the Quarterly meetings of the Executive Committee of the Ulster Women's Unionist Council in towns other than Belfast. …

7 The first need is apparently a staff of Speakers. This is receiving attention by the formation of a Speaker's Class. This class should consist of picked members … As it would be impossible for ladies from distant parts of the province to attend classes in Belfast, it is hoped than in the larger towns, at any rate, an effort will be made to get up little Debating Societies which would give the members practice in speaking and arguing political questions, and would thereby in time provide a supply of new speakers.

8 One winter of preliminary work of this kind should result in greatly increased membership, and the next winter it should be possible to reduce the entertainment and increase the education, and in time we may have a strong body of loyal women with a real interest in and a sound knowledge of the political questions of the day.

9 It cannot be too strongly emphasised that if this or any other scheme of 'rejuvenation' is to be successful, it is necessary that great personal effort should be made. Nothing can be accomplished by gathering together in Committees and passing Resolutions or uttering pious aspirations to be carried into effect by other people.

30 October 1923

A meeting of the Sub-Committee was held … Lady Craig (in the Chair)[331] … The Committee … proceeded to consider in detail the draft Scheme of re-organisation.[332]

331 Twenty members were present at this meeting and there were five apologies for non–attendance.
332 No further details are given in the minutes of this meeting.

4 January 1924

The Quarterly Meeting of the Executive Committee was held … in the Old Town Hall … Lady Craig (in the Chair)[333] … Lady Craig read a letter she had received from Captain Herbert Dixon[334] thanking the women for their hard work during the elections in North and West Belfast [stating] Both the Members have informed me that they largely owe their Victories to the unselfish and magnificent work which the Women's Organisations in the Constituencies performed … as you know I have the greatest belief in the Women Electors; they stand for Peace and Stability which are the two most needed things for the Country at the present time. Whilst the Women are properly organised in their own Organisations, I have no fear for the future of Ulster.

1 April 1924

The Quarterly Meeting of the Executive Committee was held … in the Old Town Hall … Lady Craig (in the Chair)[335] … A letter from Miss Entrican asking that the Unionist candidates in the forthcoming Poor Law Elections should receive official and financial support from the Council was read … the Secretary was instructed to write [to] Miss Entrican, [stating that] the Committee would ask the Belfast Associations to give all the possible assistance in the way of canvassers etc[.], but could not recommend the giving of any financial assistance … The Secretary stated that he would be glad to receive the names of any ladies who would undertake to speak at meetings as he had received several requests for speakers … the Handbooks were now ready and could be obtained at the Office at 3d each; also that the last page 'Reasons for joining the Women's Unionist Association' had been printed separately and would be distributed to the Associations …

REPORT OF SPEAKERS CLASS …

Nine classes were held extending from 12th November to 24th March, the total attendance being 299, making an average of slightly over 33 each day … The object aimed at by the promoters was to get Members to overcome their timidity in rising to ask questions; afterwards to give short addresses and so gain confidence … the

333 Forty–two members were present at this meeting and there were twenty–nine apologies for non–attendance.

334 Captain Herbert Dixon, later 1st Lord Glentoran (b. 1880), OBE and Deputy Lieutenant for Co. Down. He was also a JP and High Sheriff for Co. Kildare, a member of the Imperial Parliament from 1918–39 and a member of the Parliament of Northern Ireland for East Belfast from 1921–29 and for the Bloomfield Division of Belfast from 1929. He was Parliamentary Secretary to the Minister of Finance for Northern Ireland from 1921 and Minister of Agriculture for Northern Ireland from 1941–43. Captain Dixon was also Chief Whip of the Northern Ireland Government. *Burke's Genealogical and Heraldic History*, pp 876–7; *Thom's Irish Who's Who*, p. 62. The letter is dated 8 December 1923.

335 Forty–two members were present at this meeting and there were thirty–three apologies for non–attendance.

Members were encouraged to speak on and study pressing questions of the day, such as Tariff Reform, Free Trade, the Education Act, Child Welfare, Socialism, concluding with a broad view of our beloved province of Ulster ... Should there be a call for Election work, the response will be found quite satisfactory.

20 May 1924

A Special Meeting of the Executive Committee was held ... Lady Craig (in the Chair)[336] ... Lady Craig said that she had received a request from the Chief Whip, Rt. Hon. Herbert Dixon, that the Council should appoint a Woman Organiser to act in co-operation with an Organiser appointed by the Ulster Unionist Council.

Captain Dixon attended and explained that a redistribution of seats throughout the Six Counties would take place shortly and that it is most essential that all Unionists, both men and women[,] should be thoroughly organised. He emphasised the need for a Special Woman Organiser and confirmed the willingness of the Ulster Unionist Council to bear the expense[337] ...

26 May 1924

A meeting of the sub-Committee was held ... Lady Dixon (in the Chair)[338] ... [The meeting was called] to consider the appointment of a Woman Organiser ... [and] Miss Edith Gregg was appointed ... subject to the approval of the Chief Whip[.]

12 June 1924

The Quarterly Meeting of the Executive Committee was held ... in the Y.M.C.A. Hall, Londonderry ... Lady Craig (in the Chair)[339] ... Lady Craig ... hoped that the meeting would be the means of promoting even a more friendly feeling between the various Members of the Association than already existed ... The Secretary reported that he had called a meeting of the Belfast Secretaries to meet the Candidates for the Poor Law Elections, and that Associations had given assistance in the way of canvassing.

16 October 1924

The Quarterly Meeting of the Executive Committee of the Ulster Women's Unionist Council was held ... in the Orange Hall, Enniskillen ... Lady Craig (in the Chair)[340] ... Lady Craig ... believed that the arrangement to hold Executive

336 Fifty members were present at this meeting and there were twenty apologies for non–attendance.

337 The Executive Committee appointed a sub–committee to choose a woman suitable for the position of Special Woman Organiser.

338 Seven members were present at this meeting.

339 Twenty–seven members were present at this meeting and there were forty apologies for non–attendance.

340 Forty–two members were present at this meeting and there were twenty apologies for non–attendance.

meetings in the country was having good results and that the Belfast Members were most grateful for the hospitality that had been shewn[*sic*] them in Derry and Enniskillen ... A letter was read from Mrs Murray (Comber) suggesting that Propaganda work should be carried out in some of the English Constituencies. The Secretary stated that Captain Dixon had informed him that it was not the intention of the Ulster Unionist Council to send large delegations to England for the coming election, but small delegations would be sent if specially asked for, that the intention was to concentrate as much as possible here on the contested seats in North and West Belfast and in Tyrone and Fermanagh ... Subsequently a very large and influential meeting [,] representative of all parts of Tyrone & Fermanagh, was held, presided over by Lady Brooke[341] ... and addresses were delivered by Lady Craig, Mrs T.J. Andrews, Mrs Chichester,[342] Sir Charles Falls,[343] Mr Pringle,[344] Mr Cooper[345] M.P. and others.

13 January 1925

The Quarterly Meeting of the Executive Committee of the Ulster Women's Unionist Council was held in the Old Town Hall, Belfast ... Lady Craig (in the Chair)[346] ... The President explained that the Arrangements Committee had decided on organising a Luncheon to be given by the Office-Bearers of the Council and the Members of the Belfast Association after the Annual meeting, and to invite the Duchess of Atholl M.P. to be present; that it was also thought well to take advantage of the Duchess of Atholl's visit to have a public demonstration for women in the Ulster Hall to be addressed by her and other speakers[.]

341 Lady Cynthia Mary Brooke, 2nd daughter and co–heir of Capt. Charles Warden Sergison, Deputy Lieutenant of Cuckfield Park, Sussex. In 1919 she married Sir Basil Stanlake Brooke, later Viscount Brookeborough. Born in 1888 in Co. Fermanagh, Basil Brooke was elected to the Northern Ireland Senate in 1921, but resigned in 1922 to become Commandant of the Ulster Special Constabulary. He became a unionist MP for Co. Fermanagh in 1929 and a Privy Councillor of Northern Ireland in 1933. He was Minister of Agriculture for Northern Ireland from 1933–41 and Minister of Commerce and Production for Northern Ireland from 1941–45. Brooke became Prime Minister of Northern Ireland in 1943. He was a leading member of the Orange Order and was made first Viscount Brookeborough in 1953. Brooke resigned as Prime Minister of Northern Ireland in 1963 due to ill health and died in 1973. *Thom's Irish Who's Who*, p. 24; *Dod's Peerage*, pp 116–7.

342 Dehra Chichester, see footnote 275 above.

343 Major Sir Charles F. Falls (1860–1936), MP, unionist solicitor of Dublin and Enniskillen and the Secretary of N. Fermanagh Loyalist Registration Association in 1893. He was elected as a unionist member of the Imperial Parliament representing Fermanagh in October 1924. *Who Was Who, 1929–40*, vol. 3 (London, 1941), p. 430.

344 James Alexander Pringle (1874–1935), qualified as a solicitor in 1900, was called to the Bar in 1912 and to the Inner Bar (Northern Ireland) in 1921. He was elected as a unionist MP in the Imperial Parliament representing Tyrone in October 1924. He held this seat until 1929. *Who Was Who*, vol. 3, p. 1106.

345 James Cooper (b. 1882), MP for Fermanagh and Tyrone from 1921 and a member of Fermanagh Urban District Council. He was a solicitor and director of several companies, including Erne Manufacturing and Repair Boot Co. Ltd. He was also Post Master General of the Grand Orange Lodge of Ireland. *Thom's Irish Who's Who*, p. 46.

346 Sixty–six members were present at this meeting and there were eleven apologies for non–attendance.

1 April 1925

The Quarterly Meeting of the Executive Committee, of the Ulster Women's Unionist Council, was held in the Synod Hall, Armagh … Lady Craig (in the Chair)[347] … [The Executive Committee unanimously passed a resolution:]

That this meeting of the Ulster Women's Unionist Council desires on the eve of the Election to appeal to every Unionist voter in the Six Counties to strike a decisive blow for our rights and liberties, and show their confidence in our Prime Minister by giving him an overwhelming majority at the Poll …

The President reported that Mr J.C. Lendrum had sent the Prime Minster a cheque for £100 to be handed by him to whatever Unionist Association he considered was doing the best work, and that the Prime Minister had handed over the money to this Council.

The President also announced that a number of ladies in Mid-Antrim had expressed the intention of reforming the Women's Unionist Association there and she had gladly promised them every possible assistance … Mrs Hume reported that during the winter the Speakers class had been carried on … Miss Armstrong and Mrs D'Arcy strongly urged the importance of anti-Socialist work.

Miss Corry suggested the formation of a Social Club in Belfast which she thought would be particularly valuable for country members who at present were badly off for some place where they could meet friends or rest or wait for trains … It was decided that the matter should be put on the agenda for the next meeting … The Committee were entertained to Luncheon by the members of the Armagh Associations, after which a large Public meeting was held in the Town Hall at which the Prime Minister, Mr Best K.C.[348] and Major Shillington[349] spoke.

29 May 1925

A meeting of Office Bearers and Belfast Branch Secretaries was held in the Old Town Hall … Mrs McMordie (in the Chair)[350] … The Secretary stated he had received a letter from the Secretary of the Wigan Constitutional Association saying that a party of Women Unionists from Wigan would visit Belfast on the 9th June … when it was unanimously decided that the party be entertained.

7 July 1925

The Quarterly meeting of the Executive Committee of the Ulster Women's

[347] Sixty–four members were present at this meeting and there were thirty–seven apologies for non–attendance.

[348] Rt. Hon. Richard Best, a barrister in King's Inns from 1895 and a Bencher from 1918. Richard Best was also a JP in Co. Armagh, a member of the Parliament of Northern Ireland and Attorney General for Northern Ireland from 1921. *Thom's Irish Who's Who*, p. 17.

[349] Major David Graham Shillington, a JP for Co. Armagh and a member of the Parliament of Northern Ireland from 1921. *Thom's Irish Who's Who*, p. 231.

[350] Eleven members were present at this meeting and there was one apology for non–attendance.

Unionist Council was held in the Old Town Hall, Belfast ... Mrs Cunningham (in the Chair)[351] ... [The] Secretary reported that he had received a letter from Miss Corry saying that there seemed to be no general desire for the formation of a Social Club at present as a number of members had joined a recently opened ladies Club in Belfast ... The Secretary reported that the National Union of Conservative and Unionist Associations (Women's Unionist Organization) had invited the Council to send three delegates to the Annual Conference in London on the 14th and 15th May, that Mrs Cunningham, Miss H. Johnston and Miss E. Corry had attended on behalf of the Council ... [it was decided that] the opportunity should be taken of distributing literature to the large number of tourists at present visiting Ulster especially in the seaside towns of Larne and Portrush.

Miss Houston (Portrush) supported the proposal and undertook to distribute a parcel of literature if it were sent to her.

15 October 1925

The Quarterly Meeting of the Executive Committee of the Ulster Women's Unionist Council was held in the Northern Counties Hotel, Portrush ... Lady Craig (in the Chair)[352] ... The President drew the attention of the Members that a Branch of the Junior Imperial League had been formed in Belfast, and said that she had first wished to start a Junior Branch in connection with the Ulster Women's Unionist Council, but that Captain Dixon[,] the chief whip thought it better to take advantage of the existing organisations in England. The inaugural meeting had already been held and the President hoped that all members would support the new venture.

The President showed the Committee a copy of a Magazine entitled 'Home & Politics' issued by the Kilmarnock Unionist Association. She explained that this Magazine was printed and issued in bulk by Unionist Head Quarters in London with the idea that different Associations would add pages of local news and advertisements ... She understood that if 1,000 copies were sold at 1d. it would meet the expense of publication while 2,000 copies would show a profit ... passed that the paper be tried, and the title be 'Northern Ireland Home & Politics a Journal for Women' ... Mrs Montgomery asked the Committee to consider the advisability of organising Summer Schools to be addressed by Public men and experts on various subjects, and to be run as far as possible on non party lines.

19 January 1926

The Quarterly Meeting of the Executive Committee of the Ulster Women's

351 Twenty–five members were present at this meeting and there were twenty–nine apologies for non–attendance.

352 Sixty–six members were present at this meeting and there were forty–three apologies for non–attendance.

Unionist Council was held in the Old Town Hall, Belfast ... at 11.30 a.m. ... Lady Craig (in the Chair)[353] ... [The Annual Report for 1925 was discussed, which stated] The year 1925 has been an eventful one in the history of our Province. The action of the Labour Government at Westminster, when in power in 1924, in setting up a Boundary Commission[354] despite the protests of Northern Ireland seemed likely to plunge our country into fresh horrors of civil strife; and almost to the end of the year we were filled with anxiety by the uncertainty of the outcome. At last, when it seemed almost certain that an adverse decision would be promulgated by the Commissioners an amicable agreement was reached between the three Governments concerned, confirming the Boundary exactly as defined by the Act of 1920,[355] thus freeing Ulster from the dark shadow overhanging her for so long, and justifying the policy of the Government – 'Not an inch.' Once more we acknowledge with heartfelt gratitude that statesmanship and patriotism of our Prime Minister.

The Boundary has now been settled, and we hope and pray that continued peace and increasing prosperity may bless our land.

The result of the General Election held in the month of April showed that there is no weakening in our allegiance to the Empire and no breach in our united front.[356] The various affiliated Associations and their members played no small part in the success of the Election.

20 April 1926

The Quarterly Meeting of the Executive Committee of the Ulster Women's Unionist Council was held ... at 11 a.m. at Strabane ... Lady Craig (in the Chair)[357] ... The Secretary reported that the Old Town Hall[358] is being taken over by the Belfast Corporation and that new headquarters have been obtained in Glengall Street [Belfast] ... the following Motion ... 'That affiliated associations do all in their power to encourage their members to buy Home and Dominion goods' ... [was discussed]. The Secretary was instructed to communicate with the Chambers of Commerce in Northern Ireland with reference to difficulties about freight, due to all goods being sent to Liverpool in the first instance instead of direct to Belfast ... The Secretary reported than an invitation had been received from The National Union of Conservative and Unionist Associations – Women's Unionist

353 One hundred and ninety members were present at this meeting and there were twenty–four apologies for non–attendance.

354 The first meeting of the Boundary Commission was held on 6 November 1924. When the commission reported in 1925 the boundaries between Northern Ireland and the Irish Free State remained unaltered.

355 The Government of Ireland Act of 1920.

356 A Northern Ireland general election was held on 3 April 1925 and resulted in a unionist majority.

357 Forty–one members were present at this meeting and there were forty–nine apologies for non–attendance.

358 This was the location of Unionist Headquarters in Belfast.

Organization – to send three representatives to their Annual Conference in London on 29/30th April … arrangements had been made by the Ulster Unionist Council for a Summer School in Portrush and the Secretary read letters from Mrs Huey (North Antrim) and Mrs Shaw (North Down) guaranteeing £10 and £5 respectively towards the expenses of the school if required.

6 July 1926

The July Executive Meeting of the Ulster Women's Unionist Council was held … at 11.30 a.m. in the Unionist Headquarters[,] Glengall Street, Belfast. Lady Dixon, D.B.E. (in the Chair)[359] … Mrs Andrews said she hoped it would be possible to improve the papers now that there was a balance in hand[360] … It was proposed that a copy of Dr. Shadwell's Book on Socialism should be obtained for the Office.

A letter was read from Mrs Montgomery J.P. suggesting a plan whereby working class members could be helped to attend 'Summer Schools' and saying that she would raise the matter at the October Meeting … The Secretary read a letter from Lady Craig enclosing a letter from the General Manager of the 'Morning Post' asking for support in the effort to provide a Conservative 1d. paper. It was decided to order a copy for the office as soon as the new rooms are ready.

19 October 1926

The October Executive Meeting of the Ulster Women's Unionist Council was held … at 1.45 p.m. in the Dufferin Hall, Hamilton Road, Bangor. Lady Craig (in the Chair)[361] … [The Executive Committee discussed the use of British Empire products and] Lady Craig said that … now that our domestic troubles are happily at an end, the Council might with advantage turn its attention to further the purchase of Dominion products. She had spoken to the Lord Mayor of Belfast about holding an Empire shopping week and hoped that something of this kind would be done … The Magazine continued to be successful and … there is now a profit of £58 … Miss Edith Gregg[362] stated that, as the Redistribution Bill had been indefinitely postponed, she did not feel justified in retaining her position as Travelling Organizer, and she therefore wished to resign. She would continue to take a deep interest in the work of the Council and would be ready to help at any time.

21 January 1927

The January Executive Meeting of the Ulster Women's Unionist Council was held

359 Forty–five members were present at this meeting and there were twenty–eight apologies for non–attendance.

360 The UWUC 'Northern Ireland' magazine made a £47 profit in the first five months of its existence.

361 Seventy–three members were present at this meeting and there were thirty–nine apologies for non–attendance.

362 She was appointed as a Travelling Organiser of the UWUC in May 1924.

... at 11 a.m. in 3 Glengall Street, Belfast ... Lady Craig (in the Chair)[363] ... In connection with the Empire Products campaign, the President mentioned that the Lord Mayor was arranging a special Empire Shopping Week to begin on 26th January, and she hoped it would be well supported ... [The UWUC Annual Report for 1926 is attached to the minutes and states] During the year 1926 our country has fortunately been free from political strife or civil disturbances ... It was hoped that this welcome change might be tuned to good account by affording opportunities for increased effort and renewed progress in industrial and social affairs. Unfortunately, the General Strike[364] in Great Britain followed by the protracted and unhappy disturbance in the coal trade, though they did not extend to this country, re-acted upon it very severely. The settlement of the strike has been followed by renewed hopes of reviving trade and prosperity, and we look forward with confidence in the year which lies before us ... The exchange visits between the city and country [associations of the UWUC] ... has maintained and cemented feelings of personal friendship between members from different parts of the country ... The advantages of closer co-operation between different parts of the Empire has been prominently before your Committee during the year, and efforts have been made to interest Unionist women in the subject and to induce them to purchase Empire products on preference to foreign importations whenever possible ... during the first 11 months of its existence ... [the] magazine has been an unqualified success ... The income derived from the subscription of members and affiliated associations is barely sufficient to meet the ordinary needs of the Council, and unless Associations assist the funds by additional contributions ... there is no margin available to meet expansion or sudden emergencies.

It is earnestly hoped that our expectations of a prolonged period of peace and mutual good feeling throughout Ulster will be amply fulfilled, but that no false sense of security will tend in any way to induce the relaxation of those efforts necessary to maintain our splendid organisation at the highest state of perfection. All should bear in mind that if a time of crisis should again arise the loyal women of Ulster must be well prepared, and with this end in view should see that the necessary machinery is kept in smooth working order, so as to be able to repeat the magnificent help they rendered in past hours of anxious trial.

5 April 1927

The April Executive Meeting of the Ulster Women's Unionist Council was held ...

363 Sixty–two members were present at this meeting and there were twenty apologies for non–attendance.

364 The first British national strike lasted from 4–12 May 1926. The strike was organised by the Trades Union Congress (TUC) and began with the lock–out of 1 million miners on 3 May 1926. On the following day 1.5 million transport and railway workers came out on strike, alongside printers, some building workers and those employed in heavy industry and gas and electricity supply in support of the miners' strike to resist wage cuts. In the next week engineering and shipbuilding workers also took strike action. The TUC called off the strike, although the miners continued striking until November 1926.

at 11.30 a.m. in 3 Glengall Street, Belfast … The Viscountess Craigavon (in the Chair)[365] … In connection with the Empire Products Campaign it was reported that the 'At Home' Committee were running a Cake Competition on the 17th May. All the Cakes and Bread were to be made entirely from Empire Products … A letter was read from the Secretary of the National Union of Conservative and Unionist Associations (Women's Unionist Organization), inviting the Council to send 3 representatives to the Annual Conference in London on May 26/27th … Mrs McDonald J.P. drew the attention of the Committee to the Revision of the Prayer Book which is taking place at present and suggested that the Affiliated Associations should be advised to bring pressure to bear on their Members of Parliament to oppose some of the changes. The President said that she was doubtful if a discussion of this kind would be in order or would come within the terms of the Constitution and asked Mrs McDonald, if she wished to raise the matter, to give Notice of Motion for the next meeting and in the meantime she would look into the point of order … Mrs Barr, C.B.E., and Mrs Hume[,] O.B.E. reported that the Ulster Unionist Council had arranged to hold a Summer School in Portrush on 30th May and following days, and had invited Professor Dudley J. Medley, M.A. of Glasgow University to speak. A registration fee of 2/6d. would be charged to admit to all classes and lectures.

5 July 1927

A Meeting of the Executive Committee of the Ulster Women's Unionist Council was held … at 11.30 a.m. in 3 Glengall Street, Belfast … Mrs McMordie, C.B.E., J.P. (in the chair)[366] … On behalf of the Magazine Committee, Mrs R.H. Macauley reported that, owing to lack of advertisements and lack of support from several branches of the Council, it had been found impossible to carry on the Magazine any longer except at a heavy loss, and the Committee had therefore reluctantly discontinued publication.

11 October 1927

A Meeting of the Executive Committee of the Ulster Women's Unionist Council was held … at 2.45 p.m. in the Victoria Orange Hall, Larne … The Viscountess Craigavon (in the Chair)[367] … Miss Gregg said that the Committee in Charge of the 'At Homes' would be prepared to carry on this Winter again, and suggested that Meetings should begin at 3 o'clock on the 3rd Wednesday of each month. Miss Gregg also reported that she has prepared a new lecture on 'China and its Relation

365 Seventy members were present at this meeting and there were eighteen apologies for non–attendance.

366 Forty–two members were present at this meeting and there were thirty–four apologies for non–attendance.

367 Forty–five members were present at this meeting and there were fifty–one apologies for non–attendance.

to the British Empire' ... [It passed that] The Council Meeting be held in the forenoon, followed by a Luncheon, and a Public Meeting in the evening, and that the Advisability of holding an Afternoon Conference be discussed at the Council Meeting ... the Public Meeting be arranged and run entirely by the Ulster Women's Unionist Council and not jointly with the Men's Council.

17 January 1928

A Meeting of the Executive Committee of the Ulster Women's Unionist Council was held ... at 11 a.m. in 3 Glengall Street, Belfast ... The Viscountess Craigavon. (in the chair)[368] ... The draft Annual Report for 1927, [a] copy of which is appended, was read by the Secretary [stating] Your Committee rejoices to know that during the year there has been a steady advance in the prosperity of the Province and signs are not wanting of an improvement in Trade and Commerce ... A new and valuable activity was inaugurated during the past year in the form of an 'At Homes' held monthly in the Club Room in 3 Glengall Street. Interesting addresses were given and discussions took place on various important subjects, and tea was provided at a nominal charge for those who attended ... Your Council was asked by the Ulster Unionist Council to assist in clearing off the debt incurred in the purchase and equipment of the new Headquarters in Glengall Street. The committee gladly acceded to this request, and many of the Affiliated Associations threw themselves heartily into the project. Already the sum of £219 17s 3d has been raised, and it is hoped that further contributions will come in. In addition to this a very successful dance was held in the Plaza, Belfast, on 23rd November ... many ... members of the Council took an active part. Bridge Tournaments and small Dances arranged by Affiliated Associations have also been held and have resulted in substantial contributions to the fund ... In the month of December your President handed to the Finance Committee a cheque for £250, given to her as a donation to the Funds of the Council by a friend and well-wisher, who desires to remain anonymous. This magnificent gift is much appreciated and very welcome ... Your Committee wishes to point out that Affiliation Fees and Members' Subscriptions – in themselves – are not sufficient to meet the current expenses of the Council and provide a necessary reserve for emergencies; and your Committee, therefore, earnestly appeal to the Associations to help in this direction, by sending contributions whenever possible.

If this record of our activities during the year seems somewhat uneventful and merely routine work it should be none the less pleasing on that account. There have been no elections, no great controversies to arouse excitement and call for special effort. Peace and tranquillity have been the keynote of the year and have afforded a much needed opportunity to our country of recovery from the disturbances and excitements which so sorely tried us in the past. Let us not, however, be lulled into any feeling of false security. We must never relax our vigilance, as no one can tell

[368] One hundred and fourteen members were present at this meeting and there were twenty–five apologies for non–attendance.

when a fresh crisis may arise demanding our best efforts to meet it. Our organizations must be in the fullest efficiency and readiness, and we must train the members of the younger generation to come forward and take their place in the fighting line. In this connection your Committee has noted with great pleasure the success of the Junior Imperial League ... The great enemy lurking in our midst at the moment is Socialism, and your Committee hope that all members will strive in every way possible to expose the fallacies and dangers of its doctrines. The Council starts off a new year determined to render full assistance in defending the rights and liberties of the loyalists of Ulster.

4 April 1928

A Meeting of the Executive Committee of the Ulster Women's Unionist Council was held ... at 11.30 a.m. in Brownlow House, Lurgan ... The Viscountess Craigavon (in the Chair)[369] ... A letter was read from the National Union of Conservative and Unionist Assocns. – Women's Unionist Organization, inviting the Council to send 3 Delegates to [a] Conference on 10th/11th May, 1928 in London ... A letter was read from Miss E. Blair, resigning her position as Assistant Secretary in view of her forthcoming marriage ... hearty congratulations be extended to Mrs McMordie C.B.E., J.P. on her election as High Sheriff of the City ... Mrs McMordie, in acknowledging the congratulations, said that she had always been very kindly treated during her Public Life, and that no woman need have any fear of not being well received by public bodies. She urged younger women to come forward and take their part in public life.

3 July 1928

A Meeting of the Executive Committee of the Ulster Women's Unionist Council was held ... at 11.30 a.m. in 3 Glengall Street, Belfast ... Mrs Hume O.B.E. (in the Chair)[370] ... The Secretary read a letter from Mr. Hungerford, Secretary to the Unionist Council, enclosing particulars of a Summer Camp for girls between the ages of 18 and 30, which is being organized by the Scottish Unionist Council, Eastern Divisional Council, to be held in Edinburgh ... It was unanimously decided to ask all affiliated Associations if each of them would try to send one, or if possible two or more representatives to the Camp ... The Secretary read a letter from Mrs Bell of Newry, applying for affiliation on behalf of the newly formed Newry Women's Association ... It was unanimously decided to grant Newry's application ... the 'At Homes' Committee be congratulated on their successful work, and that they should be asked to continue them for the Winter 1928–1929.

Miss E. S. Corry was asked to try and arrange for an 'At Home' on the day after

369 Forty–nine members were present at this meeting and there were fifty–three apologies for non–attendance.

370 Forty–one members were present at this meeting and there were twenty–nine apologies for non–attendance.

the Public Meeting in October, so as to give the country members an opportunity of attending.

Mrs Hume, O.B.E. said that she hoped the Belfast members would try to arrange hospitality for those coming up from the country.

30 October 1928

A Meeting of the Executive Committee of the Ulster Women's Unionist Council was held … at 11.30 a.m. in 3 Glengall Street, Belfast … The Viscountess Craigavon (in the Chair)[371] … Miss E. S. Corry gave a most interesting account of the Summer Camp held by the Eastern Division of the Scottish Unionist Council in August. She said that a party of 12 had attended from Ulster. They had all enjoyed the proceedings and had benefited greatly, and would all be anxious to go back … Lady Craigavon urged upon those present the importance of re-organization and of trying to restart Associations in those districts where there are none at present.

17 January 1929

A Meeting of the Executive Committee of the Ulster Women's Unionist Council was held … at 11 a.m. in 3 Glengall Street, Belfast … The Viscountess Craigavon (in the Chair)[372] … The Annual Report was read by the Asst. Secy … The exchange of visits between city and country has continued to meet with approval, and has maintained feelings of personal friendship from different parts of the country … On 19th May, the Foundation Stone of the new Houses of Parliament was laid.[373] Your President secured a number of Tickets which were distributed amongst our members, many of whom witnessed this interesting ceremony … It is with pleasure your Committee reports that the 'At Homes' inaugurated in 1927 were again held this year. Interesting addresses and musical programmes were given, and tea was provided at a nominal charge … As there is still a large portion of the debt incurred in the purchase of the new Headquarters unpaid, your Council is endeavouring to assist in clearing this off … A very successful and enjoyable Dance was held this year again in the Plaza … Bridge Parties, Whist Drives, Concerts and small Dances arranged by Affiliated Associations have also resulted in substantial contributions to this Fund … Your Committee again wishes to point out that Affiliation Fees and Member's Subscriptions – in themselves – are scarcely sufficient to meet the current expenses of the Council and to provide a necessary reserve for emergency … Now that the Franchise has been extended to women of 21, it is more important than ever that Women Unionists should be organized and take an active part in

371 Sixty–four members were present at this meeting and there were twenty–one apologies for non–attendance.

372 Eighty members were present at this meeting and there were twenty–one apologies for non–attendance.

373 The location for the new houses of parliament was Stormont in East Belfast.

upholding the rights and privileges which we now enjoy.[374] The Council starts off a new year determined to render full assistance in defending these rights and liberties.

16 April 1929

A Meeting of the Executive Committee of the Ulster Women's Unionist Council was held in 3 Glengall Street, Belfast ... at 11.30 a.m. ... The Viscountess Craigavon [in the Chair][375] ... Lady Craigavon read a letter she had written to Capt. The Rt. Hon. Herbert Dixon, D.L., M.P., regarding joint Men's and Women's Associations. She also read Capt. Dixon's reply, in which he urged the formation of separate Associations, but he stated that where Joint Associations already existed they should be carried on until after the Elections.

A short résumé was given by Lady Craigavon on the re-organisations of Branch Associations. She explained that in several districts difficulty had been experienced in trying to form Branches, but it was hoped that when the Elections were over something might be done to rouse interest in those Areas. In many districts Branches had already been formed[.]

2 July 1929

A Meeting of the Executive Committee was held ... in Headquarters ... Mrs McMordie C.B.E. took the Chair[376] ... [The] Secretary gave in a report of work carried out by Headquarters since 16th April 1929, which showed that 46 meetings had been addressed by the Secretary.[377] A successful Rally of women voters had been held in Wellington Hall, Belfast on 9th April, attended by upwards of 1000 electors. The total cost of this effort had only been £3. 0. 9 to the Ulster Women's Unionist Council ... it had been unanimously agreed to recommend to the Executive the appointment of Miss Kathleen Lawley as an extra typist in the Office ... She was willing to come at a salary of fifteen shillings per week, on the understanding that she would receive a thorough training in Politics, Economics, Public Speaking, and Office routine, with a view to ultimately taking a post in Political work, which every endeavour would be made by the Officials of the Council to procure for her after training, through probably it would be in England. This was unanimously agreed to ... Miss Martin asked permission to start Speakers' Classes in Belfast and in other centres, wherever it seemed that such a class might be most beneficial. Several ladies expressed a wish to have classes in their districts, especially in Tyrone, Fermanagh,

374 The Equal Franchise Act of April 1928 lowered the voting age for women from 30 to 21 years of age, and granted them the same residential qualification as men.

375 Seventy–seven members were present at this meeting and there were twenty–six apologies for non–attendance.

376 Fifty–five members were present at this meeting and there were twenty–nine apologies for non–attendance.

377 Miss Jeanette Martin was the Organising Secretary of the UWUC from 1929–34.

and Mourne areas ... The Executive warmly approving the suggestion and expressing the hope that this might be the means of providing a greater number of women speakers.

The Secretary also suggested holding a Unionist Luncheon Club to meet in Belfast once a month during the winter. This idea was approved of.

15 November 1929

A Meeting of the Executive Committee of the Ulster Women's Unionist Council was held ... in 3 Glengall Street, Belfast ... Mrs [Janet] Cunningham, J.P. presided[378] ... Re[.] Luncheon Club – The Secretary explained that it had been impossible to secure suitable premises at Lunch time, and the Committee had resolved that the Club take the form of a Supper Club. The Club was proving quite a success, over 150 girls having joined ... It was agreed [that] ... Each member of a Branch shall pay an annual subscription and receive a membership card[.]

28 January 1930

A Meeting of the Executive Committee of the Ulster Women's Unionist Council was held in 3 Glengall St., Belfast ... at 11.30 a.m. ... Mrs McMordie, C.B.E., J.P. presided[379] ... Mrs Ainsworth Barr, C.B.E. intimated that the Ulster Unionist Council wished to invite all the Women's Council to the Luncheon to be given in honour of the Rt. Hon. Stanley Baldwin,[380] but that the Unionist Council felt that their finances would not permit of this unless some assistance could be given by the Women's Council ... a small donation be given by each Council member towards the Luncheon Fund ... This was unanimously agreed to, and a minimum of 2/- was decided on ... Mrs Waring referred to the Bill at present before the Imperial Parliament to amend the Blasphemy Bill, and asked if the Ulster Women's Unionist Council were going to take any action in the matter. It was agreed to form a Sub-Committee to meet Sir Dawson Bates,[381] and ask his advice before taking any action.

25 February 1930

A [Special] Meeting of the Executive Committee of the Ulster Women's Unionist Council was held in Unionist Headquarters ... at 11.30 a.m. Mrs Hume O.B.E.

378 Fifty–eight members were present at this meeting and there were thirty apologies for non–attendance.

379 Forty members were present at this meeting and there were twelve apologies for non–attendance.

380 Stanley Baldwin (1867–1947), 1st Earl Baldwin of Bewdley, an MP from 1908–37, Parliamentary Secretary to Andrew Bonar Law, 1916–17, Joint Financial Secretary to the Treasury, 1917–21, President of the Board of Trade from 1921–22, Chancellor of the Exchequer, 1922–23 and Lord President of Council from 1931–35. Baldwin served as British Prime Minister from 1923–24, 1924–29 and from 1935–37. *The Concise Dictionary of National Biography*, vol. I (Oxford, 1992), pp 124–5.

381 Minister of Home Affairs in the parliament of Northern Ireland and legal advisor to the UWUC.

presided[382] … School of Study. The Secretary explained the object and working of this scheme, and reported that acting on instructions from the Advisory Committee, she had written to several Schools to ascertain whether the premises could be hired for this purpose. The only favourable reply received was from St. Ninian's School, Moffatt, Dumfriesshire, which could be rented … for two weeks … It was finally agreed that if a student was enrolling for the whole course the fee should be £2 per week, but if enrolling for one week only, the fee should be £2. 5. per week. This fee to be exclusive of excursions, which were optional and extra. It was agreed to send particulars to all Association Secretaries, and to ask them to bring the matter before their members … Miss Martin asked the Committee whether they wished to send a copy of the Annual Report to each Member of Parliament, and this was approved of.

14 April 1930

A Meeting of the Executive Committee was held … Mrs McMordie, C.B.E., J.P., presided[383] … The Secretary reported re[.] The Blasphemy Law Amendment Bill that a Sub-Committee had met The Home Secretary,[384] and with his approval a Petition was drawn up, which was sent to all the Unionist Members of Parliament, both in the Imperial and Ulster Parliaments, asking them to do all in their power to prevent the passing of the Bill, which was dropped on a second reading … [It was proposed]

'That representation to [the] Council should be increased in numerical proportion to the number of Branches in Association on the same basis as old representation'. It was agreed to submit this resolution to the Annual Meeting.

Mrs McCausland asked if the Ulster Women's Unionist Council could do something in regard to pushing Ulster Goods, and the Committee decided to communicate with Sir Dawson Bates, Legal Adviser to the Council, to find out whether this was within the scope of the Council's work … It was agreed to hold a Conference of all Branch Officials throughout Ulster on the day of the Public Meeting in [the] Autumn.

20 May 1930

A Meeting of the Executive Committee of the Ulster Women's Unionist Council was held in Glengall Street … The Viscountess Craigavon presided[385] … Discussion arose as to the advisability of forming a League to push Ulster Goods. Lady

382 Forty–four members were present at this meeting and there were thirty–five apologies for non–attendance.

383 Fifty–eight members were present at this meeting and there were twenty–two apologies for non–attendance.

384 Richard Dawson Bates.

385 Sixty–three members were present at this meeting and there were eighteen apologies for non–attendance

Craigavon informed the Committee that such a league, known as the Housewives' League, already existed, and that she considered it would be better to join this than to form another. Mrs McMordie referred to the Housewives' League, which was inaugurated by the Lady Mayoress, and pointed out that it was not desirable to make this a Political organisation as every woman's help was wanted. The members pledged themselves to purchase first Ulster, then Empire, and lastly Colonial goods, and by this means trade would be stimulated and unemployment relieved.[386] The Committee agreed that it would be better not to take any direct action, but recommended that all the women on the Committee should join the Housewives' League ... Miss Martin reported that a number of the mothers of the members of the Pioneer Club were anxious to have a Club on similar lines to the Pioneer Club.[387] Discussion ensued, but owing to the expense involved it was decided not to proceed meantime with the scheme. It was suggested that an Evening 'At Home' could take the place of such a Club in the Belfast Area, also that Arts and Crafts classes could be organised at the ordinary meetings of the Association.

[The minutes include a copy of a letter from Miss Jeannette Martin, Organising Secretary of the UWUC to Sir Dawson Bates, Minister of Home Affairs, dated 9 May 1930, stating:] At the Executive Meeting of our Council it was suggested that the Ulster Women's Unionist Council should take some definite steps to further the buying of Ulster Goods. As I had previously been warned that too definite a stand on this matter might be prejudicial to Ulster interests over the water, I recommended taking no immediate action and referring the question to you for your advice.

Would it be wiser to circularise our Branches asking women Unionists to ask first for Ulster, and then Empire goods in their own domestic shopping? Or would it be better to form an Empire Purchasing League within our Associations, members of which would pledge themselves to give preference to Ulster goods first, and secondly to Empire goods?

Perhaps this does not come within the scope of our legitimate activities, and we should be very grateful for your guidance in this matter.

[A copy of Dawson Bates' reply is attached to the minutes, dated 10 May 1930, stating:] This matter, it seems to me, is more in the nature of a question of policy than as to whether or not that matter comes within the scope of the activities of the Ulster Women's Unionist Council, and I think Lady Craigavon, as President of the Council, should be consulted as to a question of policy.

On the assumption that Lady Craigavon approves of the policy, I think it would be an excellent plan to circularise all Branches in the way you suggest, and I think

386 Industrial unemployment in Ulster was high as the staple industries of shipbuilding, engineering and linen entered world–wide decline in the 1930s. New industries, with the exception of aircraft production, did not relocate in the province. Unemployment in the 1930s averaged 25 per cent and was often noticeably higher.

387 This was an UWUC organisation run for young girls. The club met weekly and gave various types of classes, both social and educational, with the aim of interesting future women voters in unionism.

it would be better to do so than to form an Empire Purchasing League.

24 June 1930

A meeting of the Executive Committee of the Ulster Women's Unionist Council was held … at 11.30 a.m. in 3 Glengall Street, Belfast … Mrs McMordie C.B.E., J.P. presided[388] … [The] Secretary reported that as no adequate response had up to date been received for the proposed Summer Camp, she asked permission to return enrolment fees to those who had paid, and to definitely cancel the scheme this year. This was agreed to … The Chairman then asked the Secretary to read a letter she had received from Lady Craigavon, setting forth the scheme as approved by the Finance Committee for the winter's work … This proposal … was that Miss Wilson, at present a trainee in Central Office, should be engaged as a paid worker from 1st October 1930 at a salary of £2 per week for a period of six months; also that Miss Binns, the other trainee should still continue her studies and training as an unpaid worker, but that when employed to speak at meetings she should receive a fee of 5/- per meetings; also that Miss Lawley, Assistant in the Office, should have an increase of salary amounting to 5/- per week, which would bring her salary up to £1 per week. Lady Craigavon also expressed her regret that the state of the Council's finances did not seem to make it possible to re-engage Miss John, though her services had been much appreciated … Lady Craigavon also urged the holding of a Country Market as last Year's had been so successful, and in her opinion funds for organisation would be required during the coming winter. Lady Craigavon pointed out that Captain Dixon had kindly promised to give one fourth of the proceeds of the proposed Fete and Unionist Bazaar, to be held in June, to the Ulster Women's Unionist Council, but that she felt that it would be too long to wait until June to make a special effort to raise funds, as otherwise it would be impossible to end the financial year in a solvent condition.

Mrs Ainsworth Barr, C.B.E. then suggested that in addition to this proposal Miss Lawley, who had originally been engaged as a trainee, should also receive a fee of 5/- per meeting, if it were found that she were able to address political meetings efficiently.

Mrs McMordie, C.B.E. expressed her approval of this proposal … Miss A. McConnell pointed out that a great deal of the expense incurred by the Council last winter had been in starting Country Branches where work could not successfully be undertaken without some financial help from the Council … Miss Corry also spoke of the great benefit derived by the Party from the formation of these small Branches throughout the Council's area.

[388] Forty–six members were present at this meeting and there were thirty–five apologies for non–attendance.

28 October 1930

A meeting of the Executive Committee of the Ulster Women's Unionist Council was held … at 11.30 a.m. in Coleraine Orange Hall.

The Viscountess Craigavon presided[389] … The Secretary … reported that the Country Market had raised £375, and a further sum of £20 had been promised, which was the proceeds of a Jumble Sale organised by Gartree Branch … The Secretary reported that the scope of the Council's activities was still expanding, and … a large number of ladies were now coming to the Office for advice and help regarding their work in the various Branches. The desire for political information was still increasing, and the Secretary reported that the Chief Whip[390] and Sir Wilson Hungerford[391] had kindly agreed to print a political leaflet monthly during those months when political activity was at its height. This leaflet would be distributed gratis to the Branches of the Ulster Women's Unionist Council.

The Secretary intimated that she hoped shortly to start a class for political study in Belfast.

Miss Martin mentioned that the Pioneer Club had been re-started and was meeting in Headquarters this winter. Interest was still being maintained by all the members. Lady Craigavon asked Miss Josephine McConnell whether she would be so kind as to organise 'At Homes' again this winter in Headquarters, Belfast. Miss Connell very kindly consented.

27 January 1931

A meeting of the Executive Committee was held … at 11.15 a.m. in 3 Glengall Street, Belfast. The Viscountess Craigavon presided[392] … [The] Secretary reported that she was starting the class in current politics on Thursday 5th February.

Lady Craigavon then read a letter she had received from Sir Wilson Hungerford, stating that the Central Committee of the National Union of Conservative and Unionist Associations[393] had offered to affiliate the Ulster Women's Unionist Council. In this letter an invitation was extended to the Organising Secretary to attend meetings in London in a representative capacity … The Executive Committee warmly approved of this suggestion … The Secretary then reported re[.] School of Study, that she had advertised in the principal northern papers, but had only received one reply, and as this was from Co. Donegal, the district was unsuitable.

14 April 1931

A meeting of the Executive Committee of the Ulster Women's Unionist Council

389 Sixty–one members were present at this meeting and there were fifty–nine apologies for non–attendance.

390 Captain Herbert Dixon.

391 Secretary to the Ulster Unionist Council.

392 Sixty members were present and there were twenty–eight apologies for non–attendance.

393 This committee was based in London.

was held at Magherintemple, Ballycastle … The Viscountess Craigavon presided[394] … Mrs Hume, O.B.E. then proposed the following Resolution …

> 'That in future the expenses of delegates from the Ulster Women's Unionist Council to the London Conferences [of the National Union of Conservative and Unionist Associations] should not be paid, except in special circumstances, but that ladies should attend at their own expense'.

Considerable discussion ensued, and Mrs Noble expressed her opinion that many very loyal Unionist workers who could not afford to defray their own expenses to London, would, if this Resolution were passed, be debarred from the privilege of participating in the Conference. Mrs Innis, J.P. expressed her strong disapproval and said it was most unfair to deprive loyal working women the chance of attending these Conferences. The opinion of the majority of those present was that loyal work for the Unionist Party is carried out by all social classes represented on the Council and is not by any means confined to one class or section. Mrs Molly, M.B.E., Lady Allen J.P., Mrs Lawson and others spoke against the Resolution from the point of view that it would limit representation in London, and deprive less wealthy members of Council the opportunity of attending the Conferences … [The resolution was withdrawn.] The Secretary then reported on the work carried out since the last meeting of the Executive Committee, and mentioned the activity of the Belfast Pioneer Club, and those more recently formed in Portadown and Newtownards Clubs, and the chances of interesting girls in politics in these Clubs was stressed.

The Secretary then stated that she had received permission from Lady Craigavon to suggest that following the plan of the English organisation for interesting speakers, a speakers' competition should be held in Belfast in the Autumn … The Committee warmly assented to this scheme … The Secretary in her Report also advocated the holding of fetes as far as possible in each Association during the Summer in order to unite the members and to stimulate enthusiasm. It was also reported that classes for Political study were being held in Belfast and were proving most successful, also that a new class was being held in Mourne. The Secretary also reported the formation of a Branch of the Women's Unionist Association at Clough.

Lady Craigavon then explained that Miss Wilson, Staff Speaker, had been appointed from 1st October, 1930, for a period of six months … and spoke in favourable terms of the excellent political knowledge possessed by Miss Wilson … Miss Wilson's appointment was renewed on a permanent basis.

The Secretary then explained that an application had been received from Miss Bell, Whitehouse, asking to be taken as a trainee. Lady Craigavon said that this applicant had been interviewed by the Secretary and had been considered satisfactory, and asked the Committee for permission to receive her as a trainee, which was unanimously granted.

394 Seventy–six members were present at this meeting and there were twenty–eight apologies for non–attendance.

Lady Craigavon then asked [if] it was the wish of the Committee that a Mass Meeting should be held in the Autumn, and if she should secure a speaker from London to address the gathering. This was unanimously agreed to … Lady Craigavon … [raised] the question as to whether the Committee wished to lay down a definite proportion for the number of L.O.L.[395] representatives on the Executive Committee of an Association. After considerable discussion … it was decided unanimously to leave this question to the decision of the various Associations.

7 July 1931

A meeting of the Executive Committee of the Ulster Women's Unionist Council was held at 11.30 a.m. … Mrs Hume presided[396] … Mrs S. Cunningham, J.P. proposed the following resolution –

> 'The Finance Committee suggests that owing to the state of the finances of the Council, the Executive Committee should consider the advisability of continuing to maintain the Pioneer Club during next winter.'

Mrs Cunningham in speaking to this resolution expressed her appreciation of the work done by the Pioneer Club in interesting girls politically, but at the same time pointed out the fact that the funds of the Council were not in a satisfactory state, and that the expenditure exceeded the income … Mrs Cunningham then read a letter from the Hon. Treasurer, Mrs Ainsworth Barr, C.B.E., in which she showed the state of the finances to be such as to cause anxiety, and stated that she had received a letter from the Auditors warning her that the expenditure was out-running the income, and that capital was being eaten into.

Lady Allen, J.P. seconded the Resolution, and advised the giving up of the Club, especially on the ground that it caused dissatisfaction in some country districts that this money subscribed for Headquarters purposes should be expended upon a Club which only benefited Belfast … Miss Montgomery then spoke in favour of Girls' Clubs, and said that her experience of the last few months' work in Newtownards had been that the Club had given her entrance into all the factories in the town, and in them about 1,200 girls were employed. She considered this one of the best methods of preparing for an election. Mrs Casement expressed her opinion that it would be a great pity to stop the Pioneer Club in Belfast, and Mrs MacDonald spoke of her experience in the Portadown Girls' Club, which she said had not only been most successful as regards to interesting the members, but had been an actual financial help to the Party as the girls had raised £10 for Unionist Funds by the sale of daffodils, and by another effort had raised £13 for Unionist funds … Mrs Hume … deprecated the closing down of any Unionist work once begun as a very bad precedent. Mrs Jas. Thompson expressed her opinion that it was unnecessary

[395] Loyal Orange Lodges.

[396] Forty–three members were present at this meeting and there were forty–one apologies for non–attendance.

expenditure of money to pay the expenses of delegates to the London Conference and then to economise on such an object as the Club which had for its aim the interesting of young girl voters on whom so much would depend in the future … [It] passed unanimously that 'The Pioneer Clubs be continued under the auspices of the Ulster Women's Unionist Council, but be made self-supporting.'

28 July 1931

An emergency meeting of the Executive Committee was held … at 11.30 a.m. The Chair was taken by Lady Dixon, D.B.E.[397] … The Chairwoman requested the Secretary to explain the proposal from [Edith] the Marchioness of Londonderry to assist in the financial support of the Girls' Unionist Pioneer Clubs in Northern Ireland provided the management were vested in a special Committee and not in the Ulster Women's Unionist Council … The Secretary explained that one great difficulty in running these Clubs was that of finding a leader, prepared to give up definitely one night a week to the work, and said that Lady Londonderry suggested engaging a lady for this purpose, whose duty would be to supervise all the Clubs already started and such as might be started in the future. This would be an additional expense besides the rent of premises, payment of choir leaders, dancing instructors etc. and meant that the total cost of running Clubs would be very considerable, if the movement caught on and Clubs were established in other places as was hoped. In the present state of unemployment in Northern Ireland it was hopeless to make Girls' Clubs self-supporting. Lady Londonderry hoped to obtain financial assistance from new sources, and from persons not at present active in Unionist work … The general feeling was that it would be a pity to sever the direct connection of the Girls' Clubs with the Council, but that the financial help would be of great assistance … [it was passed] That the proposal of the Marchioness of Londonderry to assist in the financial support of Girls' Unionist Pioneer Clubs in Northern Ireland be accepted. The management to be vested in a special Committee affiliated to the Ulster Women's Unionist Council … At least 15 minutes to be devoted to some kind of Unionist propaganda at each ordinary meeting of a Club. That representatives from the Ulster Women's Unionist Council … be on the Committee of the Girls' Unionist Pioneer Clubs, and that two representatives of the Girls' Unionist Pioneer Clubs be appointed to the Ulster Women's Unionist Council each year.

9 November 1931

A meeting of the Executive Committee was held … at 11.30 a.m. in 3 Glengall Street, Belfast. The Viscountess Craigavon presided[398] … [It] was reported that

[397] Fifty–five members were present at this meeting and there were forty–two apologies for non–attendance.

[398] One hundred members were present at this meeting and there were eleven apologies for non–attendance.

since the Emergency Committee had been held a letter had been received from Lady [Edith] Londonderry, declining to undertake the responsibility of the Belfast Pioneer Club and any other Girls' Pioneer Clubs which might be formed, under the conditions laid down by the Executive Committee. More recently still, however, Lady Londonderry had intimated to the Secretary that she would supply the sum of £33 in order that the Belfast Pioneer Club might be run for this year on the same conditions as last year … The Executive Committee accepted this very generous offer of Lady Londonderry's … The Secretary then reported re[.] the Mass Meeting, that this had been cancelled owing to the fact that it coincided with the date fixed for Polling Day for the General Election[399] … The Secretary then reported re[.] Election Work, that she had concentrated chiefly on Co. Tyrone, that Miss Wilson, Miss Watt and Miss Bell had canvassed in East Belfast, and that on Polling Day Miss Blair had worked in West Belfast, Miss Watt and Miss Wilson in East Belfast; also that owing to the shortage of motor-cars in Tyrone for Polling Day, Miss Bell had kindly taken her own car and had taken voters to the Poll throughout the whole day. The Secretary had also addressed one meeting in West Belfast, and Miss Wilson several in Co. Tyrone, and one in Belfast.

Mrs Ainsworth Barr, Hon. Treasurer, then reported that owing to the depression in trade the Committee in charge of the Unionist Bazaar had decided to postpone this. They also felt that to hold the Bazaar so soon after the General Election would have been inadvisable, but hoped to hold it sometime during 1932 … The Secretary then reported that Speakers' Classes had been started in Belfast, and were being arranged in Cookstown and Portrush … The Secretary reported that Miss Blizzard and Miss Gregg were willing to undertake speaking during the winter[.]

26 January 1932

A Meeting of the Executive Committee of the Ulster Women's Unionist Council was held in Unionist Headquarters, Belfast … at 11.30 a.m. The Viscountess Craigavon presided[400] … Viscountess Craigavon expressed in sympathetic terms the regret of the Ulster Women's Unionist Council at the death of Miss Connor, O.B.E., J.P. who had been Hon. Treasurer of the Council for so many years … Miss Connor had left a sum of £2,000 to the Council … Mrs Ainsworth Barr, C.B.E., Hon. Treasurer, made a statement showing that various economies were being effected in the expenditure of the Council for 1932, which would amount to approximately £160. These economies were to include a saving of one month's salary for the Secretary of the Ulster Women's Unionist Council as the Secretary had offered to take her holiday month in 1932 without salary; a saving of £104 per annum on the salary of the Staff Speaker as Miss Wilson had resigned on 1st January 1932, and it was agreed that her place should not be filled [in the] meantime. Several small

399 The date of the United Kingdom general election was 27 October 1931.

400 One hundred and fifteen members were present at this meeting and there were twenty–nine apologies for non–attendance.

savings in printing, travelling expenses made up the balance … Lady Craigavon expressed her pleasure at the satisfactory expansion, great progress and increased interest in the work of the Council … The Secretary then reported that she had received an application from Miss Kathleen Entrican, Cookstown, to be received later in the Spring as a Trainee in Headquarters. This was unanimously agreed to[.]

5 April 1932

A Meeting of the Executive Committee was held in the Minor Hall, Town Hall, Ballymena … at 2 p.m. The Viscountess Craigavon presided[401] … The Secretary … gave a report of the work since the last Executive Meeting. She touched on the Speakers' Classes which had been carried on in Belfast, Cookstown, Portrush and Coleraine, and outlined the arrangements which had been carried out in the Speakers' Competition held the previous day.

Lady Allen then said that she had a message from Sir Wm. Allen, Hon. Secretary of the Ulster Unionist Council, in which he conveyed his great appreciation of this movement for educational political propaganda … The Secretary then reported that one of the Competitors, who had gained second place in the Individual Speakers' Section at the Competition, Miss Joan Adair of Cookstown, was desirous of taking the Women's Organisers' Examination in London in September in order to obtain a professional status. The Secretary explained that to do this, Miss Adair must have been in receipt of a salary for six months prior to the Examination, and asked whether the Executive would consider giving Miss Adair a very small sum per week simply in order to qualify her for this Examination … it was agreed to give Miss Adair the nominal sum of 5/- per week … The Secretary then reported that the members of several Speakers' Classes were anxious to continue the course of instruction by attending a residential School of Study … the Secretary had made preliminary investigations, and found that a limited number of students could be received in a small hotel at Heversham, Westmoreland, at the sum of £2.10. per head per week, also that Professor Wilson[,] Chair of International Law in Edinburgh, had kindly consented to attend the School if the time could be arranged to suit his convenience and lecture without fee. The President … explained that of course Professor Wilson's expenses, and those of his wife[,] would require to be defrayed by the Council; also those of the Organising Secretary, but that apart from these items, the School would be self-supporting.

2 May 1932

An Emergency Meeting of the Executive Committee was held … at 11.30 a.m., the

401 Seventy–eight members were present at this meeting and there were thirty–four apologies for non–attendance.

Viscountess Craigavon presiding[402] … The Viscountess Craigavon [explained] the object of the meeting, which was, she said, to present to the Executive Committee the scheme of the Chief Whip, Capt. The Rt. Hon. Herbert Dixon, to run conjointly of the Country Market … and a two-day Bazaar, to take the place of the proposed Unionist Bazaar which had been postponed. Lady Craigavon pointed out that the Country Market was absolutely essential if funds were to be provided for the work of the Ulster Women's Unionist Council, and therefore nothing could be allowed to interfere with the scheme this year, the postponement last year having involved the Council in financial difficulty. She also pointed out that the Prime Minister had pledged his word to organise a Bazaar or other effort next year for the funds of Ex-Service men, and therefore the Unionist Bazaar could not be postponed to 1933.

Lady Craigavon intimated that the Chief Whip had made a most generous promise, namely, that £350 should be given to the Ulster Women's Unionist Council out of the proceeds of the joint Bazaar and Country Market in order to make up for the sum which would probably have been realised had the Country Market been run as a separate scheme by the Women's Council. In addition to this the Chief Whip promised to hand over to the Ulster Women's Unionist Council, after deducting £350, one-fourth of the total raised by the Bazaar and by all preliminary efforts to raise funds.

5 July 1932

A Meeting of the Executive Committee was held … at 11.30 a.m. in Unionist Headquarters, Belfast … Mrs McMordie C.B.E., presided[403] … [The] Secretary explained re[.] the proposed School of Study in Westmoreland, that as sufficient numbers of students had not enrolled, the scheme had been abandoned for this year, although just after the last day on which applications could be received sufficient numbers of students had enrolled, but by that time the Committee in charge had intimated to the Hotel that accommodation would not be required. It was hoped, however, that in view of this fact the scheme might be carried out on a future occasion … Mrs Waring proposed that the [public] meeting should be held as in her opinion there was a great need at the moment for political propaganda … [It] passed unanimously:–

'That a public Meeting be organised by the Ulster Women's Unionist Council, in

402 Fifty–three members were present at this meeting and there were thirty–one apologies for non–attendance.

403 Forty–eight members were present at this meeting and there were forty–four apologies for non–attendance.

January, and addressed by Lady Maureen Stanley,[404] if the finances and general political situation rendered this course desirable'.

6 October 1932

A Meeting of the Executive Committee of the Ulster Women's Unionist Council was held in the Town Hall, Magherafelt … at 12 o'c[lock] … Mrs McMordie, C.B.E., J.P., presided[405] … [The] question of continuing the Pioneer Clubs was raised and debated. The Secretary explained that the difficulty of the Belfast Club was that it did not belong to any Association and therefore could not claim help from any special quarter. Owing to the unemployment in Belfast, the members are quite unable to support the Club financially. Mrs Callender Bullick spoke strongly on the importance of continuing this Branch of work, as in her opinion work amongst girls is vital to the Party. After considerable discussion, MrsHume said that she had just been handed a note from the audience, stating that Windsor Association would be responsible for £10 towards the expense of Belfast Pioneer Club this winter … On behalf of Bloomfield Association Mrs Carey also promised some assistance. The Secretary was instructed to write to Lady [Edith] Londonderry, asking whether she could see her way to give some financial assistance to the Club this year, as she had so kindly done last year. In the event of Lady Londonderry's refusal … some effort should be organised by the Belfast Associations to cover the expenses of the Belfast Pioneer Club, and so continue it this year … After discussion it was agreed … that a Mass Meeting in connection with the Ulster Women's Unionist Council should be organised in January … The Secretary then reported as to the work carried out during the Summer, including the holding of two Country Markets in Headquarters by Co. Antrim, which had realised a considerable sum towards the Unionist Bazaar … The Secretary also reported that assistance had been given to Co. Tyrone ladies in organising a Country Market in Dungannon. She mentioned that meetings had been carried on till quite late in the Summer, and that a new Branch had been started in Antrim town. The Secretary intimated that one of the trainees, Miss Mary Watt, M.A., had successfully passed her Woman Organisers' Examination in London, and had received her Diploma … The Secretary also suggested that an efficiency competition should be held at the same time as the Speakers' Competition. It would then be decided which Branch had made the greatest progress in new methods of work, business procedure, increase in membership etc. … It was agreed that … [At

[404] Lady Maureen Helen Stanley (1900–40), was a daughter of Edith, 7th Marchioness of Londonderry and Charles, 7th Marquis of Londonderry. In 1920 she married Oliver Frederick George Stanley (1896–1950), second son of the 17th Earl of Derby and a Conservative MP from 1924–50, Minister of Transport from 1933–34, Minister of Labour, 1934–35, President of the Board of Education, 1935–37. He was also President of the Board of Trade, 1937–40, Secretary of State for War in 1940 and for the Colonies from 1942–45. *Who Was Who, 1941–50*, vol. 4 (London, 1952), p. 1093.

[405] Thirty–four members were present at this meeting and there were fifty–eight apologies for non–attendance.

Homes] should again be organised for the third Wednesday in each month, except December ... The chairman then intimated that she wished to ask permission to engage the services of Miss Marjorie Lyle, Portrush, as an extra speaker for conducting Political classes when necessary, especially in regard to economic subjects. Miss Lyle being a trained expert, it would be desirable to offer her a small fee, and the sum of 10/6d was mentioned, with travelling expenses ... A Public Meeting was held in the afternoon, at which Mrs Chichester-Clark presided, the speakers being Capt. The Rt. Hon. Herbert Dixon, M.P.[,] Sir Basil Brooke, Bart., Capt. Chichester-Clark, M.P.,[406] and Miss Jeannette Martin.

26 January 1933

A Meeting of the Executive Committee was held ... in Unionist Headquarters, Belfast, at 11.30 a.m. ... Mrs McMordie, C.B.E. presided[407] ... The following resolution ... was put forward ...

> 'That in future Transfer Forms be printed by Headquarters and that a supply be sent to each Branch Secretary, in order that Unionist women and girls leaving to reside in another district may not be lost sight of, but a Transfer Form be immediately forwarded through Headquarters to the Secretary of the Branch, in whose Area they will be resident'.

This was unanimously agreed to ... The following Resolution was proposed ...

> 'That in future two meetings of the Ulster Women's Unionist Council be held annually, in order that the delegates may attend one meeting at which a Political speech is delivered by one of the Northern Parliament members, or other outstanding speaker, as the January Council is purely for business purposes'.

... Much discussion ensued about the Resolution ... Two points of view were presented, firstly that it was a financial burden to members of the Council to attend two meetings in Belfast during the year, and on the other hand a number of ladies felt that one Council meeting which was only a business meeting did not keep them sufficiently in touch with the work, and they felt that in comparison with members of the Executive Committee, they were debarred from many interesting opportunities for meeting and discussion.

Mrs Montgomery then proposed that the experiment of two meetings should be tried for one year in order to ascertain whether or not it was a success ... The following Resolution was proposed ...

406 Captain James Lenox–Conyngham Chichester–Clark (1884–1933), a JP and Deputy Lieutenant for Co. Londonderry and a unionist member of the Parliament of Northern Ireland for S. Londonderry from 1929. He was the son–in–law of Dehra Chichester. *Who Was Who,* vol. 3, p. 247.

407 One hundred and six members were present at this meeting and there were forty–five apologies for non–attendance.

> 'That whenever possible, Annual Area Conferences be arranged in convenient districts so that members may get to know one another and discuss problems of work …'

This was unanimously passed … the Sec[retar]y. then outlined the proposal for an Efficiency Competition for Branches of the Ulster Women's Unionist Council, to be held on the same day as the Speakers' Competition. The following points of efficiency were agreed on –

1 Greatest increase in membership during the year.
2 Best methods of work.
3 Newest methods of work.
4 Best kept minute book.
5 Best financial report.
6 Best educational methods adopted during the year.

It was agreed that voting as to the most efficient Branch should be decided by the audience on the day of the Competition … the Executive Committee of the Ulster Women's Unionist Council … [sent] a resolution to the Women's National Unionist Conference, to be held in London in May … as follows:–

> 'That this meeting records its grateful appreciation of the triumph of the National Government in overcoming the recent grave financial crisis, tenders cordial congratulations on the measure of success which attended the Ottawa Conference,[408] and pledges the members of the Women's Unionist Organisation represented at this Conference to the whole-hearted support of such further legislation as his Majesty's Ministers may deem necessary to secure the revival of prosperity throughout Great Britain and Northern Ireland.'[409]

… Mrs Casement raised the question as to whether it would not be an advantage to the interests of the Unionist Party in Northern Ireland if leaflets issued by the Opposition were answered by the printing of leaflets on the Unionist side, as the circulation of these Opposition leaflets was very large. The following resolution was then agreed on –

> 'That this Committee recommend that leaflets issued from time to time by the Opposition, making statements detrimental to Unionist interests in Northern Ireland, should be answered by the publication of literature on the Unionist side'[.]

[408] At the Imperial Economic Conference held in Ottawa in 1932 agreements were drawn up whereby dominion foodstuffs and produce received preferential treatment in the UK market.

[409] This was due to the economic depression of 1929–33, the cause of which lay mainly outside Britain, principally in the general reliance on American loans and prosperity, which ceased in October 1929 with the crash of the American stock market.

4 April 1933

A Meeting of the Executive Committee of the Ulster Women's Unionist Council was held in the Dufferin Hall, Bangor ... at 12.15. The Viscountess Craigavon presided[410] ... [The] proposed Branch Efficiency Competition had fallen through as only, two Branches had entered, as the others felt that more time was required for the preparation for this competition ... After considerable discussion, it was agreed not to hold a Country Market in the Summer or early Autumn, in order to leave the forthcoming Bazaar for Ex-service Men free from competition. It was finally decided ... that a Xmas Fair be organised later in the Winter, and if necessary, The Hon. Treasurer would kindly arrange to advance funds necessary to carry on the work until such times as the proceeds of the effort had been realised.

The Secretary then read a letter from Miss Spencer, London Headquarters, asking that a lady from Ulster should propose the vote of thanks to Mr. Stanley Baldwin at the Mass Meeting to be held in the Albert Hall on the 12th May ... Lady Craigavon be asked to propose this vote of thanks ... a Public Meeting was held in the Dufferin Hall, at which Mrs Coleman presided, the speakers being –

The Viscountess Craigavon, Lady Brooke, Mrs Knox-Browne, and Mrs Hume.

7 July 1933

A meeting of the Executive Committee of the Ulster Women's Unionist Council was held at 3 Glengall Street ... at 11.30 a.m. The Viscountess Craigavon presided[411] ... The Secretary ... read the financial report of the Pioneer Girls' Club for the past session ... The total expense to the Executive Committee had worked out at only £1.16. 8, which was considered most satisfactory ... The Chairman then mentioned that an invitation had been received from the English Northern Area to Ulster Women Unionists, to join a School of Study to be held in the North of England, probably Blackpool, in the Autumn. She explained that the Finance Committee recommended that the Organising Secretary should be sent in charge of the party and her expenses paid up to five pounds, if the School did not clash with the date of the forthcoming Ulster Division Bazaar, and if at least twelve students from Ulster were willing to attend ... The Viscountess Craigavon said that she had received a letter from the Secretary of the Ulster Women's Christian Temperance Union asking that the Council would consider that fact that Lord Carson's name 'was being used for the purpose of furthering liquor propaganda'. Lady Dixon said that in her opinion this subject was entirely outside the area of the Council's jurisdiction and suggested that no steps be taken ... Lady Craigavon then gave a few valuable points on the India White Paper and strongly urged members of the Ulster Women's Unionist Council, to suspend their judgement until the

410 Seventy–five members were present at this meeting and there were forty–six apologies for non–attendance.

411 Forty–seven members were present at this meeting and there were forty–two apologies for non–attendance.

Committee sitting on the question had issued its report. She emphasised that Party Unity was of paramount importance at this time, as any split might result in the return of a Socialist Government at Westminster, which would be fatal, not only to British interests in India but to the general prosperity of the Nation.

17 October 1933

A Meeting of the Executive Committee was held in Unionist Headquarters … at 11.30 a.m. The Viscountess Craigavon presided[412] … The Secretary … reported that the Pioneer Club meetings had begun for the winter, and the attendance for the first evening was most encouraging. The following Resolution was then proposed by The Viscountess Craigavon …

> 'That in future Women Unionist Members of [the] Imperial Parliament representing Constituencies in Northern Ireland, and Women Unionist Members of the Senate and House of Commons of Northern Ireland, be Ex-Officio members of the Executive Committee of the Ulster Women's Unionist Council [and] … be incorporated in the Constitution of the said Council'.

The Resolution was carried unanimously without discussion … Lady Craigavon from the Chair urged Miss McConnell to organise the 'At Homes', which she said were thoroughly appreciated by a large number of Unionists [in] Belfast and surrounding districts. Miss Josephine McConnell kindly agreed to undertake this duty.

The Secretary then reported that she had received a communication from Miss Joyce, Organiser for 'Trade Talks', London, offering a series of lectures in Northern Ireland, preferably in January. There would be no expense to the Council, except local travelling and hospitality, as the Government of India would defray return fare of [the] Speaker from London to Belfast … it was decided to book the speaker from the 2nd. to 12th Jan. [1934] inclusive.

The Organising Secretary reported that she had received offers of voluntary help from two very capable men speakers, i.e. Councillor F. G. Anderson, M.A., I.C.S., and Alfred Coulter Esq., J.P. The former would be suitable for Educational work, Speakers' Classes, Debates etc. and the latter for large Public Meetings. It was unanimously agreed to take advantage of these most kind offers of Assistance … Lady Craigavon then asked whether it was the wish of the Committee that a Public Meeting should be held this year on the same lines as last year, and it was pointed out that the organisation of such a meeting entailed a great expenditure and although the attendance of last year's meeting had been good, the Hall was not full, although thousands of tickets had been sent out … After discussion [it was decided that] … no Public Meeting should be held this year. This was unanimously agreed to.[413]

412 Seventy–eight members were present at this meeting and there were twenty–four apologies for non–attendance.

413 This public meeting was held in Bangor on 4 April 1933.

5 December 1933

A Special Meeting of the Executive Committee was held … at 12 noon. The Viscountess Craigavon presided[414] … Miss Martin pointed out that the post of Organising Secretary to the Ulster Women's Unionist Council was one of the fifteen important posts in the Unionist Party in the United Kingdom.[415]

28 January 1934

A Meeting of the Executive Committee was held in Unionist Headquarters … at 11.30 a.m. The Viscountess Craigavon presided[416] … [The] Financial Report … [showed] that the balance was on the right side because of a cheque for £500 given to the Ulster Women's Unionist Council by the Prime Minister … Discussion followed re[.] the apathy shown in the recent Municipal Elections, especially on the part of men voters. Lady Craigavon promised to mention this matter to Sir Wilson Hungerford.[417]

19 April 1934

A meeting of the Executive Committee was held in the Orange Hall, Portadown … at 11.30 a.m. The Viscountess Craigavon presided[418] … Lady Craigavon congratulated Miss Maclean upon the success of the Speakers' Competition … After discussion … it was moved … that the Belfast Pioneer Club be closed for the present[419] … After discussion it was moved … that a Country Market be held this year … A ballot was taken for the delegates to represent the Council at the London Women's Conservative Conference on 10th and 11th May … four delegates, whose expenses are being defrayed by the Council, up to £8, were successful[420] … Mrs McMordie spoke shortly upon the subject of awakening young people to a sense of political responsibility … It was decided that the Belfast Associations hold a meeting early in the Autumn to discuss further this matter.

It was reported by Mrs Inglis, J.P., that the Catholic Truth Society had made an application for the use of the Ulster Hall [Belfast] for the first week in July. Discussion followed.

It was moved … that the Secretary write to the Lord Mayor, Alderman and

414 Seventy–seven members were present at this meeting and there were thirty–six apologies for non–attendance.

415 Miss Helen A. Maclean from Edinburgh was appointed UWUC Organising Secretary at a salary of £275 per annum.

416 Ninety–six members were present at this meeting and there were thirty–nine apologies for non–attendance.

417 Secretary of the Ulster Unionist Council.

418 Eighty–nine members were present at this meeting and there were forty–five apologies for non–attendance.

419 This was most probably due to financial considerations.

420 These delegates were picked by ballot. Other delegates were free to go if they did so at their own expense.

Councillors of the Belfast Corporation and protest on behalf of the Council against the building being let to any body of persons whose loyalty to the King [George V] and the Government of Northern Ireland was in doubt, and at the same time to explain that the protest was made not on any religious ground but only in the interests of the Loyalists of the Province. This was carried unanimously[.]

3 July 1934

A Meeting of the Executive Committee was held at 11.30 a.m. ... Lady Dixon D.B.E. presided[421] ... [A special U.W.U.C. meeting to be held in October 1934 was discussed, as was the council's Ashridge Scholarship Fund to send U.W.U.C. members to the Bonar Law College. This fund] was still open, so that if any member wished to send in a subscription, however small, it would be very acceptable.

26 October 1934

A Meeting of the Executive Committee was held ... at 11.30 a.m. The Viscountess Craigavon presided[422] ... Lady Craigavon mentioned that £70 odd had been raised for the Ashridge Scholarships and expressed gratitude to the individual Branches and Associations which had subscribed so generously.

The question of the 'At Homes' was then raised. After discussion it was decided that the arrangements should be left to the 'At Homes' Committee ... Lady Craigavon gave a short report on the Country Market, and thanked all Associations and Branches for their great help. She mentioned that over £200 had been raised.

17 January 1935

A meeting of the Executive Committee was held ... at 11.30 a.m. in 3 Glengall Street, Belfast. The Viscountess Craigavon presided[423] ... MrsMontgomery congratulated the council on a year of good work and steady progress ... It was unanimously decided to again hold a Speakers' Competition ... Miss Corry reported that the speaking work of the Ashridge Students was giving much satisfaction over the Six Counties and greatly helped the work of the Ulster Women's Unionist Council. After discussion it was proposed ... that a Resolution be sent in from the Ulster Women's Unionist Council to the London Conference [of the National Union of Conservative and Unionist Associations] pledging their continued loyal support of the National Government.[424]

421 Forty–nine members were present at the meeting and there were forty–six apologies for non–attendance.

422 Forty–two members were present at this meeting and there were thirty–four apologies for non–attendance.

423 One hundred and twenty–three members were present at this meeting and there were thirty–three apologies for non–attendance.

424 The National Government remained in power until June 1935.

9 April 1935

A meeting of the Executive Committee was held … in the Parish Hall, Cookstown, at 12 noon. The Viscountess Craigavon presided[425] … It was moved … that a Country Market be again held. After discussion it was moved … that the Market be held [for] one day only … The ballot for the London Conference [of the National Union of Conservative and Unionist Associations] was then drawn … Lady Craigavon put forward as a recommendation from the Finance Committee that the Secretary's salary be raised from £275 to £300. This … passed unanimously.

2 July 1935

A Meeting of the Executive Committee was held … at 11.30 a.m. Lady Dixon, D.B.E. presided[426] … The message of Loyalty and Congratulations from the Ulster Women's Unionist Council to Their Majesties the King and Queen on the occasion of their Silver Jubilee, also the reply from the Secretary of State, were then read … The arrangements made for the Country Market were then reported … It was decided to get Market prices for the various commodities on the day of the Market and to charge accordingly … The Chairman reported that a Special Scholarship for the 8 weeks' Course beginning on October 28th had been offered to the Ulster Women's Unionist Council by the Scholarship Committee of the Bonar Law College, Ashridge … it was decided to send a letter to each Association Secretary, giving details about the Scholarship and asking each Association to nominate a suitable candidate … Mrs Stowell Taylor suggested that the Ashridge Scholarships should not be given only to those who had done speaking work for the Council, but also to those who would be willing to speak after training and do work for the Unionist Cause.

MrsFerguson reported that a delegation from the Wigan Women's Unionist Association had paid a visit to Stormont[427] and had extended an invitation to the Executive Committee of the Ulster Women's Unionist Council to visit them at Blackpool at some future date … Mrs Montgomery suggested that at the end of each Executive Committee 10 minutes might be allocated during which time questions on current affairs could be asked and discussed.

Miss Corry suggested that when winter arrangements were being made Classes for instruction in political matters might be held in the evenings during the coming winter, as in view of an election at an early date it would be necessary for all Unionist workers to increase their knowledge on subjects such as Re-evaluation,

[425] Seventy–four members were present at this meeting and there were forty–seven apologies for non–attendance.

[426] Fifty–seven members were present at this meeting and there were forty–two apologies for non–attendance.

[427] The Northern Ireland Government Buildings [Stormont] which were formally opened by the Prince of Wales on 16 November 1932.

The Education Levy etc.[428]

Mrs Casement suggested that leaflets dealing with such subjects would be very helpful.

18 October 1935

A meeting of the Executive Committee was held … at 11.30 a.m. The Viscountess Craigavon presided[429] … Lady Craigavon reported that up to the present £325 odd had been raised at the Country Market. She expressed her great gratitude to all those who had made this Market such a great success, most especially mentioning the country members.

As no names had come from the Branches or Associations for the Eight Weeks' Ashridge Scholarship [at the Bonar Law College], Lady Craigavon explained that the Finance Committee had appointed Miss Kathleen Entrican, as if the Scholarship was not accepted it would not again be offered to the Council … Lady Craigavon explained that the Secretary was going to hold a Speakers' Class in Belfast in the evening as well as the usual afternoon Classes … It was decided that the 'At Homes' be continued and the following Associations most kindly undertook the arrangements for a Speaker and Programme … Shankill … Carrick … South Antrim [and] … Duncairn-Clifton … The following Resolution … 'That the Constitution of the Ulster Women's Unionist Council shall be altered by having 3 Executive Meetings in the year instead of 4, i.e. in January, May and October. The May Meeting to be held in the week following the London Conference' [of the National Union of Conservative and Unionist Associations] … was approved. Miss Johnston decided to have it brought up at the next Executive and Council to give time for further thought on the subject.[430]

The following Resolution … [was discussed] 'That young speakers who have taken training and are working for the Unionist Cause by speaking at Meetings, should become Ex-officio members of the Ulster Women's Unionist Council on payment of the ordinary 10/– subscription to the Council'.

It was decided that this Resolution should also be further discussed at the January Meeting.

20 February 1936

A meeting of the Executive Committee was held … at 11.30 a.m. The Viscountess Craigavon presided[431] … Lady Craigavon reported that there was the possibility of

428 In May 1934 an education levy at the rate of 6d. in the £ was introduced. This was operative for 1934–35 and thereafter the education levy was fixed at 1s. in the £. The provision aimed to place more of the cost of education in Northern Ireland onto the ratepayers. The levy was much criticised and very unpopular.

429 Sixty–five members were present at this meeting and there were thirty–four apologies for non–attendance.

430 This resolution was passed unanimously at the Executive Committee meeting of 20 February 1936.

431 One hundred and thirteen members were present at this meeting and there were thirty–six apologies for non–attendance.

another 8 Weeks' Scholarship [to the Bonar Law College, Ashridge] being given to the Ulster Women's Unionist Council, and she expressed the hope that the Associations would bear this in mind and be on the look-out for a suitable candidate, age 17 to 27 ... Proposed ... 'That the Ulster Women's Unionist Council change the method of selecting delegates to attend the London Conference [of the National Union of Conservative and Unionist Associations], so that every Association shall in turn send a delegate. As nine Associations have not yet been represented they shall be asked to forward names of those willing to go to London, after which the Associations will be represented in alphabetical order. This does not apply to delegates paying their own expenses'.

After discussion this was passed unanimously ... Lady Craigavon then referred to the idea ... that the Council should renew and maintain a floral tribute on Lord Carson's Grave in the Cathedral [in Belfast] ... and after discussion it was decided that each Association should pay from 10/- per annum towards this floral tribute.

22 May 1936

A meeting of the Executive Committee was held at Aughentain Castle[432] ... at 12 noon. The Viscountess Craigavon presided[433] ... Lady Craigavon explained the difficulty of keeping flowers fresh [on Lord Carson's grave] in the hot atmosphere of the Cathedral. She also pointed out that in the opinion of the members of [the] Finance Committee who had visited the Grave, it was not fitting to have flowers on the granite slab ... The Chairman reported that until some permanent arrangement could be made, the Sub-Committee had decided to have a wreath of Cypress palms hung on the wall beside the Grave. This was approved ... the following Resolution:–

'That addresses be given at the Special Council meeting in October on work done by Local Authorities in N. Ireland'... [was] passed unanimously.

30 October 1936

A meeting of the Executive Committee of the Ulster Women's Unionist Council was held at Unionist Headquarters ... at 12 noon. The Viscountess Craigavon presided[434] ... Lady Craigavon explained the difficulty of keeping fresh flowers on Lord Carson's Grave. Because of this the Finance Committee asked for the approval of the Executive that they should ask the Ulster Unionist Council to co-operate with the Women's Council in putting up some form of permanent memorial ... The Secretary reported that the sum raised by the Country Market up to the present was £292. 18. 0. Lady Craigavon thanked all those who had helped make the

432 This was the home of Mrs Knox Browne.

433 Sixty–two members were present at this meeting and there were fifty–two apologies for non–attendance.

434 Forty members were present at this meeting and there were forty–two apologies for non–attendance.

Market such a success ... The following Associations most kindly promised to be responsible for the musical part of the 'At Homes' Committee ... Duncairn-Clifton ... Shankill ... St. Anne's [and] ... South Antrim ... it was reported that the Secretary was now responsible for the educational side of these meetings.

The following resolution was proposed ...

'That Associations affiliated to the Ulster Women's Unionist Council may, with the approval of the Council, form Junior Branches in the various neighbourhoods where women Unionists are already working, and so encourage the younger people to take an interest in the Unionist Cause and give them an opportunity to do so' ... [This] passed unanimously.

14 January 1937

A meeting of the Executive Committee was held ... at 11.30 a.m. The Viscountess Craigavon presided[435] ... Lady Craigavon reported that permission had been granted by the Cathedral Authorities [of Belfast] to erect a tablet to the memory of Lord Carson ... the Financial Report showed a balance of £98. 7. 7½ ...

RESOLUTION FROM NORTH TYRONE W.U.A. ...

'That Affiliation Fees payable by Constituency Associations affiliated to the Ulster Women's Unionist Council be raised to cover 10/– subscription due by representatives appointed to the Council under the present system, as we feel that members should not be expected to pay for the privilege of representing their Association.'

After discussion this Resolution was withdrawn, and it was agreed that in future all notices re[.] subscriptions should be sent to the Treasurer of each Association.

27 April 1937

A Special Meeting of the Executive Committee was held ... at 2.30 p.m. Lady Craigavon presided[436]... [The successor to Miss Maclean, the Ulster Women's Unionist Council's Organising Secretary, was discussed and Miss Molly Dickson was appointed as her successor.]

4 June 1937

A Meeting of the Executive Committee was held in the Orange Hall, Portrush ... at 11.30 a.m. The Viscountess Craigavon presided[437] ... Lady Craigavon intimated that the Committee [of Lord Edward Carson's Memorial] had empowered her to spend £120 i.e. £60 from the Men's and £60 from the Women's Council.

[435] There were forty apologies for non–attendance. From this date forward the names of members present at the Executive Committee meetings are not included in the minutes.

[436] There were twenty–three apologies for non–attendance.

[437] There were thirty–three apologies for non–attendance.

The following wording was decided upon:–

'To the memory of our Leader, Edward Carson.'
'A Tribute of affection from the men and women of Ulster'…

[Seven] students were selected to attend Ashridge, The Bonar Law College.

26 October 1937

A meeting of the Executive Committee was held in Unionist Headquarters … Mrs Ainsworth Barr presided[438] … Mrs Ainsworth Barr reported that the wording for Lord Carson's Memorial had not quite been agreed upon, but that the Sub-Committee was to meet again in a few days to make their final decision … The Secretary reported that the amount raised by the Country Market was £299 and the Committee expressed their gratitude at this result. She also referred to the Bridge Drive which was being organised … to supplement the funds of the Market, and asked for the support of the members … After discussion, it was agreed to run the 'At Home' in Jan.[,] Feb. and March. The following Associations kindly offered to undertake the programme … North Antrim … Victoria [and] … Duncairn-Clifton. The Secretary then read a letter from Sir Samuel Hoare,[439] thanking the Ulster Women's Unionist Council for the loyal address presented to the King and Queen on their visit to Belfast … The Secretary reported that four Scholarships for the four weeks Course at Ashridge had been offered to the Council, and those present were asked to send in the name of any suitable candidate for their Association … A letter was read from Miss Johnson (Organiser of [the] North-West Area) (England) suggesting that with a view to closer co-operation between Ulster and that Area, a member of the Women's Unionist Council should be asked to take a series of meetings in Manchester and District.

The Committee heartily agreed to this suggestion[.]

25 January 1938

A Meeting of the Executive Committee was held … at 11.30 a.m. The Viscountess Craigavon presided[440] … Lady Craigavon referred to the gratitude of the Prime Minister for the message of sympathy received from the members of the Committee. She reported that he was now quite well, and depending on them all to rally round at the forthcoming General Election … Lady Craigavon told the

438 There were twenty–four apologies for non–attendance.

439 Sir Samuel John Gurney Hoare (1880–1959), 2nd Baronet and Viscount Templewood, a Conservative MP for Chelsea from 1910–44. He was Secretary of State for Air from 1922–24, 1924–29 and in 1940, Secretary of State for India from 1931–35, Foreign Secretary in 1935, First Lord of the Admiralty from 1936–37. He was also Home Secretary from 1937–39, Lord Privy Seal and a member of the wartime cabinet from 1939–40 and Ambassador to Spain from 1940–44. *Dod's Peerage*, pp 435–6.

440 There were twenty–five apologies for non–attendance.

Committee that she had seen the plaster caste for Lord Carson's Plaque, and that it was a remarkable likeness … the cost to the Ulster Women's Unionist Council would be at least £60.

It was proposed that each Association should be asked to subscribe 30/–, or as much as possible towards this … The Secretary reported that the London Conference [of the National Union of Conservative and Unionist Associations] would be held on 11th and 12th May.

The Associations entitled to send delegates at the expense of the Council were:- Bannside, North Derry, South Derry, and Mid Down.

It was also reported that the Speakers' Classes would begin on 16th February, and that Belfast, Ballymena and Coleraine had asked for one in their area, also that there would be one for men held in Belfast … the Financial Report … showed a balance of £81. 3. 10.

5 May 1938

A Meeting of the Executive Committee was held in Strabane … at 12 noon. The Viscountess Craigavon presided[441] … Lady Craigavon reported that the [Lord Carson] plaque was now completed, and would be unveiled at a special service in the Cathedral on a date suitable to Lady Carson. Discussion took place as to the unveiling ceremony, and it was proposed … and passed unanimously, that the Prime Minister should be asked to unveil the plaque, and failing him, Lady Craigavon be asked … The Secretary reported that the Speakers' Competition had gone off very well … [Five women] were awarded Scholarships given by the [Bonar Law] College [and three women] were awarded Scholarships from the Council's Scholarship Fund. A letter was read from Miss Hezlet, dealing with Anti-Unionist Propaganda in England. In Miss Hezlet's absence, Mrs Casement spoke on the subject. She referred to the mis-representations published in the English Press, and asked if nothing could be done to refute these statements. Lady Craigavon then reported that the Government hoped shortly to open an Ulster Office in London. She explained that Party Politics could not be dealt with there, but that false statements published about the Government of N. Ireland would be rectified.

A letter was read from Sir Wilson Hungerford[442] on the matter of Propaganda [stating] … I have been giving a great deal of consideration to this matter and as you doubtless know I had a great many articles inserted in the English papers, as well as letters replied to. But, unfortunately, I cannot get the people who have been helping me in this matter to go on doing so as they have not got the time, no matter how willing they were.

I have suggested a small scheme … which, I think would do a lot of good and which could be economically run. It would need, however, a special Department to be set up here and all that requires finance. You will realise that after running a

[441] There were fifty–four apologies for non–attendance.

[442] Secretary of the Ulster Unionist Council.

general election, especially in the scale that the last one was run, it is difficult for the Party to launch into fresh expenditure, but I have put the scheme before the Chief Whip,[443] who is giving it especially careful consideration, and is, I understand, to consult the Prime Minister regarding it … Unfortunately, the British Press is inundated with anti-Ulster propaganda, and while objection cannot be taken to persons expressing their views in a reasonable and rational manner some of the letters and articles which are published are of a most vindictive and slanderous character.

Our State being comparatively small and not too wealthy, we cannot afford to spend large sums of money on propaganda, but I think something might be attempted on these lines:

Divide Great Britain into a certain number of areas and place prominent Ulstermen in charge of each area. He should be in close touch with other Ulstermen or sympathisers. Then when an article vilifying Ulster appears in the local or county newspapers, it should be replied to at once.

It will be readily understood that it is impossible to reply from here to all articles and letters. Many of them do not come under our notice. Besides, letters signed by one living in Ulster may be regarded as more or less one-sided. Letters written and signed by those on the spot undoubtedly carry more weight.

If the people on the spot were not able to deal with all the points they could send any articles and letters to us. We could then forward the replies to the Ulsterman in the area concerned and he could sign his name and address.

Unfortunately, Ulster is so bound up with the Government politically that many of the charges could only be answered by the Government. Such a scheme would require a special department to be set up at Headquarters, with a person of journalistic capabilities in charge, and arrangements made with the different Ministers to supply information.

18 October 1938

A meeting of the Executive Committee was held … in Unionist Headquarters. The Viscountess Craigavon presided[444] … Lady Craigavon referred to the unveiling ceremony [of the Lord Carson Memorial Plaque] by the Prime Minister, which would take place in the Cathedral on Sunday, 23rd. October, and expressed regret that owing to the limited accommodation it would not be possible for the whole Council to be present.

As the ceremony would be broadcast those who wished could listen-in … Lady Craigavon reported that the Finance Committee were preparing a leaflet about Ulster, which it was hoped would be issued shortly … Lady Craigavon reported that the Country Market had raised the magnificent sum of £731. 15. 6 … It was proposed … that the 'At Homes' be carried on as usual … The following Associations kindly undertook the programme … Windsor W.U.A. … Woodvale

443 Captain Herbert Dixon.

444 There were twenty–two apologies for non–attendance.

W.U.A. [and the] … Women's Orange Order. A letter was read from Miss Dickson, resigning her post as Organising secretary to the Ulster Women's Unionist Council, owing to her forthcoming marriage … Lady Craigavon told the meeting that there was a plan for Propaganda across the water and that the Council might be asked to help launch the appeal by subscribing towards it.

Miss McCutcheon, J.P., proposed that Lady Craigavon should convey to the Prime Minister a message expressing great satisfaction at his reply to Mr. De Valera(*sic*).[445] This … passed unanimously.

10 November 1938

A Special Meeting of the Executive Committee was held … to consider applications received for [the] post of Organising Secretary. The Viscountess Craigavon presided[446] … Lady Craigavon told the committee that the candidates had been asked to present, and if it was the wish of the members, they should be asked to make a short speech on Ulster politics.

This was agreed to … Miss [Nancy] Kinghan[447] … [was] appointed as Organising Secretary.

2 March 1939

A Meeting of the Executive Committee was held at 11.30 a.m. The Viscountess Craigavon presided[448] … After a great deal of discussion it was agreed to postpone the printing of the suggested leaflet [about Ulster] until the supply of those issued by the Propaganda Committee of the Ulster Unionist Council was exhausted. It was also decided that before printing the leaflet, the information should be checked by the various Ministries concerned … the Financial Report … showed a very satisfactory balance … this was due to the £757 raised at the Country Market, and also a donation of £500 by the Prime Minister … the following Resolution was proposed …

'That any member who has worked against the Official Unionist Party should be asked to resign from the Ulster Women's Unionist Council'.

After a great deal of discussion, it was decided to put the Resolution to the vote, and it was carried by 65 votes to 38.

5 May 1939

A Meeting of the Executive Committee was held in the Assembly Rooms[,] Lisburn

445 This is a reference to the negotiations that preceded the Anglo–Éire Treaty, a trade agreement which ended the economic war between Éire and Britain in 1938. In January 1938 Sir James Craig, Prime Minister of Northern Ireland, had pushed for economic concessions to be granted to Northern Ireland and highlighted how seriously Northern Ireland was affected by southern economic policies.

446 There were twenty–eight apologies for non–attendance.

447 Nancy Kinghan, OBE, was the Organising Secretary of the UWUC from 1938 until her resignation in 1971. She was the author of the official history of the UWUC, *United We Stood. The Story of the Ulster Women's Unionist Council, 1911–74* (Belfast, 1973).

448 There were twenty–nine apologies for non–attendance.

… The Viscountess Craigavon presided[449] … A great deal of discussion then took place as to whether or not a Country Market should be held this year or not. It was finally decided that it should be held in Unionist Headquarters on Friday 6th October. Lady Craigavon referred to the success of the Speaker's Competition … Lady Craigavon reported that she had been invited to lecture at [the Bonar Law College] Ashridge on the Ulster Question and had agreed to do so. Sir Basil Brooke had also promised to deal with this question at the same lecture. This intimation was received with applause … Mrs Ainsworth Barr proposed that a resolution of Confidence in our Prime Minister be passed for the way in which he had endeavoured to include Ulster in the Military Training Bill.[450] This was … passed unanimously.

19 January 1940

A Meeting of the Executive Committee was held in Unionist Headquarters … The Viscountess Craigavon presided[451] … Lady Craigavon said there had been a great deal of discussion on the subject of whether we should hold an Annual Meeting and it had been decided to consult our legal advisor Sir Dawson Bates [and] that he had gone into the constitution and had come to the conclusion that we would have to have an Annual Meeting and an Executive Committee with the result that the Executive was being held today (19th January) and the Annual Meeting in two months time. It was then up to the members at the Annual Meeting to decide whether they wanted to carry on as usual holding three executive meetings and an Annual Meeting or whether they would pass a resolution empowering the Finance Committee to deal with all business during the war.[452]

Miss Kinghan suggested that the Annual Meeting be held later in the year and it was decided to hold it about the end of April.

Mrs Campbell asked if the Branches would have to hold their Annual Meetings and on enquiry from Sir Dawson Bates he said it would be optional.

The following resolution was then submitted for Discussion:–

'That with the exception of any money owing for the year 1939 all Association Delegates Subscriptions to the Council shall be optional for the duration of the war but the Associations shall be asked to pay their affiliation fees.'

After a great deal of discussion … [it] passed unanimously that the resolution be approved.

449 There were fifty–seven apologies for non–attendance.

450 This bill passed into law in May 1939 and introduced conscription for men aged between 20 and 21 who were required to partake in six months' military training. However, once World War II broke out a National Service (Armed Forces) Act was passed which made all men aged between 18 and 41 liable for conscription.

451 There were forty–seven apologies for non–attendance.

452 The Second World War broke out on 3 September 1939.

26 April 1940

A Meeting of the Executive Committee was held ... at 11.45 a.m. Lady Glentoran[453] presided[454] ... Mrs Ainsworth Barr presented the Financial Report which showed a satisfactory balance. The Hon. Treasurer said she hoped to curtail the expenditure during 1940, and she hoped the Associations would all send in their Delegates Fees ... the following resolution ...

That for the duration of the War only Rule 6 Paragraph E of the constitution of the Ulster Women's Unionist Council be amended to read as follows:–

'The Committee shall meet once a year, but should any emergency arise a special meeting should be immediately summoned.'

That for the duration of the War only Rule 11 be amended to read as follows ...

'the Finance Committee shall meet when required to attend all financial matters ... and for the duration of the War shall be empowered under the designation of [the] Advisory Committee to carry on the business of the Council subject to Rule 6, Paragraph E as amended'.

After a great deal of discussion the resolution was passed. There were two dissensions.

This concluded the business.

453 The Hon. Emily Ina Florence Bingham, the 2nd daughter of 5th Baron Clanmorris. In 1905 she married Herbert Dixon, 1st Baron Glentoran, OBE. Lady Glentoran was a Vice Chairman of the UWUC from 1912–30 and a Vice President of the UWUC from 1939 until her resignation in 1952. She was widowed in 1950. *Burke's Genealogical and Heraldic History*, pp 876–7.

454 There were nineteen apologies for non–attendance.

Ballybay, Drum and Newbliss Companies of Co. Monaghan
Ulster Volunteer Nursing Corps at Glasslough, Co. Monaghan, 28 July 1914
T/3376/1/1, PUBLIC RECORD OFFICE OF NORTHERN IRELAND.

ULSTER WOMEN'S UNIONIST COUNCIL MINUTES 1912–40[455]

[455] This minute book is held by PRONI under reference number D/1098/1/3.

18 January 1912

The first Annual Meeting of the Ulster Women's Unionist Council was held in the Ulster Hall, Belfast at 11-30 a.m. ... The President, The Duchess of Abercorn was in the chair and there was a large attendance of delegates present.

The Annual Report for the year 1911 was submitted ... A draft constitution drawn up by the Executive Committee ... was presented for approval ... Mrs James Craig proposed and Lady Bruce seconded that [Mary Anne] Her Grace, The Duchess of Abercorn be re-elected President, and that [Theresa] The Marchioness of Londonderry be re-elected Vice-President. Passed unanimously.

10 April 1912

A special meeting of the Ulster Women's Unionist Council was held ... at 3 p.m. in the Minor Hall of the Young Men's Christian Association, Wellington Place, Belfast. The Marchioness of Londonderry, Vice-President was in the chair ... A recommendation from the Executive Committee that the Constitution be altered to allow of the election of two Vice-Presidents and that The Dowager Marchioness of Dufferin & Ava be elected a Vice-President ... the recommendation was unanimously adopted.

The Executive Committee also recommend that the offices of the Ulster Women's Unionist Council be moved to the Old Town Hall[456] ... Passed.[457]

16 January 1913

The second Annual Meeting of the Ulster Women's Unionist Council was held in the Minor Hall of the Young Men's Christian Association, Wellington Place, Belfast ... The Dowager Marchioness of Dufferin & Ava, was in the chair, and there was a large attendance of Members present ... The meeting was opened with the singing of 'O God Our help in Ages Past' ... Passed unanimously ... that the Constitution be altered to allow of the election of two Chairmen of Committees, and that the Marchioness of Londonderry, and the Dowager Marchioness of Dufferin & Ava be elected Chairmen of Committee ... Passed unanimously ... [that] The Executive Committee shall appoint an Advisory Committee. It shall meet weekly to superintend the general Office work and to transact any urgent business which may arise between meetings of the Executive Committee ... The following resolution was ... passed unanimously.

456 Unionist headquarters were based at the Old Town Hall, Belfast.

457 An Advisory Committee of twenty–three women was appointed at this meeting to assist the UWUC Secretary. This action was taken due to the resignation of the UWUC's three Honorary Secretaries which was caused by disagreements over the position and duties of Mr J. M. Hamill, the paid UWUC Secretary. See UWUC Executive Committee minutes of April 1912 for details (PRONI, D/1098/1/1).

'Because we are entered into times of great difficulty and stress wherein the prosperity and well-being of our beloved Country are threatened, we, as representing the Unionist women of Ulster, hereby declare our unabated loyalty to the solemn Pledge to which we unitedly and mutually subscribed our names upon Ulster Day.[458]

And we further record our resolve zealously and constantly to continue in the pursuance of our cause, and against all opposition to promote the same according to our powers. God forbid that we should part with the civil and religious freedom which our fathers won and bequeathed to us as a lasting inheritance.'

Miss Murray-Ker proposed a vote of thanks to the Chairman for her kindness in taking the chair at the meeting, and also for all her efforts to forward the work of the Council … which was passed with acclamation.

The proceedings concluded with the singing of the National Anthem.

[Attached to the minutes is a letter from Theresa, 6th Marchioness of Londonderry, dated 3 January 1913, stating:] It is with great regret that I write to say that I am unable to be present at the Annual Meeting of the Ulster Women's Unionist Association this year owing to political exigencies. Lord Londonderry and I generally spend January at Mountstewart[459] and hoped to do so this year but find owing to the political situation it is impossible. This however would not have deterred me coming to Belfast to preside at our Annual Meeting had I not hurt my foot about six weeks ago which precludes my walking.

I wish particularly to congratulate our splendid Association of 200,000[460] women on the extraordinary good work they have done in the constituencies in Great Britain, on the dissemination of literature and newspapers throughout England, Wales and Scotland, on the meetings they have held in Belfast and for the unremitting work they have done to further the cause of the Union.

Our danger is indeed great. In spite of the warnings which have been addressed to them, the Government, as was seen by their refusal to accept the amendment to leave out Ulster from the Home Rule Bill, do not realise the situation. We must force the constituencies to appreciate the position. We Unionists of Ulster do not despair, for we are sure that Great Britain in the end will not desert us. The men of Ulster know well how to defend themselves and we shall support them in all that they may do … We do not ask for privilege or preference, all we desire is to remain where we are – an integral part of the British Isles under the British Government and under no circumstances whatever will we allow ourselves to be driven out.

1 April 1913

A special meeting of the Ulster Women's Unionist Council was held in the Council Chamber of the old Town Hall, Victoria Street, Belfast … at 2-30 p.m. The

458 Ulster Day was held on 28 September 1912.

459 The Marquis of Londonderry's seat in Newtownards, Co. Down.

460 This has been altered by hand from 2,000 in the original.

Vice-President, The Marchioness of Londonderry, was in the chair and there was a large attendance of Members[461] ... The Vice President read a letter from the Dowager Duchess of Abercorn resigning her position as President of the Council ... [It passed unanimously that the Marchioness of Londonderry should succeed the Duchess of Abercorn as President. Theresa, Marchioness of Londonderry] expressed her thanks to the Council for having elected her as President ... the Right Honourable Sir Edward Carson K.C. [,] M.P. said a few words to the meeting ...

STATEMENT WITH REFERENCE TO THE CARSON FUND ...

the ladies present should recommend hearty co-operation and suggest to the Advisory Committee to advise the Executive Committee that Financial help should be given to the Carson Fund in the following way:–

By a systematic collection in the various districts covered by the Ulster Women's Unionist Council and Affiliated Associations. To facilitate this collection the Carson Fund Committee will supply the Ulster Women's Unionist Council collectors with a list of all women who signed the Women's Declaration.

Small contributions are also very welcome and much needed.

20 May 1913

A special meeting of the Ulster Women's Unionist Council was held ... at 2.45 p.m. in the Old Town Hall, Victoria Street, Belfast. The Marchioness of Londonderry, President was in the Chair and a large number of Members were present ... The following recommendation was received from the Executive Committee[.] That the following words be added to paragraph 4, of the Constitution;–

'Ladies who are anxious to support the work of the Council, and whose names are approved of by the Executive Committee may become Associate Members of Council on payment of an Annual Subscription of two guineas, and such ladies need not necessarily be residents in, or natives of Ulster. Associates shall not as such be eligible as Office-Bearers or members of the Executive Committee, who shall be chosen only out of ordinary members of Council, as provided under paragraph 8'[462] ... the recommendation of the Executive Committee received be adopted.

18 January 1914

The third Annual Meeting of the Ulster Women's Unionist Council was held in the Minor Hall of the Young Men's Christian Association, Wellington Place, Belfast, at 1.30 p.m. ... The President, The Marchioness of Londonderry, was in the chair and there was a large attendance of Members ... The proceedings were opened with the

461 There were fifty–seven apologies for non–attendance.

462 See Appendix I for a copy of the UWUC Constitution.

singing of four verses of 'O God our Help in Ages Past' ... The President read a letter from the Countess of Bandon,[463] conveying the following message of sympathy, passed at a meeting of the Bandon Women's Unionist Alliance:–

'In this time of anxiety we in the South, stretch out our hands and send you greetings and thank you for the comfort and confidence your strength has given us' ... The Right Hon. Sir Edward Carson, K.C.[,] M.P. entered the meeting and made a short speech ... The following resolution was ... passed unanimously: -

'Because we are entered into times of great difficulty and stress, wherein the prosperity and well-being of our beloved country are threatened, we, as representing the Unionist women of Ulster, hereby declare our unabated loyalty to the solemn pledge to which we unitedly and mutually subscribed our names upon Ulster Day.[464]

And we further record our resolve zealously and constantly to continue in the pursuance of our cause, and against all opposition to promote the same according to our powers. God forbid that we should part with the civil and religious freedom which our fathers won and bequeathed to us as a lasting inheritance.'

18 August 1914

A special Meeting of the Ulster Women's Unionist Council was held ... in the Minor Hall of the Young Men's Christian Association[,] Wellington Place, Belfast.

The chair was taken by the President [Theresa, Marchioness of Londonderry] ... Reported that on 12th August, the following letter had been forwarded to the Lord Mayor of Belfast[465] on behalf of the Council:– [stating] We desire on behalf of the Ulster Women's Unionist Council to explain and amplify our offer of assistance made at the meeting called by you in the City Hall on Friday last.

In every great National and Imperial crisis no part of the community has more clearly demonstrated its loyalty to the Throne and to the Empire than the people of Ulster. To-day our men are responding to the call of the King and rallying round the flag; and we feel it is our duty to see that their families and dependants are cared for, and that any want and suffering which may result shall be minimised as much as possible.

We are very glad and proud to assure your Lordship and your Committee, and also, if they desire it, the Soldiers and Sailors Families' Association, of the whole-hearted co-operation of our great organisation. It covers, as you are aware, the entire province of Ulster, and through it any individual case can be reached without delay. The Council, its Affiliated Associations and Members form a unique organization

[463] The Hon. Georgiana Dorothea Harriet Evans–Freke, CBE, the only child of 7th Lord Carbery. In 1876 she married James Francis, the 4th Earl of Bandon, a representative Irish peer from 1881. The Countess of Bandon was widowed in 1924 and died in 1942. *Dod's Peerage*, p. 48; *Thom's Irish Who's Who*, p. 10.

[464] 28 September 1912.

[465] Crawford McCullagh was Lord Mayor of Belfast at this time.

for investigating, registering and dealing with all cases of want and suffering and for dispersing such relief as may be found necessary.

Associated with us are the members of the Ulster Volunteer Nursing Corps,[466] all of whom are prepared to take up whatever duty they may be assigned or called upon to perform. We have also at our disposal numerous well[-]equipped dressing stations throughout Ulster. We will assist in the distribution where required of supplies of clothing, food and other necessaries of life. If any other means suggest itself to your Lordship in which our organization can be of use, we shall be happy to co-operate. We realize at this crisis not merely the privilege but also the duties attached to citizenship of the British Empire.

29 September 1914

A special Meeting of the Ulster Women's Unionist Council was held … at two p.m., in the Minor Hall of the Young Men's Christian Association, Wellington Place, Belfast

The Marchioness of Londonderry, President, occupied the chair … The meeting was called to confer with Lady Londonderry as to the policy and action of the Council during the present crisis.[467]

The President dealt very fully with the situation, and pointed out many ways in which women could help during the national crisis. She then informed the Council that Mr Hamill with a view to saving the Council expense, had offered the use of his Office in Ocean Buildings, and his own services in looking after any small matters which might turn up until Political work had been resumed, and would ask the Committee to defray only out of pocket expenses, such as Postage, Printing etc; that the Executive Committee recommend that Mr. Hamill's offer be accepted, and that he be paid the sum of £50 per annum, to cover out-of-pocket expenses, and for the use of his office. It was unanimously decided to accept Mr. Hamill's offer [and] … it was unanimously resolved that the number of Vice-Presidents be increased to three, and that Lady Carson be appointed a Vice-President of the Council … Decided to hold a Meeting of the Advisory Committee on the first Tuesday of each month, and to hold the Annual Meeting in the first or second week of January.

At the close of the Meeting, the President moved that the best thanks of the Council be given to Mr. Bonar Law, M.P., for his support of Ulster's cause.

The proposal was carried by acclamation, and the business concluded.

19 January 1915

The fourth Annual Meeting of the Ulster Women's Unionist Council was held in

466 The Ulster Volunteer Nursing Corps were established in 1913 under the auspices of the Ulster Volunteer Force, a trained and armed body of men intending to resist home rule by force, if necessary.

467 The 'present crisis' referred to was World War I which broke out on 4 August 1914.

the Minor Hall of the Young Men's Christian Association, Wellington Place, Belfast, at 2.30 p.m. … The Chair was taken by the President, the Marchioness of Londonderry, and there was a large attendance of members … The proceedings were open[ed] by the singing of four verses of 'O God Our Help in Ages Past' … [Passed that] We … think that during the time of the struggle in which we are now engaged between the allied forces and Germany, that a great deal may be done by our members to help our people in maintaining duty and discipline in the home and also be teaching patriotism and love of country … [Passed] unanimously that the following wives of Unionist Candidates for Ulster Constituencies: - Mrs Packenham, Mrs Weir-Johnston, and Mrs D.D. Reid, be co-opted members of the Ulster Unionist Council … The proceedings concluded by the singing of the National Anthem.

11 September 1918

A Meeting of the Council was held in the Old Town Hall, Belfast … The Dowager Marchioness of Londonderry, (President) in the Chair[468] … The future policy of the Council was considered in view of the extension of the Franchise to Women,[469] and after some discussion, it was proposed by the President[,] seconded by Lady Dufferin, and passed unanimously that the Council should continue as a separate organization.

The following recommendations of the Executive Committee were considered:–

(1) That the number of Vice-Presidents be increased to four, and [Edith] the Marchioness of Londonderry be appointed a Vice-President. Passed with acclamation.

(2) To substitute for paragraph 2 of the Constitution [with] the following:-

The objects of the Council shall be:–

(a) To secure the maintenance in its integrity of the Legislative Union between Great Britain and Ireland, and for this purpose to resist all proposals of whatever kind they may be which have for their objects the establishment of an Irish Parliament.

(b) To promote and assist all such measures as may be considered by the Ulster Unionist Council to be essential for the consolidation of the Empire, and for a closer union of the United Kingdom with the Overseas Dominions.

(c) To take such action as may from time to time in the opinion of the Ulster Unionist Council be necessary, in the interests of the Imperial Province of Ulster, in relation to questions of trade after the War, the employment and settlement of Ulstermen who have fought for their country, and generally, and

468 Sixty–eight members were present at this meeting and there were ninety–four apologies for non–attendance.

469 The vote was granted to women aged thirty and over under the Representation of the People Act of 1918.

all other matters arising out of the War which may tend to the benefit of Ulster and The Empire.

It is a fundamental principle of this Council that no other subject than those objects above described shall be dealt with by the Council, it being understood that all other questions in which individual members may be specially interested shall be subordinated to the policy of the Council as above defined.

All these recommendations were passed unanimously … [A proposal to] appoint representatives to a joint committee of the Ulster Unionist Council and the Ulster Women's Unionist Council for purposes of consultation and co-operation … Passed unanimously … That the Ulster Unionist Council be requested, in revising its Constitution, to provide for the inclusion of representatives elected by the Ulster Women's Unionist Council, in the same way as the Orange Order and Unionist Clubs have representation.
Passed unanimously …

ANNUAL REPORT

In presenting this Report to the Council, we feel, that as no regular Annual Meetings were held during the War, we should not omit some reference to the events of the past four years … The outbreak of the War in 1914 put an immediate stop to all political activity. The Ulster Women's Unionist Council, following the example of the Unionist Party, and acting on the advice of our Leader,[470] agreed to, and loyally abided by the Party truce, changing this policy only when circumstances rendered further inaction dangerous, if we were to maintain our rights and liberties unimpaired.[471]

The Council can regard with pride, the achievements of its members in many spheres of patriotic effort. In particular, mention must be made of the Ulster Women's Gift Fund, and Prisoners of War Fund, which was inaugurated, developed and almost entirely carried on by members of your Council. The achievements of that Fund will form a lasting monument to Ulster patriotism and Imperial spirit.

By the efforts of members of the Council large sums of money were raised and a fully equipped Ambulance was presented to the Ulster Division, sufficient remaining to endow three beds in the U.V.F. Hospital.[472]

For two years, the Council and its Members subscribed sufficient to support the U.V.F. Hospital at Pau which had been established by the efforts of members of the North Tyrone Women's Unionist Association, and which not only alleviated the sufferings of many gallant soldiers of France, but helped to strengthen the links which bind the two nations now so closely allied.

470 Sir Edward Carson.

471 The 'party truce' referred to was the decision taken by the Ulster Unionist Council to suspend all political work for the duration of the First World War.

472 The Ulster Volunteer Force (UVF) Hospital was situated in Ville de Pau, Cabinet du Maire, France. The Ulster Women's Unionist Council ambulance was also used in France during the war, 1914–18.

The majority of members of your Council have given themselves energetically to many and varied forms of patriotic War-work. Numbers have been occupied in nursing, munition-making, canteen work, Queen Mary's Needlework Guild, [the] Women's Legion,[473] and many other activities too numerous to mention.

The Ulster Sphagnum Moss Association sent dressings to all theatres of the war.[474] The Belfast Branch carries on its work in a room lent by your Committee. Its work has been favourably noticed by the Military Authorities and serves to enhance the credit of our Province.

The passing of the Representation of the People Act (1918) and the admission of Women to the Franchise was the occasion for a quickening of political feeling and necessitated a re-organization of the Unionist forces to meet changed conditions.

Your Committee and the Affiliated Associations took part in securing the registration of women voters and much good work has been done in this direction. The Re-distribution of Seats (Ireland) Act (1918) has rendered it necessary to re-organize several existing Associations and to form new Associations. This work is still in progress, and it is confidently hoped that the enthusiastic loyalty of the women of Ulster which rendered possible the great success of your Council prior to the War, will be again directed to furthering and enlarging the work of the Council to enable it to continue in the future, as in the past, to take a large share, not merely in the struggle to maintain the Union between Great Britain and Ireland, but in all schemes which tend to advance the prosperity of our beloved Province.

We cannot conclude without a reference of deep regret, to the noble sacrifice of those men of Ulster who fought and died in the Cause of Freedom. We revere their memory, we extend to their sorrowing relatives the deepest sympathy, and we shall ever point with pride to their achievements, as a lasting Monument to the loyalty of the Province and a glorious example to those who follow after[.]

28 January 1919

The Annual Meeting of the Council was held in the Old Town Hall, Belfast … The Hon[oura]ble Lady Kennedy, in the Chair[475] … The following letter from [Theresa] the Dowager Marchioness of Londonderry was read:–

473 The Women's Legion was established by Lady Edith Londonderry in 1914. This quasi–military organisation was designed to train women to take over the work of men who were on active military service during World War I, particularly those engaged in agriculture.

474 The Ulster Sphagnum Moss Association developed from the Sphagnum Moss Depot which was established under the control of Mrs Milliken of Donaghadee, Co. Down in 1916. The depot was initially based at unionist headquarters in the Old Town Hall, Belfast but in June 1916 was re–organised. Branches were subsequently set up throughout Ulster under the new name of the Ulster Sphagnum Moss Association. Moss was collected and made into medical dressing which were sent, for example, to British military hospitals and to France and Egypt at the rate of 5000 dressings per month.

475 One hundred members were present at this meeting and there were fifty–two apologies for non–attendance.

Women of the Ulster Unionist Council, it is with deep regret that I find it necessary owing to my changed circumstances to tender my resignation as President of the Ulster Women's Unionist Council.[476]

The Ulster Women's Unionist Council was formed in 1911 to help the Men's Unionist Council to preserve the Union between England and Ireland, which was settled by Act of Parliament in 1800 … and to express the feelings of the people of Ulster, who have fought with every means in their power to remain associated with England in a legislative union, I may say with truth that there was never a prouder moment in my life than that which I was elected President of such an influential body. I believe at the time, we were the largest number of women to band ourselves together for political work. The excellent work the two Councils and their supporters have done is shown by the fact that at this date, 1919, the union between England and Ireland still exists.

I will cursorily give a few facts quoting from a speech I made in 1911 to the Women's Unionist Association in Belfast, and much water has run under the bridge since then. The question of Home Rule was never brought forward in the English Cabinet until Mr. Gladstone[477] found himself dependent on the Irish vote in 1886. The reasons against separation which held good then, hold good now in my opinion. Ulster has fought her corner well, and I trust it will be long before any serious attempt will be made to separate England and Ireland. We banded ourselves together to see how we might best organise ourselves to impress our fellow-countrymen in England with the fact that Ulster will not consent to the tearing asunder of this country … We have always contended that the Nationalist members manoeuvred to get an English Government entirely dependent on their votes. The Nationalist Party have always spoken with two voices. One it uses in the House of Commons, and the other for Ireland and America … 73 Sinn Fein members (who boast that they are Separatists and Republicans) … have been returned to the House of Commons. They have, so to speak, taken off the gloves the Nationalists wore from 1886 to the present time. Both Political Parties in England have lavished money upon Ireland in the hopes that she would be contented. They disestablished the Church of Ireland to please her, bought the Landlords to please her, and gave her far more money than she returns in taxation. Is she content now with the return of 73 Sinn Fein members to Parliament? We must remember that since the union she has prospered commercially in every way.

476 The 'changed circumstances' referred to were the death of Theresa, Marchioness of Londonderry's husband, the 6th Marquis of Londonderry in 1915. After being widowed Theresa, now Dowager Marchioness of Londonderry, moved permanently to England.

477 William Ewart Gladstone (1809–98), a Tory MP from 1832–45 who gradually moved towards liberalism whilst an MP for Oxford University from 1847–65. He was a Liberal MP from 1865–95, Chancellor of the Exchequer from 1852–55 and 1859–66. He was British Prime Minister from 1868–74, 1880–85, 1886 and from 1892–94. His last premiership was dominated by his attempts to secure the passage of an Irish home rule bill through parliament. *Concise Dictionary of National Biography*, vol. III (Oxford, 1992), pp 1154–5.

I depreciate the opening of old sores, but I cannot help quoting Lord Seaton[478] when he was discussing the invasion of the United Kingdom and Ireland by Napoleon – 'I did not think he would attempt it, as there was only one vulnerable spot - meaning Ireland – which was the heel of Achilles.' We have only to look back on the last four years to see the truth of his words. We can all remember how the south and west of Ireland conducted themselves during the war, and I trust England will never forget it.

Until last summer women could only work for our cause by inciting others to express their principles, but now they have the vote and I trust they will always use it for the preservation of our rights as an integral part of England.

I was extremely sorry not to be in Ireland for the General Election last December, and to help in the work done by members of our Council, but I feel sure they all registered their votes in favour of the Unionist candidates and endeavoured to persuade others to do the same. I know our great Leader, Sir Edward Carson will fight our cause, should it be necessary from his place in Parliament, in addition to standing as a member of Parliament for this great city of Belfast, as our Leader. Times change, new generations grow up, and new idea[s] and different methods may be required, but one thing is certain, the North East corner of Ulster will never allow herself to be coerced, (as we dreaded at one time might be the case) to sever ourselves from the Mother country.

It is with great sorrow that I resign my position as President of this magnificent Association. I have worked as hard as any woman could do, for the preservation of the Union and for the settlement of North East Ireland, ever since I first took part in public life, 44 years ago. I am quite sure that union with England is necessary for the prosperity of Ireland, or any part of it. It is not that my interest has abated one jot or one tittle, but that I am resigning, or that my convictions are changed in any way, but because owing to altered circumstances I no longer live for a portion of the year in the north of Ireland. I shall always help forward our cause with my voice, (as hitherto) and also with my vote, to the best of my ability … I want to thank all those from every portion of the Province who have worked so loyally with me, and though I sever my connection with them in my public capacity, I feel sure to the end of my life, I earnestly hope and firmly believe that this Association will continue to do good work in the future as in the past …

On the proposal of the President[479] the following Resolution was passed:– …

That we the members of the Ulster Women's Unionist Council have received with deep regret the resignation of our President the Dowager Marchioness of Londonderry. Since her election as President in 1912 Lady Londonderry has displayed a constant and unflagging interest in the affairs of the Council, and by her

[478] John Reginald Upton Elliot–Drake–Colborne, 3rd Baron Seaton (b. 1854), Deputy Lieutenant and a JP for Co. Devon who served in the S. African War, 1899–1902, and in World War I from 1914–17. *Dod's Peerage*, pp 776–7.

[479] Rosalind, 3rd Duchess of Abercorn, was appointed President of the UWUC as successor to Theresa, 6th Marchioness of Londonderry.

untiring energy has largely promoted its welfare and the success of its work. Her great ability and wide political experience have proved of inestimable value to the Council … we assure the Dowager Marchioness of Londonderry that we will long remember her help to the Women of Ulster.

ANNUAL REPORT FOR 1919

This is the first complete year of work since the outbreak of the War, the Office having been re-opened in October 1918 … The Executive Committee has met eleven times during the year.

The Finance Committee has met frequently. The Suggestion Committee, appointed early in the year, met six times, and after discussing a number of methods of work, recommended that the Branches should be visited from Headquarters, that the revival of Membership Cards should be recommended, and that a Monthly Newspaper should be published under the auspices of the Council. This Report having been adopted by the Executive, the Suggestion Committee was re-appointed as the Newspaper Committee and as such has met twenty times since May.

In response to the suggestion to the Branches, all have revived their Membership Cards and the following have been visited by the Secretary or Assistant Secretary.

North Antrim	North Derry	Duncairn	South Tyrone
East Antrim	South Derry	Portadown	Woodvale
East Cavan		South Down	Pottinger

These Branches all showed a gratifying revival of activity against the renewed threats of Home Rule.

The Monthly Newspaper known as 'The Ulsterwoman' was first published as a Special Number for the 12th July. Owing to circumstances which could neither be foreseen or avoided, it was not all the Committee could have desired and it was brought out in September in an enlarged and more attractive form. Numerous articles by well-known writers have appeared from time to time … The Council received with sorrow the news of the death of its former President, The Dowager Marchioness of Londonderry … During the strenuous times before the War, Lady Londonderry took an active and valued part in the campaign against Home Rule, and it was largely owing to the influence which she was able to exert amongst Leaders of the Unionist Party in England, and her unceasing efforts that the Council was able to obtain so many openings in Great Britain for its workers.

The approaching departure of [Mary Anne] the Dowager Marchioness of Dufferin and Ava from our midst, to reside in England, will leave a vacant place in our ranks which it will be impossible to fill. In spite of her numerous activities, which may be said to include every good cause which has been promoted in Ulster, Lady Dufferin was always ready to preside, assist, and advise, on every occasion that she was called upon by the Council or Executive.

Instruction classes … have been held every month since June (August…

excepted), and the subjects discussed have been:– Labour Unrest, Proportional Representation, The House of Commons as seen by a new Member, Propaganda, Ireland and America, and the Educational Scheme … Those who have attended, have received the greatest benefit from these classes.

A Class for Speakers and Canvassers has been organised by Mrs G. H. Wheeler, and has met weekly since October. Some promising new speakers have been discovered by this means, and a band of canvassers provided for the Municipal Elections … The work of sending Unionist Newspapers and Leaflets to Great Britain, the Dominions, and the United States of America has also been revived.

The text of the new Home Rule Bill has not yet been published, but, thanks to the efforts of our trusted Leader[480] and our representatives in Parliament, a great step has been made, by the recognition of the fact that Ulster must be given separate terms, as she is different to the other Provinces [of Ireland], in religion, race, and politics.

As the new Home Rule Bill will appear after the opening of Parliament, your Committee would urge the members of the Council to impress upon those whom they represent all over Ulster, that there must be no slackening of effort during the coming critical months, when we must be fully prepared to take up the struggle against the forces of Sinn Fein and Separation.

In conclusion, your Committee desires to acknowledge the assistance received from the Unionist Press, in reporting the numerous meetings of Associations and Branches throughout the year.

20 January 1920

The Annual Meeting of the Ulster Women's Unionist Council was held in the Old Town Hall … [Rosalind] The Duchess of Abercorn (President) in the Chair[481] … The Hon[.] Treasurer stated that more funds were urgently needed to meet the increased expenditure … the Finance Committee be instructed to consider the fixing of a minimum subscription for members, of the Council and Executive … Proposed by Miss F. H. Whitaker:– 'That the Women's Loyal Orange Order be given representation on the Council.' It was unanimously decided that the proposed representation should be granted, and after discussion, the number of representatives was fixed at three to the Council and two on the Executive Committee, from each District.

Proposed … 'That any member of the Executive Committee, living in Belfast, or within twenty miles of Belfast, failing to attend seven meetings of the Committee in the year; and any member living more than twenty miles from Belfast, failing to attend four meetings shall automatically cease to be a member of the Executive Committee, and shall be ineligible for election the following year. There shall be no

480 Sir Edward Carson.

481 One hundred and twenty–two members were present at this meeting and there were forty–six apologies for non–attendance.

exception to this rule except in the case of illness.' After some discussion the motion was carried with five dissentients [*sic*].

A recommendation from the Committee of Cromac Women's Unionist Association:– 'That the Literature Committee be revived, and literature sent to Great Britain, America, and the Dominions as before 1914,' was passed unanimously ... The meeting was then addressed by Major O'Neill[,] M.P.

9 March 1920

A special Meeting of the Ulster Women's Unionist Council was held in the Old Town Hall ... Lady Kennedy (in the Chair)[482] ... The Proceedings opened with the singing of the first verse of 'Oh God our Help in ages past' ... The question of the three counties of Cavan, Donegal and Monaghan, under the Home Rule Bill was considered[483] ... The majority of the meeting was of the opinion that Ulster should remain intact, and abide by the Covenant.

Mrs Allworthy proposed a vote of confidence in Sir Edward Carson's leadership, which ... passed unanimously.

During the discussion on the Bill, Lady Dixon said that she considered that it would be inadvisable to restrict the action of the delegates to the Ulster Unionist Council.

It was proposed ... 'That the delegates from this Council to the meeting of the Ulster Unionist Council, tomorrow, shall be left free to vote as their consciences direct them.'

This was passed unanimously.

The Proceedings concluded with the signing of the National Anthem.

5 February 1921

The Annual Meeting of the Ulster Women's Unionist Council was held ... in the Y.M.C.A., Minor Hall, Belfast ... [Rosalind] The Duchess of Abercorn (in the Chair)[484] ... The Meeting opened with Prayer and with two verses of the Hymn, 'O God, our help in ages past' ... The Duchess of Abercorn announced that she had asked Sir Edward Carson and Sir James Craig to speak at the meeting which they had promised to do ... Sir Ed. Carson who was warmly welcomed spoke as to the responsibilities now laid upon women by the franchise and urged upon them the necessity of using the vote and thanked them for the loyalty and help he had always received from them, and expressed the hope that the women of Ulster would give to their new Leader, Sir James Craig the same loyalty and individual support they

482 Ninety–eight members were present at this meeting and there were fifty–two apologies for non–attendance.

483 These counties were excluded from the Home Rule Bill, as Ulster was defined as a six county unit, comprising of counties Down, Tyrone, Fermanagh, Antrim, Armagh and Londonderry.

484 One hundred and twenty–five members were present at this meeting and there were thirty–three apologies for non–attendance.

had always given to him, that although he had resigned the leadership he was not saying 'Good-bye' as he hoped to retain a close connection with Ulster and hoped to represent her in the Imperial Parliament.[485]

Sir James Craig spoke of the encouragement he had always received from the President and also spoke of the work of the women and urged them to use their vote, to stand united and so secure a good majority to make the new Parliament a success.

Lady Carson, and Lady Craig, who was introduced as the new Vice-President, also spoke ... The Duchess [of Abercorn] read a Resolution which she had put before the Ulster Unionist Council at their meeting on the 4th February and which had been unanimously accepted by them, and explained that the proposed scheme of election and registration work, and stated that she would write to the Chairmen and Secretaries of all Parliamentary Associations asking them if they required our help ... the Resolution in question [read] ... That in view of the approaching Elections for the Northern Parliament and the necessity for organised and energetic efforts to secure a Unionist majority, the Ulster Women's Unionist Council is prepared to undertake Election work with the Ulster Unionist Council and the various Parliamentary Associations, and the new Central Bodies which it is proposed to set up.

As a means to successful co-operation, the Ulster Women's Unionist Council suggests that each Unionist Parliamentary Association throughout the new Parliamentary area should give to Women voters representation proportioned to the number of women voters in their local area, not only on its own Committees, but also as delegates to the Ulster Unionist Council and to the County Selection Conferences, or any other such bodies ... passed 'That the Attendance Rule passed at the Annual Meeting of the Council on 20th January 1920, be rescinded'.

It was strongly recommended that each Branch should send at least one representative to each meeting ... passed.

'That a minimum subscription of 10/- be fixed for each Member of Council, which may be paid by the Member herself direct or by the Association which she represents, at her option'.

It was decided to amend Paragraph 4 of the Constitution by adding:– The Council shall consist of (b) 'Three representatives from each District Lodge in Ulster of the Association of Loyal Orangewomen of Ireland, and of such District Lodges as may hereafter be formed, such representatives to be approved of by the Grand Lodge of the Association and to be already members of the Women's Unionist Association in the Constituency in which they respectively reside'.

It was also decided to amend Paragraph 8 of the Constitution by adding:- 'The Executive Committee shall consist of (b) 'Representatives of the Association of Loyal Orangewomen of Ireland to be nominated by the Grand Lodge of the

[485] Sir Edward Carson resigned the unionist leadership on 4 February 1921 and was succeeded by James Craig.

Association, out of, and in the proportion of two for every three of the representatives of the Association on the Council' … passed … 'That the representation on the Ulster Women's Unionist Council and on the Executive be increased by two members on each, making ten instead of eight on the Council and five instead of three on the Executive Committee of the Council'.

6 December 1921

A Special Meeting of Council was held … in the Old Town Hall … [Rosalind] The Duchess of Abercorn (in the Chair)[486] … The meeting opened with Prayer … The meeting was called to consider and pass the Recommendations from the Sub-Committee which were approved of by the Executive Committee at their meeting on November 1st,[487] and also the changes which were approved [by] the Executive Committee at their meeting on 6th December.

The President stated that owing to the situation created by the Agreement between the British Government and Sinn Fein[488] which had appeared that day in the papers, she had suggested to the Executive Committee … that no alterations or changes be made in the Office until March; that the Executive Committee had approved of this suggestion … The President stated that a Deputation from the Loyalist Relief Fund had waited on the Executive Committee that morning and appealed for the support of the Members of the Council; that a hearty response was given and an immediate donation of £21 from the funds of the Council … This was unanimously approved of.

The following Resolution was passed unanimously:–

'That we desire to express to the Prime Minister[489] and Government of Northern Ireland, our whole-hearted appreciation of their courageous and patriotic stand against the campaign of treachery and misrepresentation which has sought to deprive us of our Civil and Religious liberties and of our place in the British Empire, and we pledge ourselves to support to the utmost of our ability such future measures as may be necessary to maintain our position against the designs of our enemies.' [The resolution was sent to Sir James Craig and a letter of thanks from R.H. Blackmore[490], dated 9 December 1921, included in the minutes, states:] The

486 One hundred and thirty–five members were present at this meeting and there were twenty–seven apologies for non–attendance.

487 The Sub–Committee recommended 'in the interests of efficient working and for the promotion of the Unionist Cause, that separate Women's Unionist Associations be continued in all Constituencies, but that a scheme of close affiliation with the Men's or Parliamentary Associations be adopted for the purpose of election work … That the Ulster Unionist Council be asked to appoint representatives to meet representatives from the Ulster Women's Unionist Council to decide the best means of affiliation … That as the importance of the Imperial union was never greater than at present, that name 'Unionist' be retained by the Council and its Affiliated Associations … the Executive Committee meet only quarterly, except where special business makes more frequent meetings necessary.'

488 The Anglo–Irish Treaty of 1921.

489 Sir James Craig.

490 Private Secretary to Sir James Craig.

Prime Minister of Northern Ireland and his colleagues ... appreciate more than they can say the splendid stand that the women of Ulster have always taken, and this strengthens them to face the future with all its difficulties. They all feel that they owe a deep debt of gratitude to the women for all the help they have always so ungrudgingly given and for the many sacrifices they have made for our beloved Province, and they are confident that should ever the need arise they will not look in vain to the women of Ulster in future ...

Proposed ... and passed, all members standing.

'That the sympathy of the Council be extended to the relatives of those who had been killed or injured in the recent riots in the City'[491]

The President thanked all the members for their work in the past and for the large attendance at the meeting.

The meeting concluded with the signing of the National Anthem.

20 January 1922

The Annual Meeting of the Ulster Women's Unionist Council was held ... in the Old Town Hall ... [Rosalind] The Duchess of Abercorn (in the Chair)[492] ... The meeting opened with Prayer ... A letter was read from the Secretary, Ulster Unionist Council[493] saying they had appointed a sub-Committee to meet members of the Ulster Women's Unionist Council in regard to co-operation between the two bodies[494] ... The President stated that the Ulster Trades Defence Association had written asking for permission to attend the meeting and place their views and objects before the Members, that the Deputation consisting of Brig. General C. Prescott Decie, D.S.O.,[495] Major H.R. Maslett, and Mr. John McCaughey had arrived. It was decided to hear the Deputation.

The members of the Deputation then addressed the meeting explaining the objects of the Association, and how the Council and its individual members could help.

Proposed ... 'That a Committee be appointed to meet the Members of the Ulster Trades Defence Association with a view to co-operating with it in its work'.[496] Passed.

It was decided to appoint the six Vice Chairmen and one Representative from each of the Belfast Associations [to this Committee].

491 Serious sectarian disturbances were occurring in Belfast at this time.

492 One hundred and forty members were present at this meeting and there were thirty–five apologies for non–attendance

493 A. Wilson Hungerford.

494 The Ulster Unionist Council increased the number of delegates from each unionist association from 8 to 10 'to allow of women Delegates [*sic*]. Also the wives of Peers, Senators and Members of Parliament will, if they so desire, be Members of the Ulster Unionist Council.' Letter from A. W. Hungerford, UUC Secretary to John Hamill, UWUC Secretary, 11 January 1922.

495 Brigadier General Cyril Prescott–Decie (1865–1953), a veteran of the S. African war and World War I. *Who Was Who, 1951–60*, vol. 5 (London, 1961), p. 292.

2 March 1923

The Annual Meeting of the Ulster Women's Unionist Council was held … in the Old Town Hall[497] … The meeting opened with Prayer … Mrs McMordie took the Chair and explained that the Duchess of Abercorn had to resign her position as President owing to the appointment of His Grace, the Duke of Abercorn as Governor of Northern Ireland … and stated that it was the unanimous wish of the Executive Committee that Lady [Cecil] Craig be asked to become President … the following Resolution be sent to the Duchess of Abercorn … It is difficult to express, or even to estimate, the loss to the Council and its work. Since her election as President Her Grace has devoted herself whole-heartedly to the work of the Council. By her attendance at our meetings and by her influence in other places, she has guided and directed the efforts of our members along wise and prudent lines. She was at all times ready and willing to consider any suggestion made to her for the well-being and prosperity of the Council, and her warm heart and great personal charm made it easy for anyone to approach her in the assurance of a sympathetic and appreciative hearing. Her great qualities of head and heart are too well known beyond the limits of this Council to require elaboration … Lady Craig who was received with great applause then took the Chair and thanked the Council for electing her.

22 January 1924

The Annual Meeting of the Ulster Women's Unionist Council was held in the Old Town Hall … Lady Craig (in the Chair)[498] … The Meeting opened with Prayer … The Chairman … dwelt upon the usefulness of the Council and the necessity for enrolling new members and trying to educate the women up to their responsibility as voters. She thought the Council should aim at having more sub-branches than at present to bring the meetings nearer the people. The President referred to the work which had been done by the Delegates in the recent General Election, and the Speakers Class … The meeting concluded with the singing of the National Anthem[.]

13 January 1925

The Annual Meeting of the Ulster Women's Unionist Council was held … in the Old Town Hall … Lady Craig (in the Chair)[499] … The Meeting opened with Prayer … Letters were read from Sir Charles Fall, M.P., Mr Pringle M.P., Miss H. Johnston

496 This association aimed to promote the purchase of Ulster–produced goods.

497 One hundred and fifty–nine members were present at this meeting and there were twenty–four apologies for non–attendance.

498 One hundred and sixty–nine members were present at this meeting and there were forty–four apologies for non–attendance.

499 One hundred and ninety–three members were present at this meeting and there were thirty–one apologies for non–attendance.

(Fermanagh) and Miss Stockdale (South Tyrone) referring to the work done by the women in the recent General Elections, and thanking the members of the Council for their help and support which had contributed largely to the success of the Unionist Campaign in Fermanagh and Tyrone. The President … referred to the Scheme of re-organisation which had been working very successfully in some of the Branches but that other Branches had not taken it up; that she considered it better not to press them to make any change just yet as it was possible the Government would introduce a Redistribution Bill which would sub-divide the counties into so many separate constituencies, that the Council would probably have to decide on some changes in the existing system so as to aim at having a Women's Branch in every such newly constituted constituency … The President referred to the meetings of [the] Executive Committee held in Derry and Enniskillen, which had cemented feelings of cordiality and friendship between members of different parts of the country and suggested that if the Council approved of the experiment being carried on this year, that County Armagh and County Antrim should be visited … The Meeting concluded with the signing of the National Anthem … A Public Meeting of Women Unionists was held in the Ulster Hall [Belfast] the same evening at which Her Grace the Duchess of Atholl, the Prime Minister of Northern Ireland and others addressed the meeting …

[A programme of this meeting is attached to the minutes. In it Lady Cecil Craig, the UWUC President, stated:] while naturally proud and thankful that the Province has prospered during the past year, I do not feel that it would be fitting for me to make any further comment than that. The general election was a great triumph both here in our own smaller way, and in England. We here were able to return every candidate that stood, and the Conservative Party across the water [in England] certainly got in with a majority that far exceeded the most sanguine expectations. We had been faced with various difficulties during the tenure of office of the Labour Party and it is certainly a great relief to us and to our leaders to feel that our friends are once more in power … I hope all the Branches will do their utmost to enrol many new members during the coming year, and that our Council will flourish[.][500]

19 January 1926

The Annual Meeting of the Ulster Women's Unionist Council was held … in the Old Town Hall … Lady Craig (in the chair)[501] … [It was] Proposed … That a Summer School of Conference on questions of Public Interest be held in the early summer of 1926 in Portrush, under the auspices of the Women's Unionist Council … it was proposed … that the suggestion be adopted provided no charge would be

500 Ramsay MacDonald's first Labour Government was formed in January 1924, but was replaced by Stanley Baldwin's second Conservative Government in June 1924. It lasted until June 1929, when it was replaced by MacDonald's second Labour Government.

501 One hundred and fifty–three members were present at this meeting and there were seventy–one apologies for non–attendance.

thrown on the funds of the Council, which was … agreed to … It was unanimously decided to continue the arrangement of holding two meetings of the Executive Committee in Belfast and two in other towns … Mrs Hume, on behalf of Cromac W.U.A. [Women's Unionist Association], handed a donation of £20 to the Treasurer. The Meeting concluded with the singing of the National Anthem[.]

21 January 1927

The Annual Meeting of the Ulster Women's Unionist Council was held … at 3.30 p.m. in 3 Glengall St., Belfast … The Viscountess Craigavon (in the chair)[502] … Lady Dixon D.B.E. proposed that the Viscountess Craigavon be re-elected President, and expressed the pleasure felt by the Members of the Council and by all Women Unionists throughout Northern Ireland at the honour conferred upon the Prime Minister and Lady Craig[503] … Lady Craigavon thanked the members for their continued confidence in her, and hoped the year upon which they had just entered would be a successful and prosperous one … the Report of the Magazine Committee … showed a profit on 10 months work of £57, after making allowance for bad and doubtful debts. The President congratulated the Magazine Committee very heartily on the successful result of its efforts, and again urged upon those present the importance of supporting the Magazine and increasing the sales in their different districts.

A discussion took place as to Meetings of the Executive Committee … the point of view of Belfast members … [was] that the Meetings in the Country were looked forward to with a great deal of pleasure and that their success had fully justified the arrangement, but at the same time it was felt by the Belfast members that it was too great a tax upon any single Association to have to entertain members of the Committee in the lavish manner which had hitherto been adopted … [the] country members, stated that these visits were very much appreciated in the country and did a great deal of good and that it had been a great pleasure to those of them who had the opportunity of entertaining the Committee … it was unanimously decided to continue to hold two meetings in the country and two in Belfast, but that it should be understood that entertainment is not to be provided by the country associations … Proposed … 'That monthly At Homes be held in the Unionist Headquarters at 3 Glengall St. [Belfast], for informal discussion on Unionist work'[.]
Passed unanimously.

502 One hundred and seventy–one members were present at this meeting and there were twenty–eight apologies for non–attendance.

503 The UWUC presented Lady Cecil Craig with a silver tray and a diamond watch bracelet in honour of the Viscounty conferred on her husband. 'Lady Craigavon, in reply, expressed great appreciation of the feeling which prompted the Presentation and hoped that the members and she would be spared many years to enjoy the happiest ties of friendship and to still further increase the usefulness of the Council', UWUC Minute Book, 29 January 1927 (PRONI, D/1098/1/3).

17 January 1928

The Annual Meeting of the Ulster Women's Unionist Council was held … at 11.30 a.m. in 3 Glengall St., Belfast … The Viscountess Craigavon (in the chair)[504] … Lady Craigavon, on taking the Chair, again thanked the members for their continued confidence in her and expressed the hope that the work of the Council would go on and flourish … Mrs Montgomery (N. Antrim); Mrs R.K. Gilliland (Londonderry) and Mrs D. Stevenson (N. Derry) said that there were matters of great and urgent importance which should be discussed by the Council without delay … it was decided to summon a special meeting of the Council in February and notice of all subjects for discussion to be sent to the Secretary before 1st. February … Before dispersing, the members joined in singing the National Anthem.

21 February 1928

A special Meeting of the Ulster Women's Unionist Council … was held … in 3 Glengall St., Belfast … at 11.30 a.m.[505] … The Meeting opened with Prayer … Proposed … 'That a Public Meeting be held in October on the evening of the Executive Committee Meeting instead of in January after the Annual Meeting when it is so difficult to get speakers'[.]

Considerable discussion took place … The Resolution was then put to the Meeting and Passed Unanimously … Proposed … 'That in order to increase the attendance at Executive Meetings, Associations should be asked to elect small lists of substitute delegates, with power to represent their Associations at Executive Meetings when the original delegates are unable to attend' … After the matter had been thoroughly discussed, it was decided that a list of attendances of Members of the Executive Committee should be published at the end of the present year and the discussion brought up at the next Annual Meeting.

Mrs Waring gave a brief but very interesting account of Communist Propaganda, particularly as it is being carried on amongst young people. She gave some startling facts as to the kind of teaching that is being given in Communist Schools. Miss Lowry (Victoria W.U.A. [Women's Unionist Association]) stated that Victoria Association is starting a Junior Branch in the hope of dealing with this particular danger.

Miss Lyle J.P. suggested 'That a speaker from Headquarters should be sent round all the W.U. Assocns.[506] to make suggestions, give advice and arouse more interest in

504 One hundred and eighty–one members were present at this meeting and there were fifty apologies for non–attendance.

505 Seventy–nine members were present at this meeting and there were forty–eight apologies for non–attendance.

506 Women's Unionist Associations.

the work'[.]
It was pointed out that Miss Gregg and other speakers are quite willing to go to any country districts where their services are required.
A letter was read from Mrs Miller, Hon. Sec., North Down W.U.Asn. enclosing [a] letter from Miss E. L. Andrews of Comber, suggesting that A Series of Lectures should be given on Political Economy. Some discussion took place and there was a general feeling that it might be difficult to get speakers to give more than one lecture in country districts. Miss Corry and Miss Gregg undertook to keep the subject in view with the possibility of dealing with it at the Monthly 'At Homes'.
Miss Connor J.P., Hon. Treasurer of the Council – drew attention to the fact that subscriptions are now due, and said that it would lighten her work and assist the Funds of the Council if members would pay promptly.
Miss Gregg announced that at the 'At Home' on 21st. March, Mrs Waring had promised to speak on the subject of Communist Propaganda.
Before the Meeting dispersed, the National Anthem was sung.

17 January 1929

The Annual Meeting of the Ulster Women's Unionist Council was held … in 3 Glengall St., Belfast … The Viscountess Craigavon (In the Chair)[507] … Lady Craigavon gave an address on the Political situation, and the aims and work of the Council for the future … In her remarks, Lady Craigavon thanked the Members for their continued support and confidence, and pointed out that without the help and sympathy of all she would not be able to carry on successfully … Miss Martin, chief Woman Organizer of the Scottish Unionist Assoc. (Eastern Divisional Council) gave a most interesting address, and the Meeting closed with the signing of the National Anthem.

17 December 1929

A Special Meeting of the Ulster Women's Unionist Council was held … in Unionist Headquarters, Belfast.

Mrs McMordie, C.B.E., J.P. presided[508] … The Revised Constitution was read and approved, with the following alterations … that the following be added to the Rules: -

'In order to further the work of the Ulster Women's Unionist Council a Cabinet Minister shall be asked from time to time to address the Executive Committee on the political topics of the day'.

This was passed … 'the Constituency Executive Committee shall meet as often as possible'.

507 One hundred and thirty nine members were present at this meeting and there were thirty–eight apologies for non–attendance.

508 Ninety–eight members were present at this meeting and there were twenty–seven apologies for non–attendance.

This was unanimously agreed to … 'That women members of Parliament, either Imperial or Northern, shall pay an Annual Subscription of £1.1.0'

This was approved … that Rule 10 [of the UWUC Constitution], Constituency Associations, should be altered, and the following was agreed to: -

'Each Branch, at its Annual General Meeting, shall elect delegates for the current year to a Central Selection Committee for the purpose of acting in conjunction with the delegates from each of the other Branches in the Association, in regard to the selection of Candidates to the Imperial and Ulster Parliaments. The delegates shall act in conjunction with a like number of delegates from the Branch of the Ulster Unionist Council in the Division … Delegates shall recommend the Candidate to a joint meeting of the Men's and Women's Unionist Association.' … The Meeting concluded with the National Anthem.

6 May 1930

The Annual Meeting of the Ulster Women's Unionist Council was held in Unionist Headquarters, Belfast … The Viscountess Craigavon presided[509] … The Meeting opened with Prayer … The following Resolution from Pottinger [Women's Unionist] Association … was discussed and unanimously passed …

'That in constituencies where Unionist women candidates are contesting as Poor Law Guardians in the forthcoming June Election, we members of the Ulster Women's Unionist Council and Associations pledge ourselves to do all we can to support and work for their return, feeling Poor Law work is women's work'.

A letter was read from Mrs McDonald, J.P., requesting that the Council should take action with regard to the persecution of Christians in Russia … the matter be put before the Prime Minister, and it was unanimously agreed to ask Lady Craigavon to report this finding to him and to leave the decision as to whether action should be taken, with the Prime Minister and the Northern Government … In moving the adoption of the Annual Report Lady Craigavon referred to the pleasure she had experienced on her return to Ulster at the great expansion of the work of the Council, and the enthusiasm shown and the splendid help given by the members during her absence … the meeting closed with the signing of the National Anthem.

27 January 1931

The Annual Meeting of the Ulster Women's Unionist Council was held … at 11.45 a.m. The Viscountess Craigavon presided[510] … The Meeting opened with Prayer … Lady Craigavon drew the attention of the meeting to the expansion and development of the work of the Council during the year and thanked all those who

509 Two hundred and fourteen members were present at this meeting and there were forty–two apologies for non–attendance.

510 Sixty–eight members were present at this meeting and there were forty–one apologies for non–attendance.

had worked so loyally in the various districts ... Lady Craigavon ... expressed the satisfaction which it gave her to preside over the Council, and her pride in the work of this organisation ... The Viscountess Craigavon then read a letter from Sir Wilson Hungerford intimating that a Central Committee of Representatives from Unionist Associations had been formed in London, and representation had been offered to the Ulster Women's Unionist Council, and an invitation extended to their Secretary to attend meetings in future, Lady Craigavon asked if it were the will of this meeting that this invitation should be accepted, and mentioned that she had also brought the matter before the Executive Committee at the meeting that day. The Committee had unanimously agreed to recommend to the Council to accept this representation. The Council unanimously agreed that in future the Secretary should attend the meetings in London on their behalf ... Resolution ... with reference to the Licensing Acts ... 'That this Council resolves to do all in its power to assist the Authorities in carrying out the Licensing Acts with a view particularly to the prevention of illegal Sabbath drinking and saving the young girls of our Province from serious moral harm.' In speaking to the Resolution, Mrs Heney urged the members of the Council to assist the Authorities in carrying out the Licensing Acts, and quoted instances of illegal Sabbath drinking and of the unwillingness in some cases of members of the Police Force to make arrests or to examine premises which had fallen under suspicion ... Lady O'Neill then took exception to the remarks made by Mrs Heney in reference to the Police Force, and proposed the following – 'That this Council regrets that wild accusations without evidence should be brought forward against towns and individuals at a meeting such as this' ... There was considerable discussion. This amendment was put to the meeting by the Chairman and carried as substantive Resolution by 73 votes to 28 ... the meeting closed by the singing of the National Anthem.

26 January 1932

The Annual Meeting of the Ulster Women's Unionist Council was held in Unionist Headquarters, Belfast ... at 2 p.m.

The Viscountess Craigavon presided[511] ... The Meeting opened with Prayer ... the Viscountess Craigavon expressed her gratitude to all the Unionist women of the Province who had worked so enthusiastically and loyally for the Cause, and also expressed her satisfaction ... at the extension of the area of the Council's activities during the past year ... it was unanimously agreed to re-elect the Viscountess Craigavon, both proposer and seconder having testified to the magnificent and self-sacrificing work of Lady Craigavon on behalf of the Council ... Mrs Waring of Lisnacree asked whether any steps could be taken to prevent the penetration of

[511] One hundred and ninety–two members were present at this meeting and there were fifty–eight apologies for non–attendance.

Roman Catholics in certain parts of the Province, and if anything could be done to prevent Disloyalists buying property over the heads of Protestants. Mrs Knox-Browne[512] testified to the prevalence of this danger in her district, and Mrs Casement spoke along the same lines. The Chairman said she was sure that in their individual capacity the members would do whatever lay in their power to check this failing.

Mrs Inglis, J.P., then asked if some information on the Revaluation of Ulster could be given, and The Chairman very clearly explained the principal reasons for this.[513]

Miss H. E. Gregg suggested that it would be helpful to the Unionist cause if more women would come forward for Local Government and Town Council work. This suggestion was approved of by the Council.

26 January 1933

The Annual Meeting of the Ulster Women's Unionist Council was held … in Unionist Headquarters, Belfast at 2.15 p.m. … Mrs McMordie presided[514] … The following resolution …

'That in future Transfer Forms be printed by Headquarters and a supply sent to each Branch Secretary, in order that Unionist women and girls leaving to reside in another district may not be lost sight of, but a Transfer Form be immediately forwarded through Headquarters to the Secretary of the Branch in whose Area they will be resident'.

This was unanimously agreed to … The next Resolution –

'That in future two meetings of the Ulster Women's Unionist Council be held annually, in order that delegates may attend one meeting at which a Political speech is delivered by one of the Northern Parliament members, or other outstanding speaker, as the January Council is for purely business purposes'.

… Much discussion ensued about this Resolution, in which a number of ladies took part. It was pointed out that it would be a financial burden to members of the Council to attend two meetings in Belfast during the year, but on the other hand some ladies thought it would increase the interest of the delegates if they could

512 Louisa Elizabeth Knox–Browne, 3rd daughter of Sir Arthur Knox–Gore, 1st Baronet. In 1867 she married Lieutenant Colonel John Hervey, a Deputy Lieutenant for Co. Tyrone. They resided at Aughtentaine Castle in Fivemiletown, Co. Tyrone. *Thom's Irish Who's Who*, p. 129.

513 No general valuation of the six north–eastern counties of Ulster had occurred since 1852, with the exception of Belfast which was revalued in 1906. The British Treasury was keen to revalue Northern Ireland to increase the yield of income tax. In the early 1930s the Northern Ireland government agreed to attempt to bring their financial system more into line with that of Britain by revaluing the province and a Valuation Act Amendment Bill was subsequently introduced in November 1931. For further details see Patrick Buckland, *The Factory of Grievances: Devolved Government in Northern Ireland, 1921–39* (Dublin, 1987), pp 98–99.

514 One hundred and fifty–five members were present at this meeting and there were one hundred and ten apologies for non–attendance.

attend another meeting during the year, as they felt that one Council meeting, which was only a business one, did not keep the delegates sufficiently in touch with the work, and in comparison with members of [the] Executive Committee, the ordinary Council members were debarred from many interesting opportunities for meeting and discussion … proposed that the experiment of holding two meetings should be tried for one year in order to ascertain whether or not it was a success … the following Resolution was unanimously passed –

'That wherever possible, Annual Area Conferences be arranged in convenient districts so that members may get to know one another and discuss problems of work, Areas being more suitable for this purpose than Constituencies'.

The need of such gatherings and their help to the Party was emphasised by several ladies … 'At Homes' are to be continued during the remainder of the winter session.

17 October 1933

A Special Meeting of the Ulster Women's Unionist Council was held in Unionist Headquarters, Belfast … at 2.15 p.m.

The Viscountess Craigavon presided[515] … Mrs McMordie proposed that a Resolution of sympathy in his illness should be sent from the meeting to Lord Craigavon. This was passed by acclamation.

The following Resolution, which had been passed by the Executive Committee … was passed unanimously –

'That in future Women Unionist Members of [the] Imperial Parliament representing Constituencies in Northern Ireland, and Women Unionist Members of the Senate and House of Commons of Northern Ireland, be Ex-Officio members of the Executive Committee of the Ulster Women's Unionist Council, and that this Resolution … be incorporated in the Constitution of the said Council' …

The Viscountess Craigavon then intimated that Major Ronald Ross, D.S.O., M.P.,[516] had travelled specially from London to address the meeting. Major Ross then delivered a most interesting and instructive address on the political situation, and touched on Home and Foreign Policy, and also on the Economic Situation … The meeting concluded by the singing of the National Anthem.

18 January 1934

The Annual Meeting of the Ulster Women's Unionist Council was held … in

515 One hundred and sixty–seven members were present at this meeting and there were one hundred and thirteen apologies for non–attendance.

516 Lieutenant Colonel Sir Ronald Ross (1888–1958), a Deputy Lieutenant for Co. Tyrone and a unionist MP in the Imperial Parliament from 1921–51, Parliamentary Private Secretary to the 1st Lord of the Admiralty from 1931–35 and Chairman of the Ulster unionist members at Westminster, 1939–41. Ross also acted as agent in Britain for the Government of Northern Ireland from 1951–57. *Dod's Peerage*, p. 743.

Unionist Headquarters, at 2.15 p.m.

The Viscountess Craigavon presided[517] … Lady Craigavon reported that the Speakers' Competition was to be held again this year … The Financial Report … showed that the finances of the Council were in a flourishing condition … due to a cheque for £500 having been given to the Council by Lord Craigavon … The council expressed their deep gratitude to the Prime Minister for his generous gift … A most interesting address on the Political situation was given by The Rt. Hon. Sir Basil Brooke, Bart., D.L., M.P.

26 October 1934

A Special Council was held … at 2.30 p.m.

The Viscountess Craigavon presided[518] … Lady Craigavon gave a report of the Country Market and thanked all those who helped. She said that next year notices of the Market would be sent to every member of Council. The sum raised was over £200 … The six students who visited [the Bonar Law College] Ashridge in September then spoke.

17 January 1935

The Annual Meeting of the Ulster Women's Unionist Council was held … in Unionist Headquarters, at 2.15 p.m. … The Viscountess Craigavon presided[519] … [It] was agreed to hold a second Council meeting again this year … the finances of the Council were sound.

20 February 1936

The Annual Meeting of the Ulster Women's Unionist Council was held … at 2.30 p.m.

The Viscountess Craigavon presided[520] … Before dealing with the business on the Agenda, Lady Craigavon referred to the loss sustained by the death of His Majesty, King George [V].

She also referred to the loss to the Unionist Party in Ulster owing to the death of Lord Carson[521] … Resolution …

'That the Constitution of the Ulster Women's Unionist Council shall be

[517] Two hundred and four members were present at this meeting and there were ninety–two apologies for non–attendance.

[518] Forty–six members were present at this meeting and there were seventy apologies for non–attendance.

[519] Two hundred and nine members were present at this meeting and there were one hundred and four apologies for non–attendance.

[520] One hundred and sixty–nine members were present at this meeting and there were ninety–four apologies for non–attendance.

[521] Carson died on 22 October 1935.

altered by having 3 Executive Meetings in the year instead of 4, i.e. in January, May and October. The May meeting to be held as soon as possible after the London Conference'.

After discussion, this was passed unanimously.

RESOLUTION …

'That young speakers who have taken training and are working for the Unionist cause by speaking at Meetings, should be eligible for co-option to the Ulster Women's Unionist Council on payment of the same subscription (10/-) as other members of the Council. Only one to be co-opted from each Association.'

This was unanimously agreed to.

RESOLUTION …

'That the Ulster Women's Unionist Council change the method of selecting delegates to attend the London Conference, so that every Association shall in turn send a delegate. As nine Associations have not yet been represented they shall be asked to forward names of those willing to go to London, after which the Associations will be represented in alphabetical order. This does not apply to delegates paying their own expenses'. This was passed unanimously.

The next item on the Agenda was – Discussion as to ways and means of carrying out the idea … of the Council undertaking to 'renew and maintain, tenderly and reverently, a floral tribute of Lord Carson's last resting place in the Cathedral' … After discussion it was decided that each Association should pay from 10/1 per annum towards this floral tribute.

18 October 1936

A Special Council Meeting was held … at 2.15 p.m.

The Viscountess Craigavon presided[522] … [A] most interesting address by the Viscountess Craigavon was given upon Jubilee Week in London. Miss Lena Irvine then made a short political speech. Addresses on aspects of educational life at [the Bonar Law College] Ashridge were given[.]

30 October 1936

A special Meeting of Council was held at Unionist Headquarters … at 2.15 p.m.

The Viscountess Craigavon presided[523] … [A] Resolution from S. Antrim W.U.A.

522 Eighty–nine members were present at this meeting and there were sixty–nine apologies for non–attendance.

523 One hundred and two members were present at this meeting and there were eighty–two apologies for non–attendance.

[Women's Unionist Association] … which read as follows:–

'That Associations affiliated to the Ulster Women's Unionist Council may, with the approval of the Council, form Junior Branches in the various neighbourhoods where women Unionists are already working, and so encourage the younger people to take an interest in the Unionist cause and give them an opportunity to do so'

… [this was] passed unanimously.

The next part of the meeting took the form of a Conference, at which Mrs Montgomery presided.

The Council listened with interest to the following speakers:–

Mr. R. Crawford, M.P. – The Framework of Local Government.
Miss McCready, P.L.G. [Poor Law Guardian] – The Care of the Sick Poor in Belfast.
Miss H. Johnston – The Care of the Sick Poor in the Country.
Miss Montgomery – Housing.
Miss D. Robertson – Education.
MrsParker, O.B.E., J.P. – Summing Up.

14 January 1937

The Annual Meeting of the Ulster Women's Unionist Council was held … The Viscountess Craigavon presided[524] … Before commencing the routine business of the meeting, it was decided to send the following telegram to Their Majesties, the King and Queen[525] … The Ulster Women's Unionist Council from their annual meeting send respectful greetings to Their Majesties, and beg to assure them of the devotion and loyalty of the women of Ulster to the Throne and Constitution.

25 January 1938

The Annual Meeting of the Ulster Women's Unionist Council was held … in Unionist Headquarters.

The Viscountess Craigavon presided[526] … Lady Craigavon reported that the cost of the Memorial Plaque [to Sir Edward Carson] to the Ulster Women's Unionist Council would be about £60. At the Executive committee held that morning it had been suggested that each Association should be asked to subscribe £2.1.0 or £1.10.1 towards this, and it was unanimously agreed to … Lady Craigavon referred briefly to the Speakers' Classes and Speakers' Competition, Ashridge, the Country market, 'At Homes' and the Junior Unit, and expressed her satisfaction at the progress made in these efforts.

524 There were sixty–eight apologies for non–attendance. A list of those present is not included in the minutes from this date onwards.

525 King George VI (1895–1952), King from 1936–52 and his wife Elizabeth, née Elizabeth Bowes–Lyon.

526 There were sixty–eight apologies for non–attendance.

527 A general election in Northern Ireland was scheduled for 9 February 1938.

She also referred at length to the forthcoming General Election,[527] and read a message from the Prime Minister, asking for the support of the loyalist women throughout Ulster … Mrs Parker, O.B.E., J.P., Parliamentary Secretary to the Ministry of Education then gave a most interesting address[.]

2 March 1939

The Annual Meeting of the Ulster Women's Unionist Council was held … The Viscountess Craigavon Presided[528] … The Meeting opened with Prayer. The Adoption of the Annual Report was then moved by the Lady Cushendun[529] who referred in her remarks to the splendid record during the past year … the Financial Report … showed a balance of £977.10.5. The Hon. Treasurer explained that the Prime Minister had given a donation of £500 and that without this donation and the Country Market,[530] the funds would be in a bad state … The Rev. Dr. Little M.P.[531] then gave an address.

25 April 1940

The Annual Meeting of the Ulster Women's Unionist Council was held … Lady Glentoran Presided[532] … The Meeting opened with Prayer … The adoption of the Annual Report was then moved by Lady Glentoran who referred in her remarks to how Ulster was placed in the present crisis.[533]

Lady Glentoran also referred to how Miss Kinghan was dividing her time between the Ulster Gift Fund and the Ulster Women's Unionist Council and wished her success in her work … the Financial Report … showed a balance of [£]282.15.1. The Hon. Treasurer said that she hoped to cut down the expenses to at least half during the coming year … Mrs C. Andrews proposed [and] Mrs D.C. Lindsay seconded, passed unanimously, the following resolution

That for the duration of the War only Rule 6 Paragraph E. of the Constitution of the Ulster Women's Unionist Council be amended to read as follows.

'The Committee shall meet once a year, but should any emergency arise a special meeting should be immediately summoned'[.]

That for the duration of the War only Rule 11 be amended to read as follows.

528 There were sixty–two apologies for non–attendance.

529 Lady Cushendun was the wife of Baron Ronald John McNeill (1861–1934), a Conservative MP for E. Kent from 1911–27, Parliamentary Secretary for Foreign Affairs, 1922–25 and Financial Secretary to the Treasury from 1925–27. Lady Cushendun was a Vice President of the UWUC from 1937. *Concise Dictionary of National Biography*, vol. II (Oxford, 1992), p. 1909.

530 This Country Market was an annual event that was organised by the Ulster Women's Unionist Council. In 1937 the market raised £717.

531 Rev. Dr. James Little (1868–1946), Minister of Castlereagh Presbyterian Church in Belfast from 1915 and a unionist MP in the Imperial Parliament representing Co. Down from 1939. *Who Was Who*, vol. 4, p. 689.

532 There were thirty–eight apologies for non–attendance.

533 'The present crisis' being the Second World War.

After the words 'The Finance Committee shall meet when required to attend to all financial matters' insert 'and for the duration of the War shall be empowered under the designation of [the] Advisory Committee to carry on the business of the Council subject to Rule 6 Paragraph E. as amended.[']

This completed the business.

The Rt. Hon. J.F. Gordon,[534] M.P. then gave an address.

[534] The Rt. Hon. John F. Gordon stood unsuccessfully as a unionist candidate in the 1918 election, but in 1921 was elected as an MP for Co. Antrim in the Parliament of Northern Ireland. Sydney Elliot, *Northern Ireland Parliamentary Election Results, 1921–72* (Chicester, 1973), p.10.

APPENDIX I

DRAFT CONSTITUTION OF THE ULSTER WOMEN'S UNIONIST COUNCIL JANUARY 1911[535]

(1) That this Association shall be called the 'ULSTER WOMEN'S UNIONIST COUNCIL'.

(2) The sole object of the Council shall be to secure the maintenance in its integrity of the Legislative Union between Great Britain and Ireland, and for this purpose to resist all proposals, of whatever kind they may be, which have for their object the establishment of any form of an Irish Parliament. It is a fundamental principle of this Council that no other subject other than the above shall be dealt with by the Council, it being understood that all other questions, in which individual members may be specially interested, shall be subordinated to the single issue of the maintenance of the Legislative Union.

(3) The object of the Council shall be carried out both by itself and by the affiliated Associations in the following among other ways: -

(a) Helping in connection with Revision sessions in having names of Unionist voters placed on the Register.

(b) Canvassing and speaking at Elections.

(c) Promoting missionary work in England by suitable personal effort, by public meetings, and by circulation of appropriate literature.

(d) By any other means approved after consultation with the Ulster Unionist Council.

To prevent overlapping it is desirable that the Women's Unionist Council should, in all its operations, keep in close touch with the Ulster Unionist Council.

(4) The Council shall consist of representatives of existing Women's Associations in the Parliamentary Divisions of Ulster, and of such Associations as may be hereafter formed. Each local women's Association shall return to the Ulster Women's Unionist Council one representative for every three hundred members. In addition, the wives of such Ulster Unionist Peers as have seats in the House of Lords, and the wives of Ulster Unionist Members of Parliament

535 PRONI document reference number D/1098/1/3.

(all these ladies being themselves, in the opinion of the Executive Committee, Unionists), shall be Members of Council.

In addition, the Council shall have power to co-opt from time to time distinguished ladies who have rendered, or are likely to render, service to the cause, being residents in, or natives of, Ulster.

(5) The Governing body of the Council shall consist of a President, a Vice-President, and twenty Provincial Representatives on Executive Committee, a Chairman, and four Vice-Chairmen thereof, together with three Honorary Secretaries, an Honorary Treasurer, and an Assistant Honorary Treasurer.

(6) The following have been nominated as Provincial Representatives:–

Lady Harvey Bruce
The Countess of Dartrey
The Dowager Marchioness of Dufferin and Ava.
The Marchioness of Ely
The Countess of Erne
Lady Ewart
The Marchioness of Hamilton
Lady Heygate
The Countess of Kilmorey
The Countess of Leitrim
The Countess of Ranfurly
The Lady Rossmore
MrsSaunderson
The Countess of Shaftsbury
The Dowager Lady Smiley
Lady Stronge

Any vacancies which may occur hereafter shall be filled by the Council at the Annual Meeting.

(7) The Honorary Secretaries, Honorary Treasurer and Assistant Honorary Treasurer shall be ex-officio members of all Committees and Sub-Committees.

(8) The Executive Committee shall consist of the following:–

(a) Two representatives from each affiliated Association, to be chosen before the Annual Meeting of the Council, by those members of such respective Associations who are Members of the Council. Any Association having more than 2,000 Members may nominate one additional Member of [the] Executive Committee for each 500 of such extra Members.

(b) The wives of Ulster Unionist Peers and of Ulster Unionist Members of Parliament, these ladies being made members of the Council as per par[agraph] 4.

(c) The Executive Committee shall, in addition, have power to co-opt a number of ladies not exceeding 20, who have rendered, or are likely to render, service to the cause.

The Committee shall meet at least once a quarter.

(9) Each Association affiliated to the Council shall pay an annual subscription of 3 guineas to the Treasurer of the Council.
It shall be the duty of the Executive Committee to collect from friends of the cause such additional funds as will be needful to meet the expenses of the Council.

(10) It shall be the duty of the Executive Committee, at the earliest possible moment, to proceed with the organisation of Women's Unionist Associations at all important centres in the various Parliamentary Divisions of Ulster. The affiliation of such Associations with the Council shall be entrusted to an Affiliation Sub-Committee of the Executive Committee, consisting of the Chairmen, Vice-Chairmen, and five members chosen by the Executive.

(11) The Annual Meeting of the Ulster Women's Unionist Council shall be held not later than the 31st of January each year. At this Meeting the Annual Report and Statement of Accounts of the previous years shall be submitted, and the election of officers for the ensuing year shall be made. Auditors for the ensuing year shall also be chosen at the Annual Meeting.

(12) Further Meetings of the Ulster Women's Unionist Council shall be held whenever the Executive Committee consider them necessary or desirable. Special Meetings shall be held upon a requisition to the Honorary Secretaries, signed by twenty-five Members. Ten days' notice of Ordinary, and at least three days' notice, when possible, of Special Meetings shall be given.

(13) Notice shall be given to the Honorary Secretaries of each Association affiliated to the Ulster Women's Unionist Council, two months prior to the Annual Meeting of the Ulster Women's Unionist Council, requesting the selection by such Association of Members of the said Council to the number specified in paragraph 4.

(14) A Finance Committee shall be formed, consisting of the Chairman of the Executive Committee, the Vice-Chairmen, and three members of the Executive Committee selected by it. It shall meet monthly to attend to all financial matters. It shall submit an Annual Statement of Accounts duly audited. This Committee shall select a Bank in which the Accounts of the Council shall be kept.

(15) Quorums shall consist of the Members as follows:–

The Council, 25; the Executive Committee, 7; and all other Committees and Sub-Committees, 3.

(16) Any member of Executive Committee failing to attend three consecutive Meetings of Committee without reasonable excuse shall *ipso facto* vacate office, and the vacancy so caused shall be filled by co-option.

(17) The Executive Committee shall have power to appoint a Standing Emergency Sub-Committee of seven members residing within twenty miles of Belfast.

(18) The Executive Committee shall have power to propose alterations or additions to above Rules, but such alterations or additions shall not take place until notified by a meeting of the Ulster Women's Unionist Council.

(19) At least four clear days' notice, when possible, shall be given of Meetings of [the] Executive Committee, and each notice shall contain a full agenda of the business to be submitted to the Meeting.

(20) The Executive Committee shall have power to employ a paid Organising Secretary, to engage a suitable Office, and to incur all expenses necessary for the conducting of the business of the Council.

APPENDIX II

DRAFT CONSTITUTION OF THE ULSTER WOMEN'S UNIONIST COUNCIL JANUARY 1929[536]

(1) That this Association shall be called the 'ULSTER WOMEN'S UNIONIST COUNCIL'.

(2) The sole objects of the Council shall be:–

To keep alive the feeling of the Union with Great Britain, and to promote and assist all such measures as may be considered desirable by the Ulster Unionist Council and the Unionist Party of the Parliament of Northern Ireland for the consolidation of the Empire, and the good government and improvement of Northern Ireland, and all classes and conditions of the people within its borders.

It is a fundamental principle of this Council that no other subjects than the objects above described shall be dealt with by the Council, it being understood that all other questions in which individual members may be specially interested shall be subordinated to the policy of the Council as above defined.

(3) The objects of the Council shall be carried out both by itself and by affiliated Associations in the following amongst other ways:–

(a) Helping in connection with Revision sessions in having names of Unionist voters placed on the Register.
(b) Canvassing and speaking at Elections.
(c) By keeping in touch with all classes and trying to raise the standard of education, morality and industry of all kinds.
(d) By supporting by Public Meetings, by circulation of Literature, and otherwise Reforms introduced by the Unionist Party in the Parliament of Northern Ireland on all subjects.
(e) By promoting Propaganda work in Great Britain, America and the Colonies by similar or other suitable means.

To prevent overlapping, it is desirable that the Women's Unionist Council should, in all its operations, keep in close touch with the Ulster Unionist Council.

536 PRONI document reference number D/1098/1/3.

(4) The Council shall consist of :–

(a) Representatives of existing Women's Unionist Associations in the Parliamentary Divisions of Northern Ireland, and of such Women's Unionist Associations as may be hereafter formed. Each local Women's Unionist Association shall return to the Ulster Women's Unionist Council not more than ten representatives.

(b) Three representatives from each District Lodge in Ulster of the Association of Loyal Orangewomen of Ireland, and of such District Lodges as may hereafter be formed, such representatives to be approved of by the Grand Lodge of the Association, and to be already Members of the Women's Unionist Association in the constituency in which they respectively reside.

(c) Women Unionist Members of the Imperial Parliament representing constituencies in Northern Ireland, and Women Unionist Members of the Senate and House of Commons of Northern Ireland.

(d) The wives of such Ulster Unionist Peers as have seats in the House of Lords, and the wives of Ulster Unionist Members of the Imperial Parliament, and of Unionist Members of the Senate and House of Commons of Northern Ireland (all these ladies being themselves, in the opinion of the Executive Committee, Unionists).

(e) In addition, the Council shall have power to co-opt from time to time ladies who have rendered, or are likely to render service to the Cause, being residents in or natives of Ulster.

A Life-Member may be expelled from the Council at a meeting of Council specially summoned for that purpose. The resolution for expulsion must be passed by not less than two-thirds of those present at the meeting.

A minimum subscription of 10/- per annum shall be payable in respect of each Member of Council. In the case of Members chosen as representatives of Affiliated Associations or District Lodges such subscriptions shall be payable by the Affiliated Associations or the Grand Lodge of the Association of Loyal Orangewomen, as the case may be; otherwise, the subscriptions shall be payable by the Member direct. Such subscriptions shall be paid not later than 1st March in each year.

Ladies who are anxious to support the work of the Council and whose names are approved of by the Executive Committee may become Associate Members of the Council on payment of an Annual Subscription of two guineas, and such ladies need not necessarily be residents in or natives of Northern Ireland. Associates shall not, as such, be eligible as Office-bearers or Members of the Executive Committee, who shall be chosen only out of ordinary Members of Council as provided under paragraph 7.

(5) The Office-bearers of the Council shall consist of a President, five Vice-Presidents, a Chairman, six Vice-Chairmen of the Executive Committee, together with an Honorary Treasurer and an Assistant Honorary Treasurer.

(6) The Honorary Treasurer and Assistant Treasurer shall be ex-officio Members of all Committees and Sub-Committees.

(7) The Executive Committee shall consist of the following:–

(a) The Office-bearers of the Council, as set out in par.[agraph] 5.
(b) Five representatives of each affiliated Association, to be chosen before the Annual Meeting of the Council by and out of those Members of such respective Associations who are members of Council.
(c) Representatives of the Association of Loyal Orangewomen of Ireland, to be nominated by the Grand Lodge of the Association out of, and in proportion of two for every three of the representatives of the Association on the Council.
(d) The Executive Committee shall in addition have power to co-opt a number of ladies not exceeding 20, who have rendered, or are likely to render service to the Cause.

The Committee shall meet at least once a quarter. Special meetings shall be held when considered necessary or desirable by the Office-bearers or on the requisition in writing to the Secretary signed by ten Members of Committee.

(8) Each Association affiliated to the Council shall pay an Annual Subscription of five guineas to the Treasurer of the Council.

(9) It shall be the duty of the Executive Committee, at the earliest possible moment, to proceed with the organisation of Women's Unionist Associations at all important centres in the various Parliamentary Divisions of Northern Ireland.

Each Association affiliated, or desiring to be affiliated, to the Ulster Women's Unionist Council shall submit the Rules and Bye-Laws shall be valid until submitted to, and approved of by, the Executive Committee of the Ulster Women's Unionist Council.

(10) The Annual meeting of the Ulster Women's Unionist Council shall be held not later than the 31st of January in each year. At this meeting the Annual Report and Statement of Accounts of the previous year shall be submitted, and the Election of Officers for the ensuing year shall be made. Auditors for the ensuing year shall also be chosen at the Annual Meeting.

(11) Further meetings of the Ulster Women's Unionist Council shall be held whenever the Executive Committee consider them necessary or desirable. Special Meetings shall be held upon a requisition to the Secretary, signed by twenty-five members. Ten days' notice of Ordinary, and at least three days' notice, when possible, of Special Meetings shall be given.

(12) Notice shall be given to the Honorary Secretaries of each Association affiliated to the Ulster Women's Unionist Council, two months prior to the Annual Meeting of the Ulster Women's Unionist Council, requesting the selection by such Association of Members of the Council to the number specified in paragraph 4.

(13) A Finance Committee shall be formed, consisting of the Chairmen of the Executive Committee, the Vice-Chairmen, and five Members of the Executive Committee selected by it. It shall meet when required to attend to all financial matters. It shall submit an Annual Statement of Accounts duly audited. This Committee shall select a Bank in which the Accounts of the Council shall be kept.

(14) Quorums shall consist of the Members as follows:–

The Council, 25; the Executive Committee, 7; and all other Committees and Sub-Committees, 3.

(15) At least four day's notice, when possible, shall be given of Meetings of [the] Executive Committee, and each notice shall contain a full agenda of the business to be submitted to the Meeting.

(16) The Executive Committee shall have power to propose alterations or additions to the above Rules, but such alterations and additions shall not take place until ratified by a Meeting of the Ulster Women's Unionist Council.

(17) The Executive Committee shall have power to employ a paid Organizing Secretary and Clerical Staff, to engage a suitable Office, and incur all expenses necessary for the conducting of the business of the Council.

APPENDIX III

OFFICE BEARERS OF THE ULSTER WOMEN'S UNIONIST COUNCIL 1911–40

PRESIDENTS

1911–1913	Mary Anne, 2nd Duchess of Abercorn
1913–1919	Theresa, 6th Marchioness of Londonderry
1919–1922	Rosalind, 3rd Duchess of Abercorn, DBE
1922–1942	Lady Cecil Craig, Viscountess Craigavon, DBE

VICE-PRESIDENTS

1911–1913	Theresa, 6th Marchioness of Londonderry
1912–1923 and 1942–1960	Lady Cecil Craig (later Viscountess Craigavon), DBE
1914–1919	Rosalind, 3rd Duchess of Abercorn, DBE
1914–1966	Lady Ruby Carson
1919–1959	Edith, 7th Marchioness of Londonderry, DBE, JP
1919–1941	Mrs Julia McMordie, CBE, JP
1921–1936	Hariot, Dowager Marchioness of Dufferin and Ava, DBE
1930–1964	Lady Dixon, DBE, JP
1937–1939	Lady Cushendun
1939–1952	Lady Glentoran

VICE-CHAIRMEN

1911–1914	Lady Jaffe
1911–1918	Lady Anderson
1911–1919	Mrs Julia McMordie, CBE, JP
1911–1920	Lady Ewart
1912–1919	Mrs Thomas Sinclair
1912–1930	Lady Dixon, DBE, JP
1915–1924	Honourable Lady Kennedy
1918–1930	Mrs Dehra Spencer Chichester (later Parker), DBE, MP
1919–1925	Mrs MacGregor Greer
1919–1920	Lady Richardson
1920	Mrs Mercier Clements

1921–1923 and 1933–1937	Lady W J Allen
1922–1923	Mrs J McCalmont
1922–1932	Mrs S Cunningham
1923–1925 and 1933–1947	Mrs Ainsworth Barr, CBE
1925–1939	Hon. Mrs Dixon (later Lady Glentoran)
1925–1939	Mrs B Hume, OBE
1926–1928	Mrs T J Andrews
1927–1944	Lady Cynthia Brooke (later Viscountess Brookeborough), DBE
1932–1937	Honourable Lady O'Neill (later Lady Rathcavan)
1935–1937	Honourable Mrs Henry Mulholland (later Lady Mulholland)
1937–1946	Mrs Knox Browne
1938–1961	Lady Clarke, JP
1940–1964	Mrs D C Lindsay

HONORARY SECRETARIES

1911–1912	Mrs A G Finlay
1911–1912	Miss E A M Tracey
1911–1912	Miss F Henderson
1911–1912	Mrs G H Wheeler

HONORARY TREASURERS

1911–1912	Mrs John Thompson
1912–1930	Miss E Connor, OBE
1930–1947	Mrs Ainsworth Barr, CBE

ASSISTANT HONORARY TREASURERS

1911–1920	Mrs Mercier Clements
1920–1930	Mrs Ainsworth Barr, CBE

ORGANISING SECRETARIES

1911–1929	Mr J M Hamill
1929–1934	Miss Jeanette Martin
1934–1937	Miss Helen A Maclean
1937–1938	Miss Molly Dickson
1938–1971	Miss Nancy Kinghan, OBE

APPENDIX IV

AFFILIATED ASSOCIATIONS OF THE ULSTER WOMEN'S UNIONIST COUNCIL 1911–12[537]

ASSOCIATION	DATE OF AFFILIATION
North Derry	21 April 1911
County Fermanagh	21 April 1911
Portadown	27 April 1911
Mid Tyrone	27 April 1911
Londonderry	29 May 1911
County Monaghan	29 June 1911
Lisburn	29 June 1911
Mid Armagh	29 June 1911
East Down	4 October 1911
South Down	4 October 1911
North Belfast	4 October 1911
South Belfast	4 October 1911
Antrim[538]	4 October 1911
Lurgan	4 October 1911
East Cavan	4 October 1911
East Belfast	10 January 1912
West Belfast	10 January 1912
North Down	10 January 1912
West Cavan	10 January 1912
South Armagh	10 January 1912
North Antrim	10 January 1912
East Tyrone	10 January 1912
Cookstown	10 January 1912
North Tyrone	10 January 1912
West Down	19 March 1912
South Tyrone	19 March 1912
Mid Antrim	29 April 1912

537 Extracted from Kinghan, *United We Stood*, pp 93–4.
538 Antrim and Lisburn Women's Unionist Associations amalgamated into South Antrim Women's Unionist Association on 28 March 1913.

South Derry	19 November 1912
North Donegal	19 November 1912
South Donegal	19 November 1912
West Donegal	19 November 1912
East Donegal	17 December 1912

APPENDIX V

PAPERS OF THE ULSTER WOMEN'S UNIONIST COUNCIL (UWUC) IN THE PUBLIC RECORD OFFICE OF NORTHERN IRELAND

DOCUMENT REFERENCE NUMBER	
D/1098/1/1	UWUC Executive Committee Minute Book, 1911–1913
D/1098/1/2	UWUC Executive Committee Minute Book, 1913–1940
D/1098/1/3	UWUC Minute Book, 1912–1940
D/1098/2/1/1	Minute Book of North Tyrone Women's Unionist Association, 1907 which includes sample unionist badges, tickets etc., 1907–1950
D/1098/3/1	Notes on the Women's Declaration, 1912 and newspaper cuttings re. the same
D/1327/23/4G	Minute Book of Mid Armagh Women's Unionist Association, 1929–1955
D/1327/18/9	Papers relating to the UWUC gaining representation on the Ulster Unionist Council, 1918
D/1327/1/1/96	Approximately 100 boxes of signatures to the Solemn League and Covenant and Women's Declaration, 1912
D/1327/25/2/1	UWUC Desk Diary and blotter containing a history of the UWUC, with a forward by the UWUC President, Viscountess Cecil Craigavon, 1935–1936
D/1327/25/2/2	Winter programme of the UWUC, 1946–1947
D/1327/25/2/3	Winter programme of the UWUC, 1951–1952
D/1327/25/2/4	Resolutions for debate at a women's conference organised by the UWUC, 24 November 1951
D/1327/25/2/5	Leaflet advertising an Ulster Fair organised by the UWUC
D/1327/25/2/6	Annual report of the UWUC, 1969
D/1332/5/3	Papers of East Antrim Women's Unionist Association, 1912–1923
D/1460/10–11	Papers of Dunmurry and district branch of Lisburn Women's Unionist Association, 1912–1922

D/2688/1/1	UWUC Finance Committee Minute Book, 1911–1913
D/2688/1/2	UWUC Finance Committee Minute Book, 1931–1938
D/2688/1/3	UWUC Standing Committee re. Active Workers' Minute Book, 1911–1916
D/2688/1/4	UWUC Affiliation and Newspaper Committee Minute Book, 1911–1913
D/2688/1/5	UWUC Advisory Committee Minute Book, 1913–1914
D/2688/1/6	UWUC Advisory Committee Minute Book, 1914–1916
D/2688/1/7	UWUC Advisory Committee Minute Book, 1916–1918
D/2688/1/8	UWUC Balance Sheets, 1913–1938
D/2688/1/9	UWUC Annual Reports, 1914–1971; Yearbooks 1914 and 1920; agendas, 1931–1946, 1949-1956 and 1958–1971; notices of UWUC annual meetings,1951, 1954, 1956, 1962, 1965–1971 and press cuttings re. the UWUC Executive Committee meeting of 15 July 1914
D/2688/1/10	UWUC miscellaneous papers, 1914–1940, including a copy of the first edition of *Ulsterwoman*; letters to the Southern Irish Loyalists Relief Association and lists of contributions to the Carson Fund
D/2688/1/11A-F	Xerox copies of UWUC newspaper reports, 1892–1913
D/2688/1/12	UWUC Advisory and Finance Committee Minute Book, 1938–1946
D/2688/1/13	Minute book of the UWUC Finance and Advisory Committee, 1946–1953
D/2688/1/14A	Printed Annual Report of the UWUC, 1971
D/2688/1/14B	Printed Annual Report of the UWUC, 1973
D/2688/1/14C	Printed Annual Report of the UWUC, 1973
D/2688/1/14D	Printed Annual Report of the UWUC, 1974
D/2688/15	Folder of papers re. the UWUC Jubilee Lunch in the Ulster Hall, Belfast, 1961
D/2688/1/16	Typescript copy of the UWUC prayer, c1960
D/2688/1/17	Copy of Nancy Kinghan, *United We Stood. The Story of the* UWUC, *1911–1974* (Belfast, 1975)

D/2688/2/1	Minute Book of the General Committee of St. Anne's Women's Unionist Association, Belfast, 1918-1923
D/2688/3/1	Minute Book of North Down Women's Unionist Association, 1914–1930
D/2688/3/2	Annual Meeting Minute Book of North Down Women's Unionist Association, 1924–1953
D/2688/4/1	Minute Book of South Belfast Women's Unionist Association, 1911–1918, containing some minutes of the Ulster Women's Gift Fund
D/2688/5/1	Minute Book of Ballycastle branch of North Antrim Women's Unionist Association, 1911–1934
D/2688/6/1	Minute Book of Strandtown branch of Victoria Women's Unionist Association, Belfast, 1947–1958
D/2688/7/1-5	Photographs of the Ulster Volunteer Force and UWUC functions etc., c1912–1967
D/2688/3/3	Officers and Committee List Book of North Down Women's Unionist Association, 1931–1959
D/2688/4/4	Annual Meeting Minute Book of North Down Women's Unionist Association, 1954–1969
D/2706	106 documents re. North Antrim Women's Unionist Association including an UWUC Annual Report, 1966, correspondence, auditor's printed announcements of forthcoming meetings, printed circulars re. statements, forthcoming elections, postcards, manuscript notes re. the proceedings of North Antrim Women's Unionist Association Executive Committee Meetings, circular letters and invitations, 1956–67
D/3790/4	Papers of Lurgan Women's Unionist Association, 1911–1921
D/2765/C/1–3	3 Committee Minute Books of Coleraine Division of North Derry Women's Unionist Association, 1911–1959
D/3121	Newspaper cuttings re. North Antrim Women's Unionist Association, including a typed list of officials, membership cards, etc, 1946–1970
D/3953/1	East Down Women's Unionist Association Papers, 1950–1961, including an agenda for executive committee meetings, letters, leaflets, newspaper cuttings, notes etc.
D/892/8A-B	2 copies of the UWUC Women's Declaration, 1912 (1 copy signed, the other is blank)

D/3027/6/13 Press cutting book, including UWUC draft constitution of 1912 and manuscript comments regarding home rule

SELECT BIBLIOGRAPHY

BOOKS

A Dictionary of Twentieth Century World Biography (Oxford, 1992).

Bardon, Jonathan, *A History of Ulster (*Belfast, 1992).

Boyce, D. G., *The Northern Ireland Question, 1886-1986* (London, 1987).

Boylan, Henry, *A Dictionary of Irish Biography* (Dublin, 1978).

Buckland, Patrick, *Irish Unionism: One. The Anglo-Irish and the New Ireland, 1885-1922* (Dublin, 1972).

______________, *Irish Unionism: Two. Ulster Unionism and the Origins of Northern Ireland, 1886–1922* (Dublin, 1973).

______________, *Irish Unionism, 1885-1923. A Documentary History* (Belfast, 1973).

______________, *James Craig. Lord Craigavon* (Dublin, 1980).

______________, *Lord Craigavon* (Dublin, 1980).

______________, *Factory of Grievances. Devolved Government in Northern Ireland, 1921–39* (Dublin, 1987).

*Burke's Genealogical and Heraldic History of the Peerage, Baronetage and Knightag*e (London, 1953).

Collins, Peter (ed.), *Nationalism and Unionism. Conflict in Ireland, 1885–1921* (Belfast, 1994).

Colvin, Ian, *The Life of Lord Carson* (vols. 2-3, London, 1934 and 1936).

Connolly, S. J. (ed.), *The Oxford Companion to Irish History* (Oxford, 1998).

Debrett's Peerage, Baronetage and Companionage (Surrey, 1966).

Dod's Peerage, Baronetage, Knightage, etc., of Great Britain and Ireland for 1921 (London, 1921).

Elliot, Sydney, *Northern Ireland Parliamentary Election Results, 1921–72* (Chichester, 1973).

Ervine, St. John, *Craigavon. Ulsterman* (London, 1949).

Follis, B. A., *A State Under Siege. The Establishment of Northern Ireland, 1920–25* (Oxford, 1995).

Foster, R. F., *Modern Ireland, 1600–1972* (London, 1988).

Harbinson, J. F., *The Ulster Unionist Party, 1882–1973, its Development and Organisation* (Belfast, 1973).

Montgomery Hyde, H., *Carson* (London, 1953).

Jackson, T. A., *The Ulster Party. Irish Unionists in the House of Commons, 1884–1911* (Oxford, 1989).

____________, *Sir Edward Carson* (Dublin, 1993).

____________, *Ireland, 1798-1998* (Oxford, 1999).

Kinghan, Nancy, *United We Stood. The Story of the Ulster Women's Unionist Council, 1911–74* (Belfast, 1975).

McCormack, W. J. (ed.), *The Blackwell Companion to Modern Irish Culture* (Oxford, 1999).

Newmann, Kate, *Dictionary of Ulster Biography* (Belfast, 1993).

Palmer, Alan, *Who's Who in Modern History, 1860-1980. A Biographical Dictionary* (New York, 1980).

Stewart, A. T Q., *The Ulster Crisis, 1912–14* (London, 1967).

____________, *Edward Carson* (Dublin, 1981).

The Concise Dictionary of National Biography, 3 vols., (Oxford, 1992).

The Dictionary of National Biography, 1920–30 (Oxford, 1937).

The Dictionary of National Biography, 1931–40 (Oxford, 1949).

The Dictionary of National Biography: The Concise Dictionary Part II, 1901–50 (Oxford, 1961).

The Dictionary of National Biography: The Concise Dictionary Part II, 1901–70 (Oxford, 1982).

Thom's Irish Who's Who, 1923 (Dublin, 1923).

Urquhart, Diane, *Women in Ulster Politics, 1890–1940: A History Not Yet Told* (Dublin, 2000).

Walker, B. M., *Ulster Politics. The Formative Years, 1868-86* (Belfast, 1989).

Whitaker's Peerage, Baronetage, Knightage and Companionage (London, 1935).

Who Was Who, vol. I, 1897–1916 (London, 1920).

Who Was Who, vol. II, 1916–28 (London, 1929).

Who Was Who, vol. III, 1929-40 (London, 1941).

Who Was Who, vol. IV, 1941–50 (London, 1952).

Who Was Who, vol. V, 1951–60 (London, 1961).

ARTICLES

Buckland, Patrick, 'The unity of Ulster unionism, 1886–1939', *Historical Journal*, 60 (1975), pp 211–23.

__________ , 'Irish unionism and the new Ireland' in D. G. Boyce (ed.), *Revolution in Ireland, 1879–1923* (Dublin, 1988), pp 71–90.

Fanning, J. R., 'The Unionist Party in Ireland, 1906–10', *Irish Historical Studies*, 15, no. 58 (1966), pp 147–71.

Foy, Michael, 'Ulster unionist propaganda against home rule, 1912–14', *History Ireland*, 4, no. 1 (1996), pp 49–53.

Jackson, T. A., 'Unionist history', *Irish Review*, 7–8 (Autumn 1989-Spring 1990), pp 58–66 and 62–9.

__________ , 'Unionist politics and Protestant society in Edwardian Ireland', *Historical Journal*, 33 (1990), pp 839–66.

__________ , 'Unionist myths, 1912–85', *Past and Present*, 136 (1992), pp 164–85.

Savage, D. C., 'The origins of the Ulster Unionist Party, 1885–86', *Irish Historical Studies*, 12, no. 47 (1961), pp 185–208.

Stubbs, J. O., 'The unionists and Ireland, 1914–18', *Historical Journal*, 33, 4, (1990), pp 867–93.

Urquhart, Diane, "The female of the species is more deadlier than the male'?: The Ulster Women's Unionist Council, 1911–40' in Janice Holmes and Diane Urquhart (eds), *Coming into the Light: The Work, Politics and Religion of Women in Ulster, 1840–1940* (Belfast, 1994), pp 93–123.

__________ 'In defence of Ulster and the Empire: The Ulster Women's Unionist Council, 1886–1940', *Galway Women's Studies Centre Review*, 4 (1996), pp 31–40.

INDEX